Ritual Brotherhood
in Renaissance Florence

POPULATION AND SOCIAL STRUCTURE

Advances in Historical Demography

Under the Editorship of

E. A. HAMMEL

Department of Anthropology
University of California, Berkeley

Kenneth W. Wachter with *Eugene A. Hammel* and *Peter Laslett,* Statistical Studies of Historical Social Structure

Nancy Howell, Demography of the Dobe !Kung

Bennett Dyke and *Warren T. Morril* (Editors), Genealogical Demography

J. Dupaquier, E. Helin, P. Laslett, M. Livi Bacci, and *S. Sogner* (Editors), Marriage and Remarriage in Populations of the Past.

Ronald F. E. Weissman, Ritual Brotherhood in Renaissance Florence

Ritual Brotherhood in Renaissance Florence

RONALD F. E. WEISSMAN

Department of History
University of Maryland
College Park, Maryland

ACADEMIC PRESS

A Subsidiary of Harcourt Brace Jovanovich, Publishers

New York   London
Paris   San Diego   San Francisco   São Paulo
Sydney   Tokyo   Toronto

The quotations on pages 28, 29, 30, 32, 37, 38, and 39 cited to Alberti
are reprinted by permission from *The Family in Renaissance Florence,*
a translation by René Neu Watkins of *I Libri della famiglia* by Leon
Battista Alberti, with an introduction by the translator (Columbia, S.C.:
The University of South Carolina Press, 1969). Copyright © 1969 by
René Watkins.

ACADEMIC PRESS, INC.
111 Fifth Avenue, New York, New York 10003

United Kingdom Edition published by
ACADEMIC PRESS, INC. (LONDON) LTD.
24/28 Oval Road, London NW1 7DX

Library of Congress Cataloging in Publication Data

Weissman, Ronald F. E.
   Ritual brotherhood in renaissance Florence.

   (Population and social structure. Advances in
historical demography)
   Includes index.
   1. Social structure--Italy--History. 2. Florence
(Italy)--Social conditions. 3. Confraternities--Italy--
Florence--History. 4. Florence (Italy)--Religious life
and customs. I. Title. II. Series.
HN490.S6W44   945   81-17536
ISBN 0-12-744480-7   AACR2

PRINTED IN THE UNITED STATES OF AMERICA

82 83 84 85   9 8 7 6 5 4 3 2 1

To
ARTHUR WEISSMAN
1913-1980

Contents

Preface

This book explores the meaning of fraternity in Renaissance Florence in terms of the ritual relations created in religious brotherhoods or confraternities. The confraternity was a voluntary association organized and directed by laymen. Apart from the parish mass, confraternal ritual was one of the most common forms of religious experience for southern Europeans in the early modern period. Throughout Mediterranean Europe, confraternities planned and directed much of the festive life and public charitable activities of their communities. The confraternities provided their members with certain vital forms of social insurance in life and in death. Confraternities were also commissioners of works of art, and were thereby major sources of patronage for the Renaissance artist. Confraternal activity clearly contributed in many ways to the spiritual and material needs of townsmen in the late medieval and early modern world.

But beyond being a place to pray, and an institution providing charitable distributions and other services to the community, the confraternity, like the family and guild, was one of the principal forms of sociability available to males in premodern European society. It is this sociability, revealed in patterns of membership and in forms of ceremony, that is the focus of the chapters that follow. The reader will not find in these pages a traditional institutional history of confraternities. Rather, this study of confraternities has a somewhat different goal: an understanding of the ways in which Florentines used certain forms of ritual to define, protect, and alter their relations with one another. Florence's confraternities will serve as a vehicle for examining the relationship between ritual behavior and social organization. I hope that this investigation of ritual and community will be of value to students of Mediterranean society as well as to those whose interest is the Italian Renaissance.

Two related questions are fundamental. First, what was the nature of the social relations existing among the individuals who joined religious fraternities? Second, what meanings did fraternal rituals have for individuals who chose to participate in them? Encountering such questions, the reader may well ask a third: What does the study of social relations have to do with the study of religious ritual?

Social relations have everything to do with the study of ritual practices. Society bestows meaning on all of its actions and objects, sacred and secular alike, through the process of social interaction. Rituals are structured sets of symbols that are manipulated by actors according to prescribed formulas. All of the components of ritual—the formulas, the classes of actors who will perform the ritual acts, and the symbols themselves—are social constructions, that is, their meanings are attributed to them by those who perform and observe the rituals. Rituals are commentaries about the way society organizes, categorizes, and links its persons, actions, and things. Rituals take form within human society; they even offer the possibility of transforming the society that performs them. In seeking to discover what the rituals of brotherhood meant to Renaissance Florentines, it is necessary to examine how Florentines organized and interpreted their relations with one another.

The metaphor for conceptualizing social relations in Renaissance Florence used in this book is that of social networks, that is, the pattern of bonds linking Florentines to one another. Chapter 1 offers a brief overview of the basic characteristics of Florentine social networks. In addition to its descriptions of Florentine network structures, this chapter emphasizes the social meanings that Florentine males drew from their experience in social networks.

The discussions of the structure, rituals, and cultural meanings of the Renaissance confraternity presented in Chapter 2 serve to demonstrate the variety of ways in which the confraternities of republican Florence created social relations whose network structure and meaning provided alternatives to the urban social order. Chapter 3 offers a demographic analysis of patterns of membership structure and participation. This analysis, based on data brought together from confraternal records and from Florence's richly detailed census and taxation registers, links Renaissance confraternities to particular stages in the developmental cycle of the middle-class Florentine household.

Between 1494 and the middle of the sixteenth century, the city of

Florence saw the frequently violent installation and demise of various forms of popular and princely rule. This period of prolonged civil strife witnessed the expulsion of the Medici, the rise and fall of Savonarola's charismatic leadership, a ruinous siege and foreign invasion, and the assassination of Duke Alessandro. It culminated in the elevation of the Medici as hereditary dukes of the Grand Duchy of Tuscany. The religious brotherhoods of Florence were severely damaged by these frequent disruptions of the city's *vita civile*. Chapter 4 chronicles the effects of this 50-year period of political and social turmoil on traditional confraternal life. The religious enthusiasm generated by the Catholic Reformation and the return to political stability under the Medici dukes were favorable to a reinvigoration of confraternal organization and activity. Given 50 years of decline and neglect, it is not surprising that sixteenth-century Florentine confraternities, whether newly established or recently resurrected, differed significantly from their republican antecedents. Chapter 5 describes the social foundations of confraternal reform during the Catholic Reformation and the emergence of new forms of ritual brotherhood amidst the social relations of grand-ducal Florence.

Among the rituals that are associated with publication, one of the most pleasant is thanking those institutions and individuals whose assistance made the project possible to do, and worth the doing. I am deeply indebted to William Bouwsma, Gene Brucker, Randolph Starn, and Eugene Hammel, who supervised the doctoral dissertation that formed the basis of this book. The U.S. Department of State and Italian Fulbright-Hays Commissions, and the Quantitative Anthropology Laboratory of the University of California, Berkeley, provided generous support for my research. A summer postdoctoral fellowship provided by the University of California Berkeley's Graduate Group in Demography greatly assisted in the preparation of the final version of the book.

My investigation of fraternity in Florence was enlivened and my research enriched by contact with an extraordinary group of scholars working in the Florentine archives. Anthony Molho, David Herlihy, Marvin Becker, Richard Goldthwaite, Riccardo Fubini, Richard Trexler, John Najemy, Rab Hatfield, and Gino Corti were generous in sharing their own work and archival expertise. I am fortunate, too, during two sojourns in Tuscany, to have shared in a Florentine scholarly fraternity that included the likes of Tom Kuehn, Dan Lesnick, Sam Cohn, John Henderson, Jeff Newton, Yoram Milo, David Petersen, and Jim Banker. Elihu and M. Sue Gerson, Charles S. Smith, Natalie Zemon Davis, and my colleagues at the University of Maryland provided much needed criticism, encouragement, and support. I am particularly grateful to Randolph Starn, Gene Brucker, Judith Brown, and Gabrielle Spiegel for their reviews of drafts of this work. I appreciate, too, the patience and assistance of the staff of Academic Press. To my severest critic, Emely Weissman, in whose precious company I became acquainted with Florentine life as no archive can reveal it, I remain ever grateful.

List of Abbreviations

ASF	Archivio di Stato, Florence
ASI	*Archivio Storico Italiano*
BNF	Biblioteca Nazionale Centrale, Florence
Capitoli	Archivio di Stato, Florence, *Compagnie Religiose Soppresse, Capitoli*
CRS	Archivio di Stato, Florence, *Compagnie Religiose Soppresse*
del Migliore	BNF, ms. Magliabecchiano XXV, 418, Leopoldo del Migliore, *Zibaldone*
del Prete	L. del Prete, ed., *Capitoli della Compagnia della Madonna d'Orsanmichele dei secoli XIII e XIV* (Lucca, 1859).
Meersseman	Gilles Gerard Meersseman, *Ordo Fraternitatis: Confraternite e pietà dei laici nel mondo medioevo,* 3 vols. (Rome, 1977).
MEFRM	*Mélanges de l'École Française de Rome, Temps Modernes*
Monti	G. Monti, *Le Confraternite Medievali dell'Alta e Media Italia,* 2 vols. (Venice, 1927).
Il Movimento	*Il movimento dei disciplinati nel VII centenario del suo inizio* (Perugia: Deputazione di Storia Patria per l'Umbria, 1962).
Passerini	L. Passerini, *Storia degli Stabilimenti di Beneficenza e d'Istruzione Elementare Gratuita della Città di Firenze* (Florence, 1853).
Risultati	*Risultati e prospettive della ricerca sul movimento dei disciplinati* (Perugia: Deputazione di Storia Patria per l'Umbria, 1972).
Riccardiana	Biblioteca Riccardiana, Florence
Stefani	Marchionne di Coppo Stefani, *Cronaca Fiorentina,* ed. N. Rodolico, in *Rerum Italicarum Scriptores* (Città di Castello, 1955) new ed., vol. XXX, part 1.

Chapter ONE

Judas the Florentine
SOCIAL RELATIONS
IN RENAISSANCE FLORENCE

The flatterer is truly the worst of traitors. While he charms and makes
protestations of his love, he kills the soul. He is vicious in his caresses. And so he
is like Judas, who betrayed Christ with a kiss.
                                        —*Antoninus, Archbishop of Florence*[1]

What was the nature of civic life in Renaissance Italy? Consensus or
conflict, community or faction—these are the grand questions that have
organized the historiography of Renaissance city-states for the past century. In seeking to define the nature of community, historians have chronicled the struggles that pitted groups against one another: guilds and aristocratic clans, magnates and *popolani,* Guelphs and Ghibellines. The history of
Renaissance cities has been written as the history of the shifts and realign-
ments of political and social groups.

The relations between groups is, however, only one dimension of the
social and political life of the Renaissance. Relations between individuals
were as intensely political, that is, as concerned with power and obligation,
as were relations among groups. The relations of everyday life—the casual
encounter on a *piazza,* the conclusion of a business deal, the relations of
families and friends—were as political as the struggles of guilds or the
workings of the commune. In this chapter I explore the politics of everyday
life in Renaissance Florence. The chapter opens with a brief survey of the
basic forms of power and the formal groupings of Florentine republican
society and proceeds to an analysis of the patterns and meanings of personal
relations among Florentines.[2]

---

1. Sant' Antonino, *Opera a ben vivere* (Florence, 1923), p. 62: "L'adulatore, per verità, è pessimo
traditore; però che lusingando e mostrando amore, uccide l'anima; e lisciando lorda: sicchè s'assomig-
lia a Giuda, il quale col bacio tradì Cristo."
2. My analysis of Florentine social relations and fraternal organization is derived in part from
the "Chicago School" of symbolic interactionist sociology, a tradition of research that holds that
the fundamental units of social analysis are not the individuals who inhabit the social order but the

The Structure of Social Relations

Florence was one of the great city-republics of the late Middle Ages. Republican institutions survived well into the early sixteenth century, long after most other Italian communes had adopted one or another form of princely rule. The longevity of Florentine republicanism was due, in large part, to the diffuse distribution of power in the Arno city. The political and social history of Renaissance Florence is largely the history of the distribution among Florentine social groups of three principal forms of power: economic resources, honor, and political authority. In republican Florence the distribution of these forms of power did not follow precisely the same social curves. Certain new and old Florentine merchant families might possess equal wealth, but limitations on the political authority of the new men by the men of ancient lineage ensured that the patriciate, defined in economic terms, was faction ridden and far from united. Thus, while the Florentines experienced serious conflict between status groups and classes, social trauma within such groups was frequently as severe. A relatively wide dispersion of significant forms of power prevented the accumulation of influence in the hands of a few Florentines, and the persistence of conflict within classes tended to limit, until the fifteenth century, the possibility of effective oligarchical rule.[3]

---

interactions existing among those individuals. Patterns of linkages (networks) serve as the context within which social categories are constructed and reconstructed. The units of analysis of other schools of social research, the "roles" of functionalist sociology, and the "classes" of Marxist sociology are abstractions, perceptions about behavior that take place within the context of social interaction. Such perceptions about social relations may be those of the modern analyst or the historical actor, but in either case they are of secondary importance to the social relations within which they come to have meaning. In no manner are "roles" or "classes" historical universals that predate or postdate the social relations that give them meaning. The symbolic interactionist study of society places native social categories in the context of the social linkages through which such categories were contructed.

For the interactionist, categories and meanings are socially constructed and are continually emergent. As social bonds and the situations in which people interact change, interpretations of the meaning of these and other relations may change; as interpretations of relations change, these networks of linkages may change as well. On the "Chicago School" of sociology and the tradition of social inquiry derived from John Dewey and George Herbert Mead, see, among other works, Herbert Blumer, *Symbolic Interactionism: Perspective and Method* (New York: Prentice-Hall, 1969); Berenice Fisher and Anselm L. Strauss, "Interactionism," in *A History of Sociological Analysis,* ed. Tom Bottomore and Robert Nisbet (New York: Basic Books, 1978), pp. 457-498; Bernard Meltzer, John W. Petras, and Larry T. Reynolds, *Symbolic Interactionism: Genesis, Varieties, Criticism* (London: Routledge & Kegan Paul, 1975); and David R. Maines, "Social Organization and Social Structure in Symbolic Interactionist Thought," *Annual Review of Sociology* 3 (1977): 235-259. See also, p. 21, n. 37.

3. The bibliography of Florentine studies is vast. The works that are cited in this note are bibliographically comprehensive and are analytically outstanding. On Florentine society, see Gene A. Brucker, *Florentine Politics and Society* (Princeton, N.J.: Princeton University Press, 1962), and *The Civic World of Renaissance Florence* (Princeton, N.J.: Princeton University Press, 1977); Marvin Becker,

Florentine wealth derived in large measure from international banking and the manufacture and export of textiles, and economic power in Florence was directly related to successful investment in those segments of the economy. Correspondingly, the economic elite of the city was made up of bankers and international textile merchants. Although successful ventures made their backers quite wealthy, the size of most firms, as Richard Goldthwaite has reminded historians, was small and the number of firms quite large. Even the greatest Florentine cloth firms controlled no more than 3% of the market.[4] Shopkeepers and artisans producing goods and offering services for local consumption occupied a middle position in the distribution of economic resources. At the bottom of the economic hierarchy were those who worked as skilled and unskilled laborers, most of whom produced textiles. The economy of Florence was in theory, if not in fact, controlled by 21 guilds: the 7 "major" guilds, primarily those of textile merchants, bankers, and the learned professions, and the 14 "minor" guilds, largely comprising crafts producing domestic goods and services. Wage laborers and small entrepreneurial subcontractors such as dyers and comb makers were *sottoposti,* that is, subject to the authority of the guilds but forbidden from forming or joining guilds of their own. According to census information for the year 1427, 17% of Florentine households listing occupation were headed by major guildsmen, 45% of household heads were minor guildsmen, and 38% were *sottoposti.*[5]

Florence in Transition, 2 vols. (Baltimore: Johns Hopkins University Press, 1967-1968). Concerning the Florentine economy, see Richard A. Goldthwaite, *The Building of Renaissance Florence* (Baltimore: Johns Hopkins University Press, 1980). The demographic and household patterns of Renaissance Florence have been charted by David Herlihy and Christiane Klapisch-Zuber, *Les Toscans et leurs familles: une étude du catasto florentin de 1427* (Paris, 1978). For an illuminating study of social networks and patterns of social conflict in Florence, see Samuel Kline Cohn, The Laboring Classes in Renaissance Florence (New York: Academic Press, 1980). Hans Baron's *The Crisis of the Early Italian Renaissance* (Princeton, N.J.: Princeton University Press, 1955) remains the best introduction to republican Florence's civic humanist political culture.

4. Goldthwaite, *Building of Renaissance Florence,* p. 61.

5. These figures were calculated from information given in Herlihy and Klapisch-Zuber, *Les Toscans,* p. 289. The estimates serve as a rough approximation since they exclude 4354 households, 44% of all (9820) households, which failed to list the occupation of the household head. However, the distribution of household wealth for these 44% of households is quite similar to that of the major guildsmen. Close to 50% of households failing to report occupation fell into the highest wealth category (400 or more florins) reported by Herlihy and Klapisch, whereas only 10% of those households reported 0 taxable wealth. Since those households failing to report occupation tended to be households of significant wealth, it is quite probable that the estimate of 17% underrepresents the true proportion of major guildsmen in the population of all households of at least *sottoposti* status or higher. These statistics theoretically include all lay households except for foreigners, a handful of exempt families, servants, and an inestimable floating population of the very poorest inhabitants whose vagrancy made their *Catasto* enumeration virtually impossible. See *ibid.,* pp. 140-164.

The political organization of Florence was based on these 21 guilds, and on the 4 quarters and 16 wards (4 wards in each quarter) into which the city was divided. Members of the guilds filled communal offices, the most important of which were the *tre maggiori,* the three major governing bodies: the Signoria (composed of eight priors and their chairman, the Standard-Bearer of Justice), the Twelve Good Men, and the Sixteen Standard-Bearers of the neighborhood-based militia companies. The nine members of the Signoria were, in effect, the town councilmen of this city, and the Twelve and the Sixteen served as their advisors. The members of the Signoria were drawn by lot every 2 months from a set of pouches that ensured equal representation of each of the 4 quarters of the city and ensured the maintenance of the ratio of major to minor guildsmen that gave major guildsmen, by law, a majority on the council. Below the *tre maggiori* were other councils empowered to give or withhold consent to legislation proposed by the Signoria. In addition to these councils, there existed numerous magistracies and public bodies supervising towns subject to Florentine dominion, the conduct of foreign policy, finances and taxation, public works, the grain supply, the communal prison, and the hiring of troops. Policy, made by citizens who filled these offices for short terms, was regularly implemented and monitored by a large professional bureaucracy staffed by trained notaries.

Two groups of Florentines were excluded from political office: the *sottoposti* and the magnates, who were members of patrician, often feudal, clans regarded as violent, lawless, contemptuous of communal authority, or a threat to the popular government. Although the magnates were excluded from all but a few offices, they were hardly politically powerless. Most magnate clans had intermarried with the wealthiest elements of the mercantile elite. The latter, although *popolano* (members of the guild community, including those patricians who had forsworn violent behavior and agreed to be subject to the commune), shared ties of kinship and common aristocratic outlook with those families declared to be magnates. Thus, the magnates had their own lobby within the office-holding class. During moments of public crisis the Signoria summoned special committees for consultation, *balie,* composed of prominent citizens. These *balie* offered opportunities for political participation that circumvented the antimagnate legislation of 1293, the Ordinances of Justice. The magnates were also eligible for offices in the Parte Guelpha, whose members considered themselves to be the guardians of Florentine Guelph purity. The Parte had the authority to declare suspected Ghibellines ineligible for communal office and became, in the fourteenth century, the political arm of the magnates and wealthy *popolano* families in their war against the new men—the upstart *gente nuova,* who were now wealthy enough to attempt to secure the perquisites long reserved for the most ancient clans. Most magnate families regained their political privileges in 1434 in the aftermath of the Medici revolution.

Many Florentines desired political office because of genuine patriotism, but political office holding was often sought after for less noble reasons: for the stipend that the office carried with it, or the use of that office to attempt to advance the interests of family and friends. For the upwardly mobile, office holding was a sign that a family had "arrived," for office holding was one of the major components of honor in Florence. Competition for status was as intense as competition for any other form of power. Marchionne di Coppo Stefani, a fourteenth-century chronicler, attributed all conflict in Florence to intense competition for the status conferred by public office.[6] High status was accorded to Florentines for other qualities as well, principally for membership in a family of recognized antiquity, or one of great wealth. Florentines gave pride of place to the oldest patrician clans in the city, those families descended from the Tuscan feudal nobility. Many of these families were magnates and thus, despite their high social rank, were excluded from most official forms of political power.

The types of fragmentation and conflict in the Arno republic were numerous. Florentines divided themselves into the *popolo grasso* (fat people, or wealthy) and the *popolo minuto* (thin people, or plebians)—the haves and the have-nots. Questions of communal economic policy, particularly the regulation of supplies and prices of basic commodities, divided the guild community into those who favored particular regulations and those who stood to lose by such regulation, usually members of the particular minor guild affected by the proposed action. Questions of economic policy could, during crises, unite the magnates and the *popolo minuto* against the guildsmen.[7] The governing class—the guild community—was also divided because of the ongoing struggle of the minor guilds to increase their proportion of representatives in high communal offices. The major and minor guildsmen united, however, against threats from outside the guild regime, from the *popolo minuto,* and from the magnates, although the question of magnate disqualification divided the wealthiest guildsmen from their humbler fellows. Individual guilds were divided, too, among the several unrelated trades that might make up one craft association. Ques-

6. Marchionne di Coppo Stefani, *Cronaca fiorentina,* ed. N. Rodolico, in *Rerum Italicarum Scriptores,* new ed. (Città di Castello, 1955) vol. 30, pt. 1, rubric 923, hereafter cited as Stefani.

7. See, for example, Stefani's narration (*ibid,* rubrics 590-591) of the grain riot of 1343, which pitted patricians and the *popolo minuto* against the middle-class guildsmen.

tions of prestige and honor divided magnate and *popolano* clans of great antiquity from upstart *gente nuova* families. Magnates opposed *popolani;* the *sottoposti* opposed guildsmen; poor opposed rich; and those honored opposed those seeking honor. Conflicts over the distribution of economic resources, status, and political office all fragmented the Florentines in varying ways. In addition to the continuously shifting cleavages based on struggles over the distribution of various forms of power, there were other sources of equally intense conflict and alliance. In addition to his class, guild, and status group, the Florentine was a member of more intimate groups: his family and neighborhood.

Thirteenth-century Florence was divided into sixths. Each sixth, *sesto,* was divided in turn into three or four districts, composed of a single large or several small parishes.[8] The population explosion of the thirteenth century affected the periphery of the city somewhat more than it did the center of town. In particular, Oltrarno, the area across the river opposite the older sections of the city, experienced massive immigration from the countryside. By the early 1340s popular agitation made redistricting inevitable, since Oltrarno residents comprised one-third of the population, but, under the system of *sesti,* they were entitled to only one-sixth of the political offices of Florence. So outraged were the inhabitants of this *sesto* that they threatened, in the words of one contemporary, "to cut the bridges and make a city of our own!"[9] Following the expulsion of the tyrant, the duke of Athens,[10] in 1343, the city was repartitioned into 4 quarters and 16 wards (*gonfaloni*).[11] The thirteenth-century *sesti* and their successors, the *gonfaloni,* were the elemental units of political organization. Each unit was responsible for levying taxes and raising a citizen militia. Through a procedure known as the *squittino* (the scrutiny), a secret committee in each ward decided which of their neighbors would be eligible to hold political office.[12] Neighborhoods helped to select those qualified to direct

8. For an enumeration of the 6 *sesti* and 19 wards, see R. Caggese, ed., *Statuti della Repubblica Fiorentina* (Florence: Galesiana, 1910-1921), 1:292-295. On the origins of the *Sesti,* see Stefani, rubric 90, and Guidobaldo Guidi, "Sistemi elettorali del Comune di Firenze nel primo Trecento," *ASI* 130 (1972): 361ff.

9. *La Cronica Domestica di Messer Donato Velluti* (Florence, 1914), p. 165. This story was also narrated by Giovanni Villani, *Cronica,* ed. F. Dragomanni (Florence, 1844-1845), 12, 18.

10. In 1342 the French nobleman Walter of Brienne, known as the duke of Athens because he held, theoretically, the title to a defunct crusader kingdom in Greece, was placed in charge of the Florentine military campaign against Lucca. During a severe political crisis several weeks later, he was made lord of Florence for life. In 1343, having failed to remedy Florence's growing political and economic troubles, Walter of Brienne was expelled from the city.

11. Stefani, rubric 586.

12. Robert Davidsohn, *Storia di Firenze* (Florence, 1956-1968), 5:228; Anthony Molho, *Florentine Public Finances in the Early Renaissance, 1400-1433* (Cambridge, Mass.: Harvard University Press, 1971),

the political order. In the thirteenth and fourteenth centuries, neighborhoods helped to maintain that public order as well. Lay chaplains in each parish acted as informants and agents of the commune.[13]

The thirteenth-century division of Florence extended well beyond the walls of the city. The urban administration of the countryside was based on the internal division of the city, for reasons that had much to do with urban residence and immigration patterns. Florentine immigration took a variety of forms, but thirteenth-century immigrants tended to reside in the urban district closest to their ancestral residence in the countryside.[14] Ease of

---

p. 74ff., and Anthony Molho, "Cosimo de' Medici: *Pater Patriae or Padrino?,*" *Stanford Italian Review* 1 (1979): 22, for details concerning neighborhood tax assessment procedures. Even after the adoption of the *Catasto* in 1427, neighborhoods continued to be responsible to the Florentine exchequer as corporate bodies.

On neighborhood scrutinies, see Nicolai Rubinstein, *The Government of Florence under the Medici, 1434-1494* (Oxford: Clarendon Press, 1966), p. 56, and Demetrio Marzi, *La Cancelleria della Repubblica Fiorentina* (Rocca San Casciano, 1910), *passim.*

Villani, *Cronica,* 12, 17, provides one example of neighborhood military organization in his description of the manner in which the Florentines organized in 1343 to expel the duke of Athens:

> Tutti i cittadini furono armati ciascuno a cavallo e a piedi, e ciascuno alla sua contrada e vicinanza traeva, traendo fuori bandiere dell'armi del popolo e del comune . . . E di presente fu sbarrata la città a ogni capo di via e di contrade. Quegli del sesto d'oltrarno grandi popolani si giurarono insieme e si baciarono in bocca.

A description of one *gonfalone,* Leon d'Oro, home of the Medici family, has been written by Carla Sodini, *Il Gonfalone del Leon d'Oro nel quartiere di S. Giovanni a Firenze* (Florence: CLUSF, 1979). A survey of *gonfaloni* political responsibilities is found in Dale Kent, *The Rise of the Medici: Faction in Florence, 1426-1434* (Oxford: Oxford University Press, 1978), pp. 61-63.

13. Davidsohn, *Storia di Firenze,* 5:276.

14. Claudio Greppi and Marco Massa, "Città e territorio nella Repubblica fiorentina," in *Un' altra Firenze: L'Epoca di Cosimo il Vecchio: Riscontri tra culture e società nella storia fiorentina* (Florence: Vallecchi, 1971), pp. 32-34, 39. On the general characteristics of Florentine immigrants, see J. Plesner, *L'emigration de la campagne a la ville libre de Florence au XIII siècle* (Copenhagen, 1934); and Charles M. de La Roncière, *Florence: Centre Economique Regional au XIVe siècle* (Aix-en-Provence, 1977), p. 670, 682.

The terms *city* and *countryside* are somewhat misleading. The "rural" regions of Tuscany were themselves urbanized. Immigration in northern Italy customarily took the form of chain migration, wherein individuals and families emigrated from rural settlements, moved to small towns, and finally moved to large cities such as Florence or Siena.

The thirteenth-and-fourteenth-centuries pattern of emigration from neighboring towns, according to Cohn (*Laboring Classes,* chap. 4) did not extend into the fifteenth century. Cohn argues that Medicean Florence drew immigrants from places much farther removed from Tuscany, primarily from Germany. This did not, however, result in a less neighborhood-centered immigration. The Germans, culturally distinct from the Italian population, found it harder to assimilate into the larger community than had thirteenth-century Italian immigrants. The choice of residence for a German new to Florence was no more random than the choices made by earlier generations of Italian immigrants into the city. Although the similarity is not mentioned, from the evidence that Cohn presents, it appears that fifteenth-century German immigrants formed two distinct communities in a manner analogous to those communities formed by former residents of Tuscan villages who clustered together in their own Florentine neighborhoods.

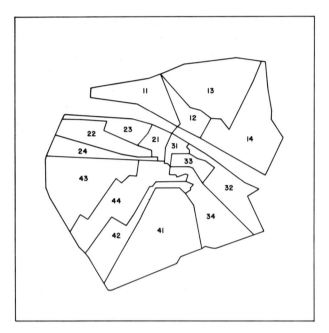

Figure 1.1. The four quarters of Florence divided into *gonfalones,* or wards. *Santa Spirito:* 11, Scala; 12, Nicchio; 13, Ferza; 14, Drago Verde; *Santa Maria Novella:* 31, Vipera; 32, Unicorno; 33, Leon Rosso; 34, Leon Bianco; *Santa Croce:* 21, Carro; 22, Bue; 23, Leon Nero; 24, Ruote; *San Giovanni:* 41, Leon Doro; 42, Drago San Giovanni; 43, Chiavi; 44, Vaio. (Map designed by the author from street confines described in *L' Illustratore Fiorentino, Calendario Storico per L'Anno 1909,* compiled by Guido Carocci [Florence, 1908], pp. 82-89.)

access to rural holdings was extremely important, especially to recent immigrants, who had strong emotional, social, and economic ties to rural Tuscany. Furthermore, since access to housing and employment was relatively difficult to obtain, one's choice of residence in the city was determined largely by one's preexisting friendship or kinship ties with those who were already residing in the city. For these reasons, urban residence patterns tended to duplicate residence patterns in the *contado.* City neighbors were commonly country neighbors as well. Much of the pattern of residence in the city thus reflects geographical and personal bonds of friendship and kinship, and even informal patronage, since northern Italian feudal nobles emigrating from the countryside frequently brought client families with them.[15] In Florence, and many another Italian city,[16] neighborhoods

15. A. Gaudenzi, "Gli statuti della società delle armi del popolo di Bologna," *Bullettino istituto stor. it.* 13 (1893): 27.

16. On the neighborhood organization of other Tuscan cities (Siena, Lucca, San Gimignano), see

and quarters resembled cities in miniature, each with its own local services, resources and solidarities. Certain crafts, to be sure, had a geographic bias; wool washers and dyers, for example, required proximity to the Arno River. But such clustering of trades was not the norm. Alfred Doren, historian of Florentine guilds, described Florence on the eve of the passage of the Ordinances of Justice in 1293 as a fragmented community in which guildsmen plying the same trade maintained far less contact with one another than with their neighbors and fellow parishioners plying different trades.[17] The patriciate did not congregate in a particular section, but resided throughout the city, as Bendetto Dei, a fifteenth-century chronicler, attests in detail.

The 50 *piazze* of Florence provided much of the structure of social life. Dei informs us that each of these *piazze* (those formally named) had "a church, and surrounding the *piazza* are the palaces and houses of the principal citizens of the regime, and the *piazze* are full of merchants and shops."[18] In a later section of the same work, Dei lists the patriciate of the city *piazza* by *piazza*.[19] In describing the richness of the city, he provides a glimpse of the self-sufficiency of its quarters. Speaking of his own quarter, Santo Spirito, which was traditionally viewed as a "poor" quarter, Dei relates that this one quarter alone had many patricians, as well as "many gardens, orchards, churches, monasteries, hospitals, *piazze,* and artisans of every craft." His listing of these crafts, craftsmen, and places of business

---

Davidsohn, *Storia di Firenze,* 5:277. For Genoa, see Diane Owen Hughes, "Kinsmen and Neighbors in Medieval Genoa," in *The Medieval City,* ed. Harry A. Miskimin *et al.* (New Haven: Yale University Press, 1977), pp. 95-111; and Eduardo Grendi, "Profilo storico degli alberghi genovesi," *MEFRM* (1975): 241-291.

A brief but suggestive treatment of the ubiquity of neighborhood social organization in Renaissance cities and of the quality of neighborhood life is found in Lauro Martines, *Power and Imagination: City-States in Renaissance Italy* (New York: Alfred A. Knopf, 1979), pp. 34-41, 74-78.

17. A. Doren, *Le arti fiorentine,* trans. G. B. Klein, 2 vols. (Florence: Le Monnier, 1940), 1:49-50.

18. Benedetto Dei, *Cronaca fiorentina,* in *Descrizioni e rappresentazioni della città di Firenze nel XV secolo,* ed. Giuseppina Carla Romby (Florence: Libreria Editrice Fiorentina, 1976). pp. 44-45:

Florentia bella à 50 piaze drento alla città nominate e in sun ogni piaza v'è cchiese ed evvi palazzi e chase d'intornno intornna de principali cittadini de reggimento e piene di merchanti e di botege al bisognio prima Piaza dela Signoria e Piaza di Merchato Nuovo e Piaza di S. Giovanni e Piaza di Santo Spirito e Piaza di Santa Chrocie e Piaza del Papa e Piazza Vecchia di Santa Maria Novella e Piaza di San Marcho e Piazza di Santa Maria Nuova e Piazza degli 'nocienti e Piaza de' Bischeri e Piaza del Charmino e Piaza di Sanfilicie e Piazza di San Pier Magiore e Piaza di Santa Filicità e Piaza de Mozzi e Piazza d'Ogni Ssanti e Piaza del Prato e Piaza di Merchato Vecchio e Piazza di Sa' Lorenzo e Piaza di Pitti e Piaza del Grano e Piaza de Castellani, Piaza degli Ablertti Piazza da Tornabuoni e Boni Piaza de Tornaquinci Piaza degli Strozi Piazza degli Agli Piaza di Madonna Piaza di San Simone Piaza de Peruzi Piaza di Santa Trinita Piazza di Sa' Romeo Piaza di San Pulinari Piaza d'Arnno Piazza de Vechietti Piaza de Freschobaldi Piazza di San Friano Piaza di Santo Nofri Piaza di Chamaldoli e altre Piaze di ch' 'i non fo menzione.

19. Benedetto Dei, *Memorie Notate,* in *Descrizioni di Firenze,* ed. Romby, pp. 56-57.

includes 40 wool shops, 30 shoemakers and barbers, apothecaries, cattle butchers, pork butchers, carpenters, 25 bakeries, kiln operators, fruit and vegetable dealers, bottle makers, corn merchants, straw sellers, haber-dashers, clog makers, textile washers, wool shearers, comb makers, secondhand-cloth dealers, artists, weavers of silk, wool, and linen, taverns, and a bordello.[20]

Other evidence corroborates the fragmentation of Florence into multiple communities. The jurisdictions of the Florentine judicial system followed the lines of the four quarters of the city, with separate courts being located in each quarter. Matriculation lists of most Florentine guilds were divided into quarters or districts, indicating a wide dispersion of members of the same trade throughout the city.[21] The distribution of major occupational groups in the city suggests the lack of economic specialization of the quarters of Florence. As Table 1.1, based on a 10% sample of household heads listed in the 1480 census and tax listing (the *Catasto*) indicates, each of the four quarters of Florence had its local shopkeepers, its major guildsmen, its members of the building trades, and its *sottoposti* wool workers. The spatial distribution of the *popolo minuto* within each quarter did change over the course of the fifteenth century, as they left the central city area, and came to be relatively segregated in the peripheral parishes of the city.[22] These figures may hide increasing social segregation between center and periphery, but this did not disturb the balance of goods and services available within each quarter, since each quarter extended from the center to the periphery.

F. William Kent's study of Florentine households, based on the examina-tion of 194 domestic groups belonging to three fifteenth-century lineages, reveals the tenacious survival of the extended patrician family, and familial neighborhood ties, well into the sixteenth century. Family houses clustered together in the same parish, or in contiguous ones, and even family dead enjoyed neighborhood ties, buried together in family chapels. In 1427 five-sixths of households belonging to the Ginori clan lived on borgo San

20. Dei, *Cronaca fiorentina*, pp. 52-53:

Somma delle somme el sopradetto quartiere di S. Spirito a 27 contrade e vie abitate e casate da ogni lato le qua sono a numero bracia 33 che vengono miglia undici vel circa a miglia tremila per miglia e da molti giardini e orti e chiese e munisteri e spedali e piazze e artieri d'ogni arte al dirimpetto e nominatamente ed a in detto quartiere 144 casati veduti. . . . 40 botteghe d'arte di lana e 30 calzolai e barbieri e speziali e beccai e legnaiuoli e pizicagnoli e 25 fornai e fornatori e fornaciai e trechoni e frabottai e zocholai e biadaiuoli e pagliauoli e purgatori e cimatori e fasteaioli e merciai e rigattieri e stufa e bordello e scuola a petinagnoli e dipintori e tessitori di drappi di seta e di lana e di lino e taverne.

21. On guild matriculation lists, see Doren, *Le arti fiorentine*, 1:20, 163, n. 1.
22. For the social geography of the *popolo minuto*, see Cohn, *Laboring Classes*, chap. 5.

Table 1.1
Distribution of Occupations by Quarter[a]

Quarter	Textile workers	Local trades	Artists, masons	Major merchants	Total
		Observed values			
Santo Spirito	27	19	5	22	73
Santa Croce	11	7	5	19	42
Santa Maria Novella	14	9	5	14	42
San Giovanni	32	32	12	31	107
Total	84	67	27	86	264
		Row percentages			
Santo Spirito	37	26	7	30	100
Santa Croce	26	17	12	45	100
Santa Maria Novella	33	21	12	33	99
San Giovanni	30	30	11	29	100
Total	32	25	10	33	100
		Column percentages			
Santo Spirito	32	28	19	26	28
Santa Croce	13	10	19	22	16
Santa Maria Novella	17	13	19	16	16
San Giovanni	38	48	44	36	41
Total	100	99	101	100	101

[a] Chi-square = 7.36 with 9 degrees of freedom; $.80 < p < .70$.

Lorenzo. One century later, in 1534, 8 of the 15 households of this lineage continued to live on the same street, and three other households remained in the same parish. The Rucellai, virtually all of whose 23 households lived in 1427 on the via della Vigna Nuova in the parish of San Pancrazio, continued this residential pattern one century later. Two-thirds of the 37 Rucellai households in 1534 continued to reside in the same *gonfalone*. Of these, 16 households resided in the traditional parish, and the remainder of those in the *gonfalone* resided in adjacent parishes. The Capponi families continued, throughout the century studied by Kent, to reside almost exclusively in the quarter of Santo Spirito. And the households of two of these three lineages retained, from the fifteenth through the sixteenth century, strong ancestral ties to the same countryside locales as other members of their families.[23]

23. Francis William Kent, *Household and Lineage in Renaissance Florence: The Family Life of the*

Samuel Cohn's study of Florentine marriage patterns reveals the centrality of parish neighborhood ties for all social classes in the fourteenth century, although, in the fifteenth century, the number of patricians selecting spouses from their own parishes decreased, whereas the parish marriages of the lower classes increased sharply. The marriage networks of fifteenth-century patricians may have become less parish centered, but this does not necessarily indicate that the importance of neighborhood ties to the patriciate had diminished.[24] The neighborhoods, with their social mélange of occupations and classes, continued to provide the Florentine patriciate with political power bases. Dale Kent has identified the several hundred families belonging to the patrician regime of the early fifteenth century. Having examined the electoral districts in which they qualified for office, she concluded that most patrician officeholders who came from the same family came from the same district. Only a small minority of members of the same family qualified in different districts, and in almost all of these cases, the different districts were located in the same quarter of the city.[25]

Although a general study of economic networks has not yet been under-

---

Capponi, Ginori and Rucellai (Princeton, N.J.: Princeton University Press, 1977), pp. 29, 227-238. He suggests that even the existence of numerous single-person households does not constitute evidence for much social isolation. These households, he demonstrates, lived near kinsmen in the same ancestral neighborhood (pp. 29, 231). One can extend Kent's argument further. If family units, of whatever size, remained for generations within the same neighborhood, then single-family households, like other types of households, enjoyed long-lasting relationships with neighbors, further diminishing the isolation of the single-person household.

For a contrasting view of the Florentine family, see Richard Goldthwaite, *Private Wealth in Renaissance Florence* (Princeton, N.J.: Princeton University Press, 1968).

24. Cohn (*Laboring Classes,* chap. 5) suggests, based on marriage patterns, that the social networks of rich and poor both changed between the late fourteenth and the end of the fifteenth centuries. It should be remembered that marriage networks are only one dimension of social networks. A social network may include, among other kinds of relations, ties based on membership in families of birth, ties of friendship, ties based on the workplace, and ties formed around certain ritual or social functions such as godparenthood. Each type of social relationship can be viewed as potentially offering a different strategy for expanding or altering social networks, and each of these types of relations did not necessarily carry the same meaning or rationale. The Florentine marriage was linked to a very specific age interval. Thus, although examination of marriage patterns provides important information about the nature of social networks, marriage relations may be descriptive of only one class of strategies used during a limited phase of the life cycle.

The examination of different types of social ties may reveal different patterns of linkage. These together make up a complete social network. See Christiane Klapisch, " 'Parenti, amici e vicini,': il territorio urbano d'una famiglia mercantile del XV secolo," *Quaderni Storici* 33 (1976): 953-982.

25. Dale Kent, "The Florentine *Reggimento,*" *Renaissance Quarterly* 28 (1975): 592. On the control of neighborhood scrutinies by a few powerful families in each ward, see Rubinstein, *Government of Florence under the Medici,* pp. 63-64.

taken, the combined research of Dale Kent and William Kent strongly suggests that business partnerships were normally formed within a common neighborhood or domestic circle.[26] In 1427 Antonio di Ser Schiatta Macci enumerated for *Catasto* officials the components of his sizable fortune of 9036 florins.[27] In addition to his substantial holdings in the countryside, Antonio Macci owned 2 houses, 11 shops, and 6 additional parcels of property that included a *loggia* and several groups of cellar storerooms and stalls. All of these properties were located in the parish of San Bartolo. Each and every one of these wool *botteghe,* storerooms, and wine shops belonged to a cluster of properties on or leading into the corso Adimari or bordered this street, next to the Macci inn and family courtyard, which formed a family enclave. Antonio was not the sole owner of this property. Much of it was owned in common with two of his immediate neighbors: his kinswoman Bandecca di Giovanni Macci and Nicola di Messer Vieri de' Medici. His debt relations reveal the complexity of his kinship and neighborhood ties. Antonio's renters frequently rented more than one property from him and often resided in these properties. His renters appeared in his list of debtors, frequently owing Antonio sums that bear little relation to their annual rent. His largest debtors were his son-in-law, Neri di Ser Viviano Franchi, whom he had loaned 105 florins, a nephew, whom he loaned 27 florins, and other nephews whom he loaned 150 florins, a debt that Antonio was forced to write off as uncollectable. Virtually all of his important urban economic relations, as revealed in his tax declaration, centered around the Macci family enclave in the parish of San Bartolo and the alleys immediately bordering Antonio's own house.

A pattern of neighborhood clustering similar to that found by Dale Kent is revealed in the social geography of Florentine family names. The results of an examination of a 10% sample of households registered in the 1480 Florentine census (*Catasto*) reveal extensive clustering of households sharing the same name within the same *gonfalone*. Whereas registration is not equivalent to actual residence, since not all households registered in their district of current residence, it does, at least, indicate a certain degree of family interest (economic, social, or political) in the affairs of that district.

In this sample, 61 distinct family names appear more than once. These clan names yield 143 pairs of households. Table 1.2 presents the results of pairing each household sharing a name with every other household sharing that name. This allows a comparison of the residence patterns of all families

26. Kent, *Household and Lineage,* p. 293; Kent, *Rise of the Medici,* pp. 191-192.
27. Archivio di Stato, Florence (hereafter cited as ASF), *Catasto,* 81, fol. 1r.

Table 1.2

Clustering of Florentine Families by *Gonfaloni*

Gonfalone	Pairs within same gonfalone		Pairs within quarter, contiguous gonfaloni		Pairs of different quarters, contiguous gonfaloni		Pairs of different quarters, non-contiguous gonfaloni		Total	
	N	%	N	%	N	%	N	%	N	%
			Membership of family group pairs by registration gonfalone							
11	8	61.5	0	.0	1	7.7	4	30.8	13	100.0
12	42	82.4	9	17.6	0	.0	0	.0	51	100.0
13	4	26.7	4	26.7	0	.0	7	46.6	15	100.0
14	10	58.8	5	29.4	0	.0	2	11.8	17	100.0
21	0	.0	0	.0	2	28.6	5	71.4	7	100.0
22	2	40.0	1	20.0	0	.0	2	40.0	5	100.0
23	16	80.0	0	.0	0	.0	4	20.0	20	100.0
24	22	76.0	1	3.4	1	3.4	5	17.2	29	100.0
31	24	75.0	1	3.1	5	15.6	2	6.3	32	100.0
32	12	54.6	3	13.6	0	.0	7	31.8	22	100.0
33	10	58.8	1	5.9	0	.0	6	35.3	17	100.0
34	6	66.7	3	33.3	0	.0	0	.0	9	100.0
41	8	72.7	3	27.3	0	.0	0	.0	11	100.0
42	2	16.7	4	33.3	0	.0	6	50.0	12	100.0
43	4	50.0	0	.0	1	12.5	3	37.5	8	100.0
44	8	44.4	1	5.6	6	33.3	3	16.7	18	100.0
Total	178	62.2	36	12.6	16	5.6	56	19.6	286	100.0

14

11	8	61.5	8	61.5	9	69.2	4	30.8	13	100.0
12	42	82.4	51	100.0	51	100.0	0	.0	51	100.0
13	4	26.7	8	53.4	8	53.4	7	46.6	15	100.0
14	10	58.8	15	88.2	15	88.2	2	11.8	17	100.0
21	0	.0	0	.0	2	28.6	5	71.4	7	100.0
22	2	40.0	3	60.0	3	60.0	2	40.0	5	100.0
23	16	80.0	16	80.0	16	80.0	4	20.0	20	100.0
24	22	76.0	23	79.4	24	82.8	5	17.2	29	100.0
31	24	75.0	25	78.1	30	93.7	2	6.3	32	100.0
32	12	54.6	15	68.2	15	68.2	7	31.8	22	100.0
33	10	58.8	11	64.7	11	64.7	6	35.3	17	100.0
34	6	66.7	9	100.0	9	100.0	0	.0	9	100.0
41	8	72.7	11	100.0	11	100.0	0	.0	11	100.0
42	2	16.7	6	50.0	6	50.0	6	50.0	12	100.0
43	4	50.0	4	50.0	5	62.5	3	37.5	8	100.0
44	8	44.4	9	50.0	15	83.3	3	16.7	18	100.0
Total	178	62.2	214	74.8	240	80.4	56	19.6	286	100.0

sharing the same family name to be made in order to determine the extent to which kinsmen clustered in the same area of the city. The last column in the table provides the number of pairs of households at least one of which resided in the particular *gonfalone* described in that row of the table. The other columns of the table classify that pair by the residence of the second member of the pairing. (In order to allow the *gonfalone* of each member of the pair to serve as the basis of comparison, each pair is counted twice, but this does not affect the percentages given in this table.) Of all pairs of households sharing the same name, 62% were registered in the same *gonfalone*. An additional 13% were registered in *gonfaloni* in the same quarter of the city—*gonfaloni* that were contiguous to the *gonfalone* of most frequent registration for that family. Another 6% were registered in adjoining *gonfaloni* belonging to different quarters of the city. Only 19% of all possible pairs of households sharing the same name were registered in *gonfaloni* that did not share a common border. Even if one allows, as one certainly must, for the approximate nature of these statistics—since the sharing of a common name is not proof of kinship, nor is registration necessarily residence—the concentration of related lineages within *gonfaloni* and quarters, even in the late fifteenth century, appears to have been substantial.

Table 1.3 disaggregates family clustering by comparing the relative extent of clustering of household pairs (sharing the same name) that were relatively wealthy and relatively poor. Did poor households tend to cluster with greater or lesser frequency than rich households? As the average wealth of the pair of households increased, the tendency to cluster in the same neighborhood increased slightly, from 74% clustering in the same ward or a neighboring one to 87% clustering for the wealthiest families. These differences are, however, statistically insignificant and suggest that neighborhood ties were only slightly weaker among poorer Florentine families (although the presence of a family name indicates that poverty, in the context of this data, is middle-class poverty.)

Let us turn to the family of Matteo Corsini, a late fourteenth-century wool merchant, for an illustration of the system of Florentine social relations in action. The choice of godparents has long been recognized as one important indicator of the range and type of important social contacts. Of the 34 godparents that Matteo Corsini chose for his children, 32 can be identified by parish.[28] Of these, 4 were neighbors of the Corsini family in

---

28. Armando Petrucci, ed., *Il libro di ricordanze dei Corsini* (1362-1457) (Rome: Istituto Storico per il Medio Evo, 1965), pp. 1-95. Similarly, the godparents of Giovanni di Pagolo Morelli were all from his father's parish. See Giovanni di Pagolo Morelli, *Ricordi* (Florence: Felice Le Monnier, 1969),

Table 1.3
Clustering of Households by Relative Wealth[a]

District	Mean wealth of household pairs											
	0-200		201-400		401-600		601-1000		1001-8000		Total	
	N	%	N	%	N	%	N	%	N	%	N	%
Identical and/or contiguous	14	74.0	25	78.0	23	79.0	26	81.0	27	87.0	115	80.0
Noncontiguous	5	26.0	7	22.0	6	21.0	6	19.0	4	13.0	28	20.0
Total	19	100.0	32	100.0	29	100.0	32	100.0	31	100.0	143	100.0

[a] Chi-square = 1.27 with 4 degrees of freedom; not significant at .95.

the Florentine countryside. Of the remaining 28 urban godparents, 4 were
clerics: 2 residing in Matteo's quarter and 2 residing elsewhere. The priest
in traditional, closely knit parish communities had access to most parish
gossip networks. Little could be hidden from him, and, in such a gossip-
ridden community, the priest was suspect as a source of gossip. It was not
unusual, therefore, for parishioners to develop ties with clerics removed
from the parishioner's neighborhood network. Confession to such extra-
parish clergymen was especially popular at Easter.

Of the remaining 24 lay godparents residing in the city, 17 came from
Matteo's own parish, San Felice in Piazza, and 5 came from two contiguous
parishes, both within his quarter of the city, bordering his own *gonfalone*.
Of the remaining 2 godparents to the Corsini children, 1 lived in a parish
directly across the river from Matteo's neighborhood.

The Corsini godparents were almost always connected to Matteo's family through multiple ties. Lorenzo Belotti, like several other godparents, was
Matteo's neighbor in the countryside, as well as in the city. Agnola Bonagi,
a neighbor, was the daughter of a business partner. Bartolo Segnorini,
another neighbor, served as Matteo's notary for 33 years. Simone Barone,
also a neighbor, residing in a contiguous parish within Matteo's *gonfalone,*
a godparent twice, was Matteo's relation by marriage. Miliano di Bartolo
Salvini, a neighbor and a fellow guildsman, served as an occasional witness
to Matteo's notarial acts. Giovanozzo Biliotti, stationer and neighbor, served
as godparent to Matteo's son Giovanni in 1376; from 1377 onward he
became Matteo's principal supplier of stationery goods. Other godparents
are kin or affines, poor neighborhood widows, or wives of neighborhood
tradesmen. Their common neighborhood tie and their joint appearance in
Corsini account books suggest that many of the Corsini godparents were
familiars of each other as well. In almost every instance of a choice of a lay
godparent, that is, in 22 out of 24 cases (or, counting rural *compari,* in 26 out
of 28 instances), Matteo chose a neighbor, a neighbor who was also a
kinsman, a business partner, a guild colleague, or an artisan or tradesman
whom he patronized. Matteo's important social contacts, at least judging
by those he chose to be godparents, rarely extended beyond his urban

p. 195. Christiane Klapisch has written on the social world of godparents in Florence: in
"'Parenti, amici e Vicini.'"

On ritual kinship more generally, see Sydney W. Mintz and Eric Wolf, "An Analysis of Ritual
Co-parenthood (Compadrazgo)," *Southwestern Journal of Anthropology* 6 (1950): 341-368; George M.
Foster, "Cofradia and Compadrazgo in Spain and Spanish America," *Southwestern Journal of Anthropology* 9 (1953):1-28; Julian Pitt-Rivers, "Ritual Kinship in the Mediterranean: Spain and the Balkans,"
in *Mediterranean Family Structure,* ed. J.-G. Peristiany (Cambridge: Cambridge University Press, 1976).

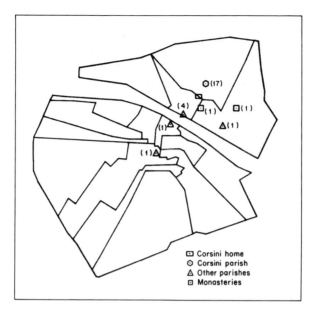

Figure 1.2. Parishes or residence of Corsini godparents. Number of godparents within parish is given in parentheses.

neighborhood, but within this restricted circle there was a considerable occupational and social range, extending throughout the social spectrum, from poor widows and wives of artisans to men of Matteo's own considerable social rank. (See Figure 1.2.)

The Florentine's sense of neighborhood varied according to his class, his status, and his sense of the utility of local bonds in the attainment of specific objectives. For members of the political class, the secular geographical divisions of the city had significant meaning. The *gonfalone* and quarter were, for this group, structures that defined obligation (being units of military assembly and taxation) and were structures of opportunity as well, since one qualified therein for office. It is not surprising, therefore, that chains of political patronage, as the Kents have revealed, operated through the quarters and *gonfaloni* of the city. Thus, for this class, the *gonfalone* and the quarter were meaningful units of ceremonial action at times of public political ritual. On the vigil of the feast day of John the Baptist, when the city was ceremonially subdivided, every member of the guild community marched in procession, each according to the *gonfalone* in which he lived.

For the artisans, local shopkeepers, and *sottoposti* of Florence, smaller units such as the parishes, dominated by *piazze,* those theaters of festive assembly and casual exchange, offered a day-to-day sense of identity and community. It was in their neighborhoods, the parishes of Sant' Ambrogio, San Paolo, San Niccolò, San Giorgio, and San Frediano, and the district of Belletri, that members of the working class organized rebellion and revolt in the late fourteenth century.[29] In the fourteenth century, and increasingly so in the fifteenth and sixteenth centuries, these same neighborhoods served as the focuses of working-class festive and religious activity. Although the parish was a basic unit of social life, the parish church was less so. The Florentine was more apt to attend mass at one of the major mendicant churches of the quarter. The parish clergy, often drawn from the ranks of the moderately prosperous, directed abuse, and at times physical violence at the poor. For this, according to the chronicler Stefani, the parish clergy were bitterly resented by the Florentine working class.[30]

Documentation is scant, but it appears that the festive life of humble Florentines was organized at the neighborhood level. In 1283, for the feast of San Giovanni, each of the six *sesti* of the city formed a festive brigade, like that of the Brigata Amorosa formed in Oltrarno. On the occasion of each major holiday during the next 2 years these brigades sponsored neighborhood dances and games.[31] Combat between rival neighborhood brigades was revived in 1304 in an attempt to pacify a citizenry torn by civil war.[32] In 1343 one again discovers six festive brigades, these formed by the duke of Athens for the celebration of the feast of San Giovanni. The brigades of 1343 were located in the neighborhoods of Sant' Ambrogio (the Grand Monarchy of the Red City); San Giorgio; the Canto alle Macine, near Ognissanti and Belletri; San Paolo; San Frediano; and Monteloro, near the via del Cocomero and the via Larga.[33] During the second half of the fifteenth century festive brigades appeared again in the entries of Florentine chronicles. Several of these brigades were located in neighborhoods identical to those mentioned in 1343: the Grand Monarchy of the Red City, in Sant' Ambrogio; the brigade (*potenza*) called Monteloro on the via Larga, and the *potenza* identified with the Canto alle Macine, the Millstone (*Macine*, 'millstones').[34] The repeated mention of these same

---

29. Stefani, rubric 804.

30. *Ibid.*, rubric 616. One of the first acts of the popular regime that came to power in 1343 following the expulsion of the duke of Athens was the passage of legislation that severely punished any member of the clergy who beat or abused laymen. This legislation, according to Stefani, was directed at the parish clergy, at the instigation of the lower and middle classes.

31. *Ibid.*, rubric 160.

32. Villani, *Cronaca*, 8, 70.

33. *Ibid.*, 12, 8; Stefani, rubric 575.

34. On the *potenze* (festive brigades) of the late fifteenth and sixteenth centuries, see Richard Trexler, *Public Life in Renaissance Florence* (New York: Academic Press, 1980), p. 400ff. Trexler disputes

neighborhoods as centers of festive life 'in 1343, of rebellion four decades later, and of festive activity in the fifteenth century suggests a continuity of working-class activity, if not necessarily in institutionalized form, in several of the parishes of the city.

The foregoing discussion of Florentine social topography suggests the following pattern of network bonding in the Arno city.[35] Neighborhoods, however perceived, provided most goods and services required in daily life. To acquire basic necessities, emotional as well as economic, one was rarely required to leave one's parish, *gonfalone*, or quarter of the city. Social networks were therefore dense; that is, they were concentrated within a restricted geographical area—the neighborhood, loosely defined—and so the citizen's contacts shared a great degree of intimacy with each other as well.[36] Little distinction was made in Florence between working and living space. Shops, modest homes, workrooms, and palaces all clustered together, horizontally and vertically. One's working community, social neighborhood, and ancestral district were likely to occupy the same geographical space. Social bonds were not only dense but also multifaceted. The social roles[37] of customer, partner, competitor, kinsman, neighbor, and

---

any continuity between the organizations of 1343 and those of the fifteenth century, despite the appearance in both centuries of several *potenze* bearing the same names in the same locations. One of these *potenze,* Monteloro, identified by Trexler (*ibid.,* p. 409) as having incorporated in 1471, was founded in 1320, according to its statutes of 1578, although this has not been confirmed. See ASF, Compagnie Religiose Soppresse, *Capitoli* (hereafter cited as *Capitoli*), 811.

35. On social networks, see J. Clyde Mitchell, ed., *Social Networks in Urban Situations* (Manchester: Manchester University Press, 1969); Jeremy Boissevain and J. Clyde Mitchell, eds., *Network Analysis: Studies in Human Interaction* (The Hague: Mouton and Co., 1973); Jeremy Boissevain, *Friends of Friends: Networks, Manipulators, and Coalitions* (Oxford: Blackwell, 1974); Claude S. Fischer *et al., Networks and Places: Social Relations in the Urban Setting* (New York: Free Press, 1977); Samuel Leinhardt, ed., *Social Networks: A Developing Paradigm* (New York: Academic Press, 1977); Elihu Gerson, "Commitment Management and Urban Morphology" (Paper presented at the Annual Meeting of the American Sociological Association, Montreal, August 1974), and "Social Objects and Social Boundaries" (MS).

36. For a different interpretation of Florentine social geography, see Trexler, *Public Life,* pp. 12-14. In contrast to the views of F. W. Kent, D. Kent, A. Molho, G. Brucker, S. Cohn, and myself, Trexler minimizes the importance of neighborhood ties and loyalties, claiming that the Florentine ultimately considered himself a member of only two groups: his family and the city of Florence. I would emphasize that the evidence drawn from the selection of marriage partners and godparents, as well as the nature of political solidarities, indicate the very real and living importance of neighborhood ties and loyalties for the Florentine. The Florentine commune certainly recognized the magnitude of neighborhood loyalties. One might mention the *Lex Contra Scandalosa,* passed in 1419, which singled out four sources of equally dangerous factional allegiance: kinship, neighborhood, patronage, and party. C. Guasti, ed., *Commissioni di Rinaldo degli Albizzi per il Commune di Firenze* (Florence, 1867-1873), 3:170-172.

37. The use of the term *role* in this book differs from that in use by structuralist-functionalist sociology. By *role* I mean the cluster of perceptions and expectations given to a social relationship.

friend frequently overlapped. The social geography of the city gave the Florentine two worlds: the world of family and neighborhood, with its dense, overlapping social ties, and a larger, not infrequently hostile, world—the rest of the city. Even the wealthiest families avoided moving into new districts, for they found that when they did, it could take many years to become fully integrated into a new neighborhood network.[38]

Three elements are central to our understanding of Florentine economic organization. First, as I have suggested, Florentine neighborhoods were commercially and socially heterogeneous. Each had its rich and poor, its own local markets, and a variety of occupations that served local needs. Second, the late medieval-Renaissance city lacked the impersonal means of communication characteristic of the modern industrial economy. News of work and investment opportunities, properties available for sale or rent, sources of credit, foreign commodity prices and market conditions—all of this vital information was not available on a uniform basis of mass distribution and access. Finally, entrepreneurs needed to integrate and coordinate their diverse activities. The various crafts engaged in particular processes of textile manufacture required interlinkage by their practitioners. The wool industry, for example, producing exportable finished cloth, employed one-third of the labor force of the city, scattered in every quarter, to execute over 30 separate stages of wool manufacture. Certain interlinkages, especially at the beginning of the process, that is, the sorting and distribution of raw material, were performed by bonded agents (*sensali*) of the guilds. Most processes, however, were left to the direction of personal networks of subcontractors, factors, and agents of individual wool exporters, as were less formal procedures, such as the extension of credit and the loan of working capital. Finally, firms within the city needed to maintain contact with associates in international markets scattered throughout the known world.

In such a fragmented world, who provided the requisite links? This was the province of the patron, whose role is so closely identified with Florentine

---

Those expectations are created by the parties to that social relationship, and by those who observe that relationship. I do not mean a fixed, predefined "slot" that predates and postdates the life of the relationship. Roles are not "slots" in the social order; they are interpretations of recurring kinds of relations, defined by those who participate in them. Roles emerge, are transformed, and cease to exist during the process of social interaction. For criticism of functionalist role theory, a theory of society that views the social order as consisting in a number of predefined roles, see Aaron V. Cicourel, *Cognitive Sociology: Language and Meaning in Social Interaction* (New York: Free Press, 1974), chap. 1.

38. Kent, *Rise of the Medici*, p. 64.

Renaissance culture. In traditional societies such as Florence the patron operated as a broker or middleman inhabiting the interstices of social systems.[39] Patrons provided clients with access to personal networks of neighbors, friends, and families. They activated third-party contacts and provided services and information for those whose access was otherwise limited. Patrons supplied clients emigrating from the countryside with housing and jobs in the city through their own network of friends and kinsmen. More powerful patrons were those whose contacts and investments permeated the entire city. The most powerful political patrons in fifteenth-century Florence, the Medici, had a useful range of contacts and, therefore, a range of favors to bestow that extended not only all over Florence and Tuscany but also throughout the Mediterranean world.[40]

A fourteenth-century Florentine, Paolo da Certaldo, advised his sons that a merchant traveling in a foreign territory needed to secure the friendship of the powerful of that region.[41] This provided protection and, in

---

39. On patronage in general, see Boissevain, *Friends of Friends, passim,* and his "Patronage in Sicily," *Man* 1 (1966): 18-33; Arnold Strickson and Sidney M. Greenfield, "The Analysis of Patron-Client Relationships: An Introduction," in *Structure and Process in Latin America: Patronage, Clientage, and Power Systems,* ed. Strickson and Greenfield (Albuquerque: University of New Mexico, 1972), pp. 1-17 (included in this volume is an excellent bibliography of recent anthropological analyses of patronage); and J. Campbell, *Honor, Family and Patronage* (Oxford: Clarendon Press, 1964), and his "Two Case Studies of Marketing and Patronage in Greece," in *Contributions to Mediterranean Sociology,* ed. J.-G. Peristiany (Paris: Mouton and Co., 1968), pp. 134-143; Michael Kenney, "Patterns of Patronage in Spain," *Antrhopological Quarterly* 33 (1960): 14-23; Eric Wolf, "Kinship, Friendship, and Patron-Client Relations in Complex Societies," in *The Social Anthropology of Complex Societies,* ed. M. Banton (London: Tavistock, 1966), pp. 1-22; A. Weingrod, "Patrons, Patronage, and Political Parties," in *Comparative Studies in Society and History* 10 (1968): 1142-1158; William T. Stuart, "The Explanation of Patron-Client Systems: Some Structural and Ecological Perspectives," in *Structure and Process,* ed. Strickson and Greenfield, pp. 19-42, sets forth many important general considerations. Esther Hermitte's contribution to the same volume, "Ponchos, Weaving, and Patron-Client Relations in Northwest Argentina," pp. 159-177, presents a picture of the place of patronage in a cottage textile industry that is compatible, in many respects, with the wool industry in late medieval Florence. Of special value are the contributions of Sydel Silverman: "'Exploitation' in Rural Central Italy: Structure and Ideology in Stratification Study," *Comparative Studies in Society and History* 12 (1970): 327-339; "Patronage and Community-Nation Relationships in Central Italy," *Ethnology* 4 (1965): 172-189; "Patronage as Myth," in *Patrons and Clients in Mediterranean Societies,* ed. Ernest Gellner and John Waterbury (London, 1977), pp. 7-19. A number of these studies, together with a bibliography, now appear in Steffen W. Schmidt, James C. Scott, *et al.,* eds., *Friends, Followers, and Factions* (Berkeley: University of California Press, 1977).

40. On the Medici as patrons and on political patronage in Florence, see Molho, "Cosimo de' Medici," *passim;* Kent, *Rise of the Medici,* pp. 16-19, 23, 64-71, 84-85; Brucker *Civic World,* chap. 1.

41. Paolo da Certaldo, *Libro di buoni costumi* (Florence: Felice Le Monnier, 1945), pp. 97-99.

A structural analysis of Sicilian proverbs has described a social code quite similar to that presented in this chapter. See Maureen J. Giovannini, "A Structural Analysis of Proverbs in a Sicilian Village," *American Ethnologist* 5 (1978): 322-333.

modern terms, a means of integration. Through powerful protectors one gained access to the networks of others. This same attitude was found in urban immigrants and those who needed to establish social contacts in other urban neighborhoods. The wealthy and powerful, who are those who link different cities and, within cities, different neighborhoods, were not the only persons who enjoyed the role of patron in Renaissance society. Patronage operated through extended chains; one man's patron was another man's client. That the patron served as a middleman between two social networks relatively distant from each other meant that the patron often linked those above him—his own patrons—and those below him— his clients. The immigrant whose employment or urban residence was secured by a neighborhood patron could in turn act as a patron for those whom he had left behind. In so doing, by providing contact between his network and his own patron, he acted simultaneously as patron and client. Many notaries, especially, functioned in this mediating role. It is uncertain, however, how far patronage extended effectively into the ranks of wool workers or the urban poor.[42]

Florentine corporations provided other means by which the experience of being a patron was diffused throughout the social spectrum. Through their participation in guilds and religious fraternities, middle-class Florentines could participate in corporate acts of patronage, patronizing artists, shopkeepers, and the souls who were dependent upon the charity of these institutions. The rapid rotation of offices in Florentine corporations allowed many Florentines to share, albeit temporarily, the formal status of patron and to direct these acts of patronage.

The chains of patronage and friendship that gave structure to the urban social economy were, above all, chains of personal relationships.[43] Sapori and Melis, historians of the Florentine economy, have noted that many rentals of urban property and many business arrangements occurred without benefit of a notarized contract.[44] This suggested, at least to Melis, that

42. Molho, "Cosimo de' Medici," p. 17. David Herlihy has, on the other hand, argued that economic exchanges between employers and employees, particularly loans between wool workers and guildsmen, were personalized and intimate. See his "Family and Property in Renaissance Florence," in *Medieval City*, ed. Miskimin *et al.*, p. 13. Goldthwaite, *Building of Renaissance Florence*, p. 314, has also commented on the personalized character of loans between employers and employees in the building trades.

43. Similar economic development in Sicily taking place within a structure of patronage networks has been termed "broker capitalism." See Peter Schneider and Jane Schneider, *Culture and Political Economy in Western Sicily* (New York: Academic Press, 1976), p. 11.

44. Armando Sapori, "Case e Botteghe a Firenze nel Trecento," in *Studi di Storia Economica Medievale* (Florence: Sansoni, 1946), p. 375; Federigo Melis, "Industria, commercio, credito," in *Un' altra Firenze*, p. 146.

economic transactions took place between persons who had strong preexisting social ties, that is, between persons for whom the requirement of notarized documents would have been a breach of honor and trust.[45] Given that economic historians generally describe the Florentine economy as one in which the inhabitants made decisions on the basis of purely impersonal, market-related considerations, I do not think that the personal characteristics of the Renaissance economy can be too strongly stressed. Business historians place great importance on the development of letters of exchange and letters of credit. The Renaissance economy depended on another type of letter of credit as well, the letter of recommendation. Much of Cosimo de' Medici's correspondence consisted of requests for favors and recommendations; the letters of Lorenzo de' Medici reveal a similar preoccupation with *raccomandazione*. The trading of influence on behalf of friends and clients makes the Renaissance letter of recommendation a subgenre in its own right, through which Florentines advanced the interests of their clients and friends.[46]

Objective qualifications, skills, and merit played only a partial role in the patronage economy of Florence. Guild matriculation (excepting the guild of lawyers and notaries) did not depend on an examination of craft qualifications. Applicants for matriculation needed, instead, personal sponsors within the guild, and admission was contingent on the applicant's personal reputation and his family's acceptability.[47] The Renaissance economy, structured around personal networks and patronage recommendations, valued reputation as much as the modern economy values skill and training. Reputation was the product of two factors: personal honor and personal shame. Renaissance moralists preached that honor was worth far more than money in advancing one's interests. In Guicciardini's words:

> You can see at every turn the benefits you derive from having a good name, a good reputation. But they are few compared to those that you do not see. These come of their own accord, without your knowing the cause, brought about by that good opinion people have of you. It was said most wisely: a good name is worth more than great riches.[48]

45. Melis, "Industria," p. 146.

46. On Cosimo's correspondence, see Molho, "Cosimo de' Medici." For examples of letters of recommendation, see G. R. B. Richards, ed., *Florentine Merchants in the Age of the Medici: Letters and Documents from the Selfridge Collection of Medici Manuscripts* (Cambridge, Mass.: Harvard University Press, 1932), p. 202; Kent, *Rise of the Medici,* p. 83ff.

47. Doren, *Le arti fiorentine,* 1:130-131, 141ff.

48. Francesco Guicciardini, *Maxims and Reflections of a Renaissance Statesman,* trans. Mario Domandi (New York: Harper & Row, 1965), p. 81.

The basic components of honor related directly to the maintenance of good patron-client relationships. Honor's first component was the proper expression of generosity and gratitude as a client, the reciprocation of favors and the demonstration of loyalty to friends and patrons. Its second component involved the potential to be a patron, that is, the control and possession of a personal network, which was a necessary condition for extending aid and repaying favors. Honor and profit accrued to the man with a large network of friends and relatives because, as Guicciardini maintained, "you will profit just from the fact that it is believed that you can use them whenever you need."[49]

Shame was attributed to those who lacked clients or failed to demonstrate gratitude, or whose exchange of favors was perceived as being less than reciprocally balanced. The ungrateful man who did not recognize the true value of his friends was said to be shameful. The man who allowed himself to be embarrassed in public was ridiculed, for he could not be trusted to manage others competently, and his masculinity was subject to scorn. Honor in men was linked to the effective exercise of authority. The greatest shame was attributed to the husband of an adulteress, for he could not control and discipline his wife and therefore could not be expected to maintain influence over anyone else. Obedience and chastity were the virtues that brought honor to women,[50] whereas generosity, loyalty to friends, the maintenance of numerous friendships, and a certain measure of power and aggressiveness brought honor to men.

The Meaning of Social Relations:
The Politics of Amity and Enmity

How did Florentines view their relations with one another? What were Florentine expectations about social encounters? What meanings did they attribute to the dense networks of personal bonds interlinking them? Was

49. Guicciardini, *Maxims and Reflections,* p. 63. On honor and shame and the structure of Mediterranean values, see J.-G. Peristiany, ed., *Honor and Shame: The Values of Mediterranean Society* (Chicago, University of Chicago Press, 1965), and Julian Pitt-Rivers, *The Fate of Shechem, or, the Politics of Sex: Essays in the Anthropology of the Mediterranean* (Cambridge: Cambridge University Press, 1977); F. G. Bailey, ed., *Gifts and Poison: The Politics of Reputation* (Oxford: Blackwell, 1971). On the difficulties inherent in the concept of honor, see J. Davis, *People of the Mediterranean* (London: Routledge & Kegan Paul, 1977), pp. 89-101.

Honor in Florence has been examined by Lauro Martines, *The Social World of the Florentine Humanists* (Princeton, N.J.: Princeton University Press, 1963, pp. 18-84, and Julius Kirshner, "Pursuing Honor while Avoiding Sin: The Monte delle Doti of Florence," *Quaderni di Studi Senesi* 41 (1978).

50. Da Certaldo, *Libro di buoni costumi,* p. 73; L. B. Alberti, *I Libri della famiglia,* English trans. *The Family in Renaissance Florence* by René N. Watkins (Columbia, S.C.: University of South Carolina Press, 1969), p. 200. (Hereafter cited as Alberti.)

the basis of their social order consensual or conflictual? As to the latter, in Florence no such dichotomy existed. For the Florentine, as for the residents of many similar Mediterranean communities, conflict and consensus were inextricably linked, practically inseparable.[51]

The essential feature of the Florentine social bond was (and perhaps still is) its agonistic character. By this I mean that personal relations were perceived as being, at one and the same time, competitive encounters occurring between adversaries and supportive encounters occurring between friends sharing numerous common interests, goals, and bonds. The lessons learned by the Florentine from his experience in the *piazze* and *palazzi* of the city were carefully recorded in family diaries and memoirs.[52] It is those memoirs and reflections that provide the basis of this discussion of the meaning of personal relations in Renaissance Florence.

The Florentine observed that society contained a limited quantity of honors and riches.[53] He believed that one man's gain was another's loss. The affairs of his world were commonly viewed as unstable and unsure. Fate and fortune, unless skillfully mastered, were always ready to transform riches into poverty, old powerful families to lesser ones or conversely, *gente nuova* into *uomini da bene*. Society openly sanctioned competition between strangers, and, indeed, it was expected that strangers would employ their resources to ensure one's downfall, if only given the chance. Renaissance moralists invariably divided the social world into two camps—friends and strangers—and avoidance of the latter was considered as important as cultivation of the former. The admonitions of Leon Battista Alberti that "there is more honor and value in helping your own family than outsiders"[54] and that "a stranger abides with you as an enemy, while a kinsman is always our friend,"[55] and Paolo da Certaldo's advice, "when you are able to have the good company of your neighbors, do not leave it for the company of strangers,"[56] are Renaissance commonplaces. Since one could

---

51. On this feature of Mediterranean social relations, see Stanley H. Brandes, "Social Structure and Interpersonal Relations in Navanogal (Spain)," *American Anthropologist* 75 (1973): 750-765; Peter Schneider, "Honor and Conflict in a Sicilian Town," *Antrhopological Quarterly* 42 (1969):130-154.

52. For an introduction to the genre of Florentine family memoirs, see P. J. Jones, "Florentine Families and Florentine Diaries in the Fourteenth Century," in *Studies in Italian Medieval History Presented to Miss E. M. Jamison* (Rome, 1956), pp. 183-205; Christian Bec, *Les marchands écrivain, affaires et humanisme à Florence (1375-1434)* (Paris: Mouton, 1967).

53. On the place of this conceptualization of the world in the social structure of traditional society, see George Foster, "Peasant Society and the Image of the Limited Good," *American Anthropologist* 67 (1965): 193-315.

54. Alberti, *I Libri della famiglia*, p. 200.

55. Ibid., p. 201.

56. Da Certaldo, *Libro di buoni costumi*, pp. 73-74. See also Alberti, *I Libri della famiglia*, pp. 114, 198-200.

not trust strangers, one always attempted to deal with friends, or failing
that, to convert strangers into friends. A high premium was placed on
friendship. For Paolo da Certaldo, "a man without a friend is like a body
without a soul"[57] and "a man who loses his friends is worse than dead."[58]
Alberti advised his kinsmen that the augmentation and cultivation of numerous friendships was essential to the development of a strong family.[59]

The Renaissance need for friendship and kinship extended far beyond
the need for companionship. The fragmented nature of the Renaissance city
and the Renaissance economy made recommendations, introductions, and
access to networks of reliable third-party contacts and networks of friends
of friends necessities. Most social services were voluntary and private; in
time of need one relied on the aid and charity of friends and kinsmen. As
one Florentine explained his domestic arrangements to the tax collector, "I
find myself living in the house of Francesco di Piero Marchi, and I do not
pay any rent, because I am poor and his brother-in-law."[60] The more
extended one's network, the greater were one's chances of worldly success.
(And, as we shall see, the danger was greater too: The more extended one's
network, the greater was one's potential web of obligations.) In this regard,
friendships with those who had access to extended networks were especially useful. As Alberti explains:

> Fortunate and affluent men are indeed extremely useful friends, not so much
> because they will help you with their wealth and power directly, but because, as I
> have found by experience. . . they can show you the way to acquaintance with all
> lesser and ordinary persons.[61]

Renaissance urban demographic patterns created an additional need for ties
of friendship and patronage. Because of delayed marriage, many fathers
died before their sons reached adulthood; such fathers therefore were
unable to integrate their grown sons into their own personal networks of
friends.[62] Renaissance family memoirs helped remedy this problem by offering sons advice on the techniques of cultivating patrons and friends.[63]

57. Da Certaldo, *Libro di buoni costumi*, p. 71.
58. *Ibid.*, p. 134.
59. Alberti, *I Libri della famiglia*, p. 110.
60. ASF, *Catasto*, 1023, fol. 77r. "Trovomi in chasa di Francesco di Piero Marchi e non pagho
nulla di pigione per che sono povero e sono suo chogniato."
61. Alberti, *I Libri della famiglia*, p. 282.
62. On Florentine demography, see David Herlihy, "The Tuscan Town in the Quattrocento,"
Medievalia et Humanistica, 1 (1970): 81-109, and "Mapping Households in Medieval Italy," *Catholic
Historical Review* 58 (1972): 1-24; Christiane Klapisch, "Household and Family in Tuscany in 1427," in
Household and Family in Past Time, ed. Peter Laslett and Richard Wall (London: Cambridge University
Press, 1972), pp. 267-281; Herlihy and Klapisch-Zuber, *Les Toscans, passim.*
63. Morelli, *Ricordi*, p. 264.

The growth of theoretically impersonal communal institutions did not create extensive trust in impartial, impersonal relationships. Although almost all Renaissance moralists counseled obedience and loyalty to the commune and impartial exercise of communal offices, they seldom placed so much confidence in bureaucratic impartiality that they failed to offer strategies for converting communal officials into partisan allies and friends.[64] Paolo da Certaldo advised petitioners to have recourse to gifts and to draw officials into one's domestic circle.[65] Goro Dati quickly converted impartial relationships into personal ones by making his fellow standard-bearers of the 16 militia companies godparents to his newborn child.[66] Giovanni di Pagolo Morelli was insistent about the need to acquire powerful neighborhood patrons, who would help to reduce taxes and secure nomination for political office for their friends.[67] The Florentine seldom placed exclusive or even extensive trust in impartial relationships and sought in a quite calculating way to transform weak, impersonal social bonds into ties of loyalty and kinship.

Ties of friendship, residence, and kinship were absolutely necessary for social and psychic survival, but such ties were not without great hazard. The dense network of Renaissance social bonds placed great strain on such relationships. One's brother, neighbor, or friend was also likely to be a business partner, competitor, client, fellow district taxpayer, and potential challenger for communal office or local prestige. Competition and animosity continually threatened to subvert friendship and kinship ties. One was lost without one's friends, but one stood to be used and abused by them all the same.[68] Alberti warned, "We find that there is really nothing more difficult in the world than distinguishing true friends amid the obscurity of so many lies, the darkness of people's motives, and the shadowy errors and vices that lie about us on all sides."[69] Family diarists never failed to stress the constant need to doubt friendships and scrutinize friends. "Test your friends a hundred times," recommended Paolo da Certaldo, for "he who

64. For examples of corruption of communal officials through patronage and friendship, see Brucker, *Civic World*, pp. 313, 480; Molho, *Florentine Public Finances*, pp. 74-75.

65. Da Certaldo, *Libro di buoni costumi*, pp. 110-111.

66. Gregorio Dati, *Diary*, trans. Julia Martines, in *Two Memoirs of Renaissance Florence*, ed. Gene A. Brucker (New York: Harper & Row, 1967), p. 127.

67. Morelli, *Ricordi*, pp. 253-254.

68. See Kent, *Household and Lineage*, pp. 159-160, and Klapisch, " 'Parenti, amici e vicini,' " pp. 960-961, for examples of kin quarrels resulting from conflicting obligations of this type. Thomas Kuehn's "Honor and Conflict in a Fifteenth-Century Florentine Family," *Ricerche Storiche* 10 (1980): 287-310, provides a rich example of intimate conflict in the Lanfredini clan. Kuehn's analysis of this conflict, unlike other, static, analyses, stresses the emergent character of social relations.

69. Alberti, *I Libri della famiglia*, p. 228. See also, *ibid.*, pp. 238-240, 266, and da Certaldo, *Libro di buoni costumi*, p. 281.

was your friend earlier has become your enemy because of the trust that you placed in him."[70] Giovanni Morelli echoes these sentiments:

> Test your friend a hundred times . . . before you trust him, and do not trust him to such an extent that he can be the cause of your undoing. Do not extend your trust easily or lightly; and all the more, he who demonstrates with his words that he is wise and faithful, trust him all the less, and he who offers to help you, do not trust him at all about anything.[71]

Alberti reflects upon the darker side of friendship:

> How can anyone dream that mere simplicity and goodness will get him friends, or even acquaintances not actually harmful and annoying? The world is so full of human variety, differences of opinion, changes of heart, perversity of customs, ambiguity, diversity, and obscurity of values. The world is amply supplied with fradulent, false, perfidious, bold, audacious, and rapacious men. Everything in the world is profoundly unsure. One has to be far-seeing, alert, and careful in the face of frauds, traps, and betrayals.[72]

The agonistic character of Florentine social relations, especially the ambiguities and dangers of friendship, fostered a particular style of personal interaction, an inquisitive and emotionally demonstrative style of interaction. This style reaffirmed fragile affective links by an outward expression of interest and concern. It was also marked by a strong hidden desire to be reassured about the motives and machinations of others. Florentine neighborhood encounters occurred in an atmosphere marked by both hidden suspicion and envy and a need for formal demonstrations of neighborliness and friendship. Each encounter became a game of wits, as each contestant sought to advance his own interest without losing honor or alienating useful friends, and as each sought to discover as much as possible about the actions and intentions of his neighbors. An awareness of the existence of constant scrutiny and the power of gossip acted as an informal mechanism of social control. Of great importance was the place where the contest occurred, usually a public street or *piazza*. The casual encounter

70. Da Certaldo, *Libro di buoni costumi*, pp. 241-243.

71. Morelli, *Ricordi*, p. 227. Richard Trexler has argued that Morelli's cynicism can be attributed to his miserable childhood. But Morelli's attitudes about human nature were not unusual. As the citations in this chapter indicate, Giovanni Morelli's bleak evaluation of human trustworthiness was the *communis opinio* among Florentine moralists from Paolo da Certaldo in the fourteenth century to Francesco Guicciardini in the sixteenth. For Trexler's interpretation, see "In Search of Father: The Experience of Abandonment in the Recollections of Giovanni di Pagolo Morelli," *History of Childhood Quarterly* 3 (1975): p. 227.

72. Alberti, *I Libri della famiglia*, p. 266. See also *ibid.*, p. 244.

became, with the addition of suspicious onlookers, a carefully observed social drama. The *piazza* on which a simple personal exchange took place became the stage upon which honor was won and lost. Paolo da Certaldo was well aware of the intensely public and visual character of neighborliness, for "neighbors . . . . are always inquiring about your activities, and in your honor and dishonor they are able to harm you and be useful to you."[73] Where honor was at stake, one avoided at all costs being victimized by gossip. Florentine moralists were acutely aware of the mechanics of neighborhood gossip chains.[74] Morelli, for example, continually warned his son that gossip about one's wealth led to ruinous tax assessments.[75]

The basic strategy for all social encounters was threefold: first, guarding one's own secrets, while, second, maneuvering one's opponent into revealing as much as possible about his own affairs, and, finally, at the same time appearing not to pry so as not to lose his trust and friendship. "Keep your eyes open and your mouth shut," counseled the Florentine.[76] San Bernardino preached against the evils of gossip and slander. Advising Tuscans to be circumspect in all conversation, he urged them to emulate the Virgin Mary, "who, in the course of her whole life spoke seven times and no more."[77] Drunkenness was also to be avoided at all costs, for it weakened one's guard and placed one in danger of revealing too much.[78] Paolo da Certaldo equated his secrets with his liberty[79] and suggested that friends who revealed their secrets were mad.[80] Guicciardini, with his characteristic precision, summarized the rules and risks of the game:

> You have everything to gain from managing your affairs secretly. And you will gain even more if you can do it without appearing secretive to your friends. For many men feel slighted and become indignant when they see that you refuse to confide in them. . . . Often it is unwise to be open in your conversations, even with your friends—I mean, on those matters that should be kept secret. On the other hand, to act with your friends in such a manner that they notice that you are being reserved is to assure that they will do the same with you. For the only thing that makes

---

73. Da Certaldo, *Libro di buoni costumi*, p. 156. See also Guicciardini, *Maxims and Reflections*, p. 44.

74. Da Certaldo, *Libro di buoni costumi*, pp. 107-108.

75. Morelli, *Ricordi*, pp. 255-256.

76. Da Certaldo, *Libro di buoni costumi*, p. 64. See also *ibid.*, p. 135, "Viso presente fa lingua tacente"; p. 225, "Chi troppo parla spesso falla"; p. 225, "Parla poco e odi assai"; p. 77 "Più volte ti penterai di parlare che di tacere—e però taci dieci volte e parla una"; p. 64, "Chi odi e vede e tace sì vuole vivere in pace."

77. San Bernardino da Siena, *Le prediche volgari*, ed. Piero Bargellini (Rome: Rizzoli, 1936), sermon 9, p. 202.

78. Da Certaldo, *Libro di buoni costumi*, pp. 215-217.

79. *Ibid.*, pp. 235-236.

80. *Ibid.*, p. 139.

others confide in you is the assumption that you confide in them. Thus, if you reveal nothing to others, you lose the possibility of knowing anything from them.[81]

In public situations the Florentine was frequently in a state of tension. Scrutinized by his neighbors, he had to hide his wealth and moderate his dress and yet not appear so humble that he lost his honor and his contacts. He had to guard his speech and yet appear trusting. He had to act in accordance with the dual demands of friendship: remaining relaxed and on guard, suspicious and effusively cordial. He had to, as Adovardo and Lionardo Alberti advised, "overcome slyness with slyness," since "shrewdness is required in dealing with shrewd people."[82]

The Renaissance neighbor, caught between the conflicting requirements of ambiguous and overlapping social roles, was acutely aware of the need to maintain separate public and private lives. The inner private counterpart to his public life on the *piazza* was of course his *casa* or *palazzo*. The contrast between the rough exterior of the *palazzo* and its airy, spacious interior suggests the contrast bewteen public self-moderation and disguise and private release, between public body and private soul. The inner, interior world of the Renaissance private dwelling provided some relaxation from the tensions of the *piazza*.[83] The private house was marked off from public space by ritual and social custom. Houses were blessed yearly, on Holy Saturday, and were guarded by cultic figures. The laws of hospitality found in many traditional peasant cultures, laws that testify to the social sanctity of the home, were not absent from "modern," "urban" Florence.[84] Admission to one's home was a traditional means of demonstrating honor and extending friendship and trust. Renaissance moralists were in complete accord in their descriptions of the honored status granted to a guest by his entrance into the household for shared food and drink—an act rich in ritual significance. This act was universally considered by Florentines to be the best way to begin or strengthen important friendships. Honoring friends with dinner was, for Alberti, "a sort of tax or tribute to preserve good will and confirm relationships of friendship."[85] Morelli suggested

81. Guicciardini, *Maxims and Reflections,* pp. 88, 101.

82. Alberti, *I libri della famiglia,* p. 240.

83. On the relationship between palaces and privacy afforded wealthier Florentines, see Richard A. Goldthwaite, "The Florentine Palace as Domestic Architecture," *American Historical Review* 77 (1972): 977-1012.

84. On hospitality in Mediterranean society, see Julian Pitt-Rivers, "The Law of Hospitality," in *Fate of Shechem,* pp. 94-112.

85. Alberti, *I libri della famiglia,* p. 159. See also da Certaldo, *Libro di buoni costumi,* pp. 116-117.

using the custom to transform impersonal relations between citizens into relations of the sort enjoyed between relatives; by honoring associates with dinner one helped to ensure the creation of a sense of obligation on the guests' part, and only in this way could one avoid being robbed by them.[86] Special rules of courtesy applied to relations between host and guest. A heightened sense of honor and obligation pertained to meetings within the household of the host, for he felt compelled to demonstrate the power and authority that he enjoyed within his own realm. Aware of this, Paolo da Certaldo advised that "when you need some favor from another, go to his house . . . since he will not deny you in his own house what he might deny you outside of it."[87]

Since ambiguous and overlapping social roles existed between kinsmen, as well as between neighbors and friends, the household was not without its own hazards and tensions. As sons progressed through the life cycle, their need for independence clashed with paternal demands for respect. And eventually brother clashed with brother over the settlement of inheritances. Wives were not to be trusted, as they were a potential source of gossip about family affairs.[88] The Florentine kinship system, stressing patrilineal descent and patrilocal residence, placed wives in a structurally weak position. Wives were denied equal importance in the kinship system, and therefore their loyalty was suspect, for it was feared that wives would foster the interests of their own families of birth.[89] Paolo Morelli's suspicion of wives extended to include servants and all members of the domestic circle.[90]

The Florentine was subject to constant strain; he guarded his personal mannerisms and his ever-present suspicions and jealousies. "The greater you feel, the less your speech should reveal," warned Paolo da Certaldo.[91] A major problem posed by the social worlds in which the Florentine lived was the proper management of commitments. How did one honor competing claims and diverse loyalties in a social world in which most of the partici-

---

86. Morelli, *Ricordi*, pp. 237-239.

87. Da Certaldo, *Libro di buoni costumi*, p. 89.

88. Alberti, *I Libri della famiglia*, pp. 210, 216-217; see also da Certaldo, *Libro di buoni costumi*, p. 136, "I tuoi segreti mai non dire a femina nè a uomo giovane."

89. The weak position of women in the patrilineal cultural world of Florentine households is discussed in Robert Wheaton, "Family and Kinship in Western Europe: The Problem of the Joint Family Household," *Journal of Interdisciplinary History* 5 (1975): 619ff.

90. Morelli, *Ricordi*, p. 232.

91. Da Certaldo, *Libro di buoni costumi*, p. 137, "Secondo che ti senti così mena i denti."

pants whose commitments demanded attention were present as actors and as observers? Morelli warned:

> If within the city or rather, within your *gonfalone* or neighborhood, one or more sects springs to life, concerning itself with the affairs of your Commune, as happens every day . . . try to stay uncommitted, and keep your friendship with everyone. Don't speak ill of anyone, whether to please one man more than another or to satisfy your anger.[92]

Morelli's advice must have been difficult to heed. Caught between the conflicting demands and obligations of overlapping social worlds, the Florentine saved his honor by resorting to lies and duplicity when opposing pressures were irreconcilable. Bernardino's analysis of the Sienese applies equally well to the Florentines:

> There are those who have two tongues, who hold one thing in their hearts while they speak another with their tongues, like he who promises something and does not make good of it in order to remain at peace with his family. He will have promised to do something worthy, and because he sees that it displeases a member of his household, in order to remain at peace with his relatives he will say, "I never promised to do it."[93]

The Florentine's home was an unsure refuge from constant scrutiny—and even sleep had its dangers, for as we read often in Boccacio, a father, husband, or friend who slept was in the state most vulnerable to trickery and betrayal.

Constantly fearing the loss of honor and friendship, and the humiliation of attendant gossip, the Florentine silently suffered slights and secretly acccumulated resentments. Renaissance moralists exalted moderation, self-discipline, and control of anger. Paolo da Certaldo declared, "He who conquers anger conquers his great enemy."[94] This suppression of pent-up animosities was perhaps the most dangerous facet of the Florentine psyche. Two seemingly dissimilar patterns of behavior have long been associated with late medieval man: extreme outbursts of cruelty and violence and extravagant demonstrations of penance, compassion, and mercy.[95] These

92. Morelli, *Ricordi,* pp. 280-281.

93. San Bernardino da Siena, *Le prediche volgari,* sermon 9, p. 203. The Florentine lost more honor in admitting that he could not keep his promise than in denying that the promise had ever been made.

94. Da Certaldo, *Libro di buoni costumi,* p. 135.

95. J. Huizinga, *The Waning of the Middle Ages* (1924; reprint ed., Garden City: Doubleday Anchor, 1954), chap. 1, *passim.*

two phenomena were intimately related. Both were the products of the small-scale, face-to-face society of the Renaissance town. When anger could not be controlled, its outbreak was magnified by the sudden expression of repressed, unresolved, and unrepaid injuries that had long been suffered in silence. The intimate scale of urban neighborhood life also helps to explain the merciful, penitent side of the Renaissance personality. Since extreme outbursts of anger and violence were, for the most part, directed against those with whom one shared multiple relationships, that is, kinsmen, friends, and neighbors, one's anger could easily and swiftly be transformed into guilt, compassion, and mercy.

Social Relations and Economic Exchange

Some historians are all too willing to credit premodern man with modern economic motivations and insights. The search for modern capitalism in early modern Europe has, for example, led to a serious neglect of facets of the Renaissance economy that are more traditional than modern. Economic activity is one type of social exchange. It can rarely be understood apart from all systems of exchange that operate within a particular culture.[96] In modern societies whose social networks are loose and single-stranded, that is, where personal contacts are widely separated from each other, social worlds are less overlapping, and where economic associations do not usually follow ties of kinship, friendship, or residence, economic behavior has greater autonomy, and economic exchanges may be stripped of some of their broader cultural significance. But there is scant reason to expect Renaissance economic exchanges, occurring within dense and multitextured social networks, to lack broader cultural meaning shared by other Renaissance exchange systems: gift giving, hospitality, the exchange of greetings, or the exchange of women. The medieval merchant, like his modern cousin, was obsessed with the calculation of profit and loss. Unlike the modern capitalist, however, the calculation of profit and loss was accompanied by another obsession, not readily observed by those who tally account books: the calculation of honor and shame. The form of economic exchange that most clearly demonstrates its dependence on the

96. On exchange systems, see Marcel Mauss, *The Gift* (1925; reprint ed., New York: Norton, 1967);Cyril Belshaw, *Traditional Exchange and Modern Markets* (Englewood Cliffs, N.J.: Prentice-Hall, 1965); Peter M. Blau, *Exchange and Power in Social Life* (New York: Wiley, 1964); Georg Simmel, *On Individuality and Its Social Forms* (Chicago: University of Chicago Press, 1971).

entire cluster of beliefs and practices embedded in the personal economy of the Renaissance is the exchange of credit.

The Renaissance merchant did not distinguish sharply between banking and merchandising, for the two activities were interdependent.[97] The Renaissance bank did not make its fortune as a lending institution. Rather, the bank made much of its profit by providing a range of services related to the exchange of money. Commissions received by the Medici bank, for example, for tax and tariff collection and for currency exchange accounted for most of its profits.[98] Commissions and appointments of this sort could be had only through ties at court. The need for court connections and court appointments made the banker something of a courtier, seeking personal ties with European heads of state. The privilege of practicing tax-farming and money management was perceived by princes as a favor granted, requiring a favor in return. The favor most commonly required to gain banking commissions at court was the granting of sizable loans. Such loans were seldom repaid in full.[99]

The extension of credit was often a precarious act, especially when credit was a favor granted to friends. The borrower was placed under an obligation to reward his friend, the lender, but the lender needed to remain in the favor and good graces of the borrower as well to ensure that the loan would be repaid. The borrower thus exercised a certain leverage over the lender and often forced him, as the English crown forced the Bardi and Peruzzi banks, to extend additional credit so as not to lose the original loan.[100] The borrower lost future leverage with the lender in subsequent negotiations once the loan had been repaid in full. Furthermore, since the loan was supposed to be a favor granted to a friend, and not to a stranger, the lender was expected to demonstrate his trust in his "friend" by not insisting on firm repayment schedules. The banker-courtier walked a political and economic tightrope. Alberti compared the precariousness of cultivating princes to the danger of training a wild hawk.[101] Honor, generosity, trust, and fear were all central to the operation of late medieval credit and commerce. Alberti commented on loans to princes, remarking,

97. Armando Sapori, *La crisi delle compagnie mercantili dei Bardi e dei Peruzzi* (Florence, 1926), pp. 17-20.

98. George Holmes, "How the Medici Became the Pope's Bankers," in *Florentine Studies,* ed. Nicolai Rubinstein (Evanston, Ill.: Northwestern University Press, 1968), pp. 374-375.

99. Sapori, *La crisi,* p. 13ff.

100. *Ibid.*

101. Alberti, *I Libri della famiglia,* p. 260.

If you offer them a trifle, you will be despised for it and lose the gift besides. If you offer them much, they will give you no payment for it. If you offer excessive bounty, still you will not satisfy their immense greed. . . . and the more you give, the more trouble you will draw down on your head. The more they hope for, the more they think they have a right to receive. The more you lend, the more you will have lost. With noble lords, your promises are obligations, your loans are gifts, and your gifts are thrown away.[102]

The personal nature of credit operated throughout the social order. The Partini brothers, partners in a wool plant and a haberdashery in Florence's neighboring city, Pistoia, reported that their business consisted entirely of purchases made on credit. They had extended credit to 824 persons, but the debts were mostly for small sums that the brothers assumed would never be repaid or, at best, would be repaid only after much time had elapsed.[103] The repayment of loans extended to princes took forms other than the repayment of hard currency. The extension of market favors, especially the granting of access to markets, was common. The Florentine wool trade depended upon this system. Access to supplies of raw English wool, which was crucial to the stability of Florence's urban economy and to the employment of the Florentine lower classes, was acquired by extending credit; repayment was accomplished by granting access to raw materials and by lifting tariff requirements.[104]

The personal economy of credit was present, as we have seen, not only at court but also at all other levels of economic and social transactions. Machiavelli reported that Cosimo de' Medici reinforced his authority by providing leading Florentine families with substantial personal loans, whose repayment was long deferred.[105] After Cosimo's death, his son Piero, fearing insolvency, considered calling in those loans extended decades before by his father. In so doing he came close to precipitating a revolution.[106] This action was not viewed by the Florentine patriciate as a purely economic activity occurring in an impersonal marketplace. Rather, as Machiavelli related the story, the attempt was viewed as a violation of the basic laws of friendship and courtesy. Medici patronage took a variety of forms: renting houses to friends at low rent, paying the back taxes or debts of friends and

102. *Ibid.,* p. 237-238.

103. David Herlihy, *Medieval and Renaissance Pistoia* (New Haven: Yale University Press, 1967), pp. 168-169. See also the discussion of Antonio Macci's economic ties, p. 13.

104. Sapori, *La crisi,* pp. 46-48, discusses the tariff and marketing privileges granted to the Bardi.

105. Niccolò Machiavelli, *Istorie Fiorentine,* in *Tutte le Opere* (Florence: Sansoni, 1971), 7, 4, p. 795.

106. *Ibid.* 7, 8-10, p. 799ff.

clients, renting houses to the poor for free.[107] Giovanni Morelli imitated Cosimo on a lesser scale, advising his sons that if they needed friends, they should buy them, with favors and loans.[108] Patrons needed to display power and liberality, to form and maintain friendships and chains of clientele. Neighbors and friends needed to reaffirm affection and trust. Efficient and impersonal credit arrangements were not always available in a society in which economic transactions often took place within the social worlds of friendship, kinship, neighborhood, and patronage. How far did one's obligations to friends and kinsmen extend? Under what circumstances should one loan friends money? All Florentine moralists debated these questions. All answered ambiguously. Giannozzo and Lionardo Alberti discussed the problem:

GIANNOZZO: If to do what my friend asked were to impose too heavy a burden on me, why should I put his welfare before my own? I certainly want you to lend to your friend, when no excessive burden is put on you by it. Do it in such a way, however, that when you want your own back, you will not have to sue him for it, and he will not become your enemy.

LIONARDO: I don't know how much approval I shall win from you wise managers of these affairs, but I myself would give a lot of latitude to a friend in any situation, would trust him, lend to him, give to him. Nothing should stand between him and me.

GIANNOZZO: And what if he did not do the same toward you?

LIONARDO: If he were my friend he would. He would communicate all things, all wishes, all thoughts to me. All our wealth would be held in common, no more his than mine.

GIANNOZZO: Could you tell me of one you have found who gave you more than words and empty chatter? Show me one whom you can trust with even the least of your secrets. The world is full of deceit. Take it from me, the person who tries by some sort of art or cunning subterfuge to take from you what is yours, that person is no friend. He

107. Kent, *Rise of the Medici*, pp. 78 n. 43, 78-79.
108. Morelli, *Ricordi*, pp. 253-354:

Be clever at acquiring one or more friends in your *gonfalone,* and do whatever good you can for him, and do not worry about using your wealth in his behalf. If you are rich be content to buy friends with your money, if you cannot get them any other way; be clever about establishing family ties with good, popular and powerful citizens; and in your *gonfalone,* cling to anyone who might be able to advance you. If you are able to do this through family ties, do it; if not this way, make use of someone [else]; do business with his relatives, be quick to serve him, offer him whatever you see that he requires. If you have the means without too much harm to yourself, present it to him; make him and your other neighbors the honor of being your guests frequently.

> asks you for gifts or loans or he wants these things by threats or comes at them by flattery—I say he tries to steal from you and he is not your friend.[109]

Morelli enumerated the possible harmful results of loaning money to friends and relations: "First, you might lose your own property, second, you might lose your relative or friend, and third, you might become the enemy of your debtor and he might treat you as an enemy if you should ask him twice or more for what is owed you.[110] Morelli admitted that one was generally obligated to loan money to friends and suggested that "from the moment you decide to help, consider your loss irretrievable, and do not be miserable or put on a long face. Do not lose both your money *and* your friend."[111] Faced with the choice between alienating friends and making ill-advised loans to friends, Giovanni Rucellai urged his sons to employ a variety of delaying tactics, without directly denying the request. But, if this failed, he, too, recommended, albeit unenthusiastically, that one should loan the money.[112] Alberti's discussion of the difficulty in obtaining a long-promised dowry illustrates the difficulties of Renaissance debt collection.

> I know not why everyone, as if corrupted by a common vice, takes advantage of delay to grow lazy in paying debts. Sometimes, in cases of marriage, people are further tempted because they hope to evade payment altogether. As your wife spends her first year in your house, it seems impossible not to reinforce the new bonds of kinship by frequent visiting and parties. But it will be thought rude if, in the middle of a gathering of kinsmen, you put yourself forward to insist and complain. If, as new husbands usually do, you don't want to lose their still precarious favor, you may ask your in-laws in restrained and casual words. Then you are forced to accept any little excuse they may offer. If you make a more forthright demand for what is your own, they will explain to you their many obligations, will complain of fortune, blame the conditions of the time, complain of other men, and say that they hope to be able to ask much of you in greater difficulties. As long as they can, they will promise you bounteous repayment at an ever receding date. They will beg you, and overwhelm you, nor will it seem possible for you to spurn the prayers of people you have accepted as your own family. Finally, you will be put

109. Alberti, *I Libri della Famiglia*, pp. 238-239. See also da Certaldo, *Libro di buoni costumi*, pp. 231-232. For family quarrels resulting from Florentine credit practices, see Kent, *Household and Lineage*, pp. 68-69.

110. Morelli, *Ricordi*, pp. 237-239.

111. *Ibid.*

112. *Giovanni Rucellai ed il suo Zibaldone*, ed. Alessandro Perosa, in *Studies of the Warburg Institute* 24 (1960): 1:10-13. Similar questions are raised about the selection of employees and the wisdom of employing kinsmen and strangers in chap. 1 of Rucellai's work.

in a position where you must either suffer the loss in silence or enter upon expensive litigation and create enmity.[113]

The ambiguities and tensions described by Alberti are characteristic of transactions that occur within a dense, multitextured social network. The leading historian of Renaissance commerce has criticized Florentine bankers for not separating economic from noneconomic considerations in their conduct of business, claiming that "political considerations," in the case of the Medici, "were often given priority over business judgment."[114] But such a separation of "economic" and "political" considerations was not always possible in the social world in which Renaissance credit was advanced.

From the foregoing discussion of Florentine social interaction several basic assumptions should be highlighted. First, exchanges between strangers were considered to be quite hazardous. To achieve necessary leverage in social interactions these relations had to be converted into personalized relations, that is, relations bound by a sense of moral obligation that was perceived as transcending the immediate business at hand.[115] There were two principal methods of achieving this: directly, by befriending the party in question, or indirectly, through the mediation of some third person who exercised influence over the other party. Second, all social exchanges had to be reciprocated, and such reciprocation had to be weighed and balanced on the scales of honor and shame. When the two persons were of unequal status, reciprocity could be achieved by the proper expression by the client of obedience and gratitude to his patron. Finally, the fear of being used and abused by one's personal contacts, that is, of extending assistance that would not be repaid, created a potential for antagonism and resentment in every relationship.

Florentine society segmented vertically into kinship groups and neighborhood patronage chains, as well as horizontally, along the fracture planes of classes and status groups. Competing for clients from below and

---

113. Alberti, *I Libri della famiglia,* p. 117-118.

114. Raymond de Roover, *The Rise and Decline of the Medici Bank,* 1397-1494 (Cambridge, Mass.: Harvard University Press, 1963), p. 373.

115. It is useful to remember that although personal relations in the Renaissance were often accompanied by demonstrations of strong affection, it was the perception of moral obligation, not the modern criteria of psychological intimacy, that distinguished relations between friends from relations between strangers. And Florentines could be cold and calculating in their acquisition and cultivation of personal relations.

favor from above, Florentines directed their hostilities as much at social equals as at inferiors or superiors. It has been estimated, for example, that well over 80% of the incidents of assault reported for the fourteenth century and 67% of those of the fifteenth century took place between persons of the same social class.[116] The agonistic character of social relations imbued all social contacts with potential danger. Suspicion, envy, and fear did not characterize just relations between different classes. All social relations had these characteristics. The fear of exploitation was present in every significant social bond.

The intimacy of contacts and negotiations in Renaissance Florence was part of an entire culture of behaviors and meanings. This chapter has examined a few components of this culture: a suspicion of social bonds not "protected" by many layers of meaning and a paradoxical fear of those relations that had been so protected; a desire to personalize relations; and a fragmentation of the social order along the lines of one's personal loyalties to kin, neighbors, and friends. But the web of one's personal loyalties was complex, and this complexity of personal commitments made loyalties appear ambiguous, obligations difficult to fulfill, and honor hard to maintain.

Pilgrimages and processions, feasts and festivals, and moments of ritual inversion and collective celebration offered ceremonial alternatives to the competitive and richly textured social worlds of Florence, allowing Florentines opportunities to reconstruct and reshape, if only for a brief, precious moment, their community. It is to one of these alternate forms of social organization—the lay confraternity—that this investigation now turns.

---

116. Cohn (*Laboring Classes,* pp. 189-190) suggests that the decline in the percentage of assaults occurring between members of the same class from 80% or 90% of all assaults in the fourteenth century to approximately 67% in the fifteenth century is probably attributable to a change in the type of crime that the government was willing to prosecute rather than to a change in the pattern of assaults themselves.

Chapter TWO

From Traitor to Brother
SOCIAL ORGANIZATION
AND RITUAL ACTION
IN FLORENTINE CONFRATERNITIES,
1250-1494

Mendicant Piety and the *Laudesi* and *Disciplinati* Confraternities

One Florentine confraternity, of undetermined origin, is known to have existed in the twelfth century.[1] Between 1224 and the end of the thirteenth century, no fewer than 20 confraternities were founded. By the sixteenth century, the number of Florentine religious brotherhoods had grown in

---

1. I am using the following terms, whose meanings are roughly interchangeable, to refer to confraternities: *confraternita, compagnia, società* (and their English equivalents: *confraternity, company, and society*).

On European confraternities, see Gilles Gerard Meersseman, *Ordo Fraternitatis: Confraternite e pietà dei laici nel mondo medioevo,* 3 vols. (Rome, 1977) (hereafter cited as Meersseman); *Risultati e prospettive della ricerca sul movimento dei disciplinati* (Perugia, 1972); *Il movimento dei disciplinati nel VII centenario del suo inizio,* (Perugia: Deputazione di Storia Patria per l'Umbria, 1962) (hereafter cited as *Risultati*); E. Delaruelle, P. Ourilac, and E. R. Labande, *Storia della Chiesa,* vol. 16, pt. 2: *Il grande scisma d'occidente e la crisi conciliare* (Turin, 1971) pp. 853-876; Gennaro Maria Monti, *Le confraternite medievali dell'Alta e Media Italia,* 2 vols. Venice, 1927) (hereafter cited as Monti); J. Duhr, "La confrérie dans la vie de l'Église," *Revue d'histoire ecclésiastique* (1939): 437-478; Gabriel Le Bras, "Les confréries chrétiennes. Problèmes et propositions," *Revue d'histoire du droit française et etranger* (1940-1941): 310-363. Le Bras's conclusions appear in the Fliche-Martin series, *Histoire de L'Église,* vol. 12, pt. 1; Gabriel Le Bras, *Institutions ecclésiastiques de la Chrétienté médiévale.* I refer to the Italian edition of this work, containing revised notes concerning Italian religious history: *Storia della Chiesa,* vol. 12, pt. 2: *Le istituzioni ecclesiastiche della cristianità medievale* (Turin, 1974), pp. 546-550.

Important regional studies include Maurice Agulhon, *Pénitents et Francs-Maçons de l'Ancienne-Provence* (Paris, 1966), pp. 1-448; Brian Pullan, *Rich and Poor in Renaissance Venice* (Cambridge, Mass.: Harvard University Press, 1971); Charles Pythian-Adams, "Ceremony and the Citizen in the Communal Year at Conventry," in *Crisis and Order in English Towns, 1500-1700,* ed. Peter Clark and Paul Slack (London, 1972), pp. 57-85.

On Florentine confraternities, see L. Mehus, *Della origine, progresso, abusi e riforma delle confraternite laicali* (Florence, 1785); Massimo D. Papi, "Le associazioni laiche di ispirazione francescana nella Firenze del due-trecento," in *I Frati Penitenti di San Francesco nella società del due e trecento* (Rome, 1977),

excess of 75.[2] The fundamental features of confraternities of the republican period (1250-1494) developed in the thirteenth century and owed much to the spread of mendicant spirituality. Of the 20 confraternities founded in the thirteenth century, at least 11 were founded in mendicant churches, sponsored by mendicant orders, or established by penitential groups informally linked to the mendicant movement.[3]

The social and religious aspirations of mendicant orders such as the Franciscans involved the rejection of that neighborhood and kin group particularism that was characteristic of the life of the ordinary late medieval townsman. The mendicant lacked a fixed geographical place and refused to own or deal in property or to provide himself with a regular income through stable social and economic ties. His practice of begging involved instability, danger, movement. His activities placed him outside the social relations of employers and employees, debtors and creditors, clients and patrons, owners and tenants, and kinsmen. The mendicants viewed involvement in traditional social structures as an obstacle to holiness. They sought especially to remove themselves from participation in society's most basic unit, the family:

> Often the brothers would beg their superior not to send them to their native places, for they wished to avoid familiarity and intercourse with their own relatives and to

---

p. 226ff.; M. Papi, "Confraternite ed ordini mendicanti a Firenze, aspetti di una ricerca quantitativa," *MEFRM* 89 (1977): 723-732. Charles de la Roncière, "La place des confréries dans l'encadrement religieux du contado Florentin: l'exemple de la Val d'Elsa," *MEFRM* 85 (1973): 31-77, 633-671; Rab Hatfield, "The Compagnia de' Magi," *Journal of the Warburg and Courtauld Institutes* 33 (1970): 107-161; Richard C. Trexler, "Charity and the Defense of Urban Elites in the Italian Communes," in *The Rich, the Well Born, and the Powerful: Elites and Upper Classes in History,* ed. F. C. Jaher (Urbana: University of Illinois Press, 1973), pp. 64-109; Richard Trexler, "Ritual in Florence: Adolescence and Salvation in the Renaissance," in *The Pursuit of Holiness in Late Medieval and Renaissance Religion,* ed. Charles Trinkaus (Leiden: E. J. Brill, 1974), pp. 200-264. Richard Trexler's *Public Life in Renaissance Florence* (New York: Academic Press, 1980) is an invaluable guide to all aspects of Florentine ritual behavior.

I have profited greatly from my conversations on republican confraternities with John Henderson and look forward to the completion of his University of London thesis.

2. Benedetto Varchi, *Storia fiorentina,* (Florence: Salani, 1963) 9, 36.

3. A listing is contained in Massimo D. Papi, "Per un censimento delle fonti relative alle confraternite laiche fiorentine: primi risultati," in *Da Dante a Cosimo I: ricerche di storia religiosa e culturale toscana nei secoli XIV-XVI,* ed. Domenico Maselli (Pistoia: Libreria Editrice Tellini, 1976), pp. 113-117. These companies were: the Compagnia della Penitenza (1224), Compagnia Maggiore della Vergine Maria (1244), Compagnia delle Laudi di Santa Maria Novella (1244), Compagnia di Sant' Agnese (1248), Compagnia di Santa Maria in Santa Croce (1255), Raccomandati di Maria (1268), Compagnia di San Gilio (1268), Societas Beate Marie Verginis (1273), Compagnia dei Pellegrini d'Oltremare (1279), Compagnia delle Laudi di Santa Croce (1290), Compagnia della Purificazione di Maria Vergine (1297). In addition to these 11 confraternities organized around major mendicant devotional centers, at least 3 other citywide confraternities were formed in this period: San Zanobi (1281), meeting in Santa Reparata the cathedral, Orsanmichele (1291), and the Misericordia (1297).

observe the words of the prophet: "I am become a stranger unto my brethren and an alien to my mother's children."[4]

The Franciscan vision was, in essence, a vision of the unity of nature, of spiritual harmony, social concord and brotherhood, and of earthly peace. Brotherhood and harmony were promoted through the suspension of traditional social relations. Through charity, men would create new social bonds based on love rather than on structured obligations. These would be the bonds of true community. Thomas of Celano, Saint Francis's biographer and younger contemporary, describes the saint's efforts toward binding men together with God and with one another:

> The Lord gave him a learned tongue, with which he confounded adversaries of truth, refuted the enemies of the cross of Christ, made peace with those in discord, and bound together with the bond of charity those who lived in concord. . . . O how often, having put aside his expensive garments and having put on mean ones, and with his feet unshod, he would go about life as one of the brothers and ask the terms of peace. This he did solicitously between a man and his neighbor as often as was necessary and between God and man always. . . . It was always Francis's anxious wish and careful watchfulness to preserve among his sons the bonds of unity, so that those whom the same spirit drew together and the same father brought forth might be nurtured peacefully in the bosom of one mother. He wanted the greater to be joined to the lesser, the wise to be united with the simple by brotherly affection, the distant to be bound to the distant by the binding force of love.[5]

The mendicants attempted to alter the ritual geography of the city. The thirteenth-century Italian city was divided into parish and administrative neighborhoods, each with its own clans and loyalties. The mendicant orders, however, were not limited to particular parishes: they claimed the entire city as their "parish." Along with the cathedral and the *palazzo pubblico,* the mendicant churches were considered to be symbols of civic unity, and the responsibility for the construction of these churches, such as the building of the Franciscan friary, Santa Croce, in Florence, was assumed by the entire community. The mendicants offered ritual unity to townsmen living in fragmented cities. By concentrating on the exaltation of Christmas, Easter, the Eucharist, the Cross, and the lives of Jesus and Mary, the friars provided a common, interrelated set of symbols around which they could organize united devotion in divided communities.[6] And just as the mendi-

---

4. *Legend of the Three Companions,* in *St. Francis of Assisi: Writings and Early Biographies,* ed. Marion A. Habig (Chicago: Franciscan Herald Press, 1972), p. 930.

5. Thomas of Celano, *First and Second Lives of St. Francis,* in Habig, *St. Francis of Assisi: Writings and Early Biographies,* pp. 314, 515.

6. On the mendicant orders in Florence, see Anna Benvenuti Papi, "L'impianto mendicante in Firenze, un problema aperto," *MEFRM* 89 (1977): 597-608.

cants were citywide in their membership, so were the lay brotherhoods in whose foundation the mendicants played an active role. These brotherhoods—confraternities—were of two principal types: *laudesi,* devoted to the cult of the saints and the cult of the dead, and *disciplinati,* devoted to pentitential practices. The commemoration of the dead, the worship of saints, the practice of penance, and the celebration of ritual unity were, of course, traditional forms of Christian piety. The innovation of the mendicant orders and the newly founded confraternities was to extend such practices, formerly reserved to the clergy, to the urban laity. The widespread and socially heterogeneous participation of lay townsmen in these pious practices gave them a profoundly civic character, and the institutionalization of this piety, lay confraternities, became part of the framework of civic life itself.

The earliest Florentine confraternities were companies of *laudesi,* laymen who sang hymns of praise to the saints and the Virgin.[7] The name *laudesi* derives from the divine office of *Lauds,* so called because *Lauds* ended with Psalms 148, 149, and 150, which contain frequent repetition of forms of the noun and verb *laus* and *laudare* ('praise,' 'to praise'). Under the influence of mendicant preachers, laymen gathered in the thirteenth century to offer hymns in the morning and evening. The earliest form of *laudesi* prayer was a simple responsive litany of praise: "Praise God. God be praised. Praise the Virgin Mary. Virgin Mary be praised." In the course of the thirteenth century this litany was translated from Latin into Italian, as were Psalms 148-150. In addition, the litany took on a more elaborate form, culminating in the *lauda,* or vernacular poem of praise, which by the 1280s was not only spoken but also sung.

The hymn of praise to the Virgin was a political as well as a religious and artistic statement. Northern Italian heretics had denied the dual nature of Jesus. Their Christ was wholly spiritual, in need of neither an incarnation nor its vehicle, Mary. The propagation of the *laude* by the mendicants, consequently, played a role both in spreading reverence for the cult of the saints and in eliminating heresy that was antipapal in nature and, therefore, often Ghibelline as well. The Compagnia delle Laudi di Santa Maria Novella, founded in 1244 by Saint Peter Martyr, and the Compagnia delle Laudi di Sant' Agnese had both objectives in mind. Each fought the Patarine

7. On the *laudesi,* see Monti, 1:155ff., 2:98-104; Meersseman, 2:942ff.; Vincenzo de Bartholomaeis, *Origini della poesia drammatica italiana* (Turin, 1952), pp. 206-219, 387-396; M. Apollonio, "Lauda drammatica umbra e metodi per l'indagine critica delle forme drammaturgiche," in *Il movimento dei disciplinati nel VII centenario del suo inizio* (Perugia: Deputazione di Storia Patria per l'Umbria, 1962), pp. 395-433 (hereafter cited as *Il movimento*); Angela Maria Terruggia, "In quale momento i disciplinati hanno dato origine al loro teatro?" in *Il movimento,* pp. 434-459.

heresy and fostered the cult of saints. Within several decades of their foundation, however, both companies lost their polemical, overtly political functions as heresy declined, and they became indistinguishable from the other *laudesi* companies of Florence.[8]

The *laudesi* sought to cultivate the protection of the saintly patrons of the community through acts of spiritual clientage. The cult of patron saints was a natural focal point of Florentine piety. Human social relationships frequently serve as models for popular conceptions of the relations between humanity and divinity.[9] It comes as no surprise that the Florentines, who were deeply self-conscious about all types of interpersonal bonds, tended to conceive of their relations with divine personages as they conceived of their relations with one another. Accordingly, just as patronage lay at the heart of the late medieval social system, so the imagery of patronage lay at the heart of Florentine systems of spiritual exchange. The conception of divine patronage is well illustrated in the writings of the fourteenth-century Florentine moralist Paolo da Certaldo.

For Paolo da Certaldo, the search for salvation was inseparable from the search for divine patronage. The supreme patron was, of course, Jesus Christ, and the proper attitude of the believer toward Christ mirrored the proper respect that clients owed their patrons:

> The first key to wisdom is to fear our Lord Jesus Christ always, because He is all powerful; therefore one should fear, revere, and honor Him. One ought to fear Him because He is the Power above all other powers; one ought to revere Him because he is the Lord of lords; one ought to honor Him because He is all gracious.[10]

Jesus was feared because of His power, revered because of His place at the head of the patronage chain, and honored because of His grace, the extension of which was conceived of as the granting of a personal favor. One had to behave toward Christ in the manner appropriate to one's status as a client; one had to express proper gratitude to God for the favors that He bestowed.[11] A proper balanced reciprocity of exchange was as important between man and God as it was between man and man. One had to respond appropriately to God's favors. Ingratitude was the worst sin; it "dries up the fountain of mercy."[12]

If God administered divine justice impartially, the sinner would not be

---

8. Monti, 1:160-164; John N. Stephens, "Heresy in Medieval and Renaissance Florence," *Past and Present* 54 (1972): 26-30.

9. See William Christian, *Person and God in a Spanish Valley* (New York: Academic Press, 1972).

10. Paolo da Certaldo, *Libro di buoni costumi* (Florence: Felice le Monnier, 1945), p. 59.

11. *Ibid.,* p. 206ff.

12. *Ibid.,* p. 67.

saved, for he merited punishment. Therefore, Paolo da Certaldo suggested, one must befriend God, whom he assumed rewarded His friends in the same partisan spirit that earthly lords rewarded theirs. He exhorted his readers to establish personal relations with God, to make God a personal friend, for "he who is a friend of God weathers every fortune."[13] The medieval burgher used letters of recommendation to advance his personal interests and those of his family and friends. Paolo urged the use of prayer to recommend oneself and one's family and friends to God:

> Make sure that you do not fail to confess once or twice a year, since he who confesses often guards himself from sin and makes himself a friend of God. And do not ever fail to go to church every morning and see our Lord and to recommend yourself to Him . . . and similarly, [to recommend] all of your relatives, friends, and neighbors.[14]

Paolo da Certaldo was fearful of placing his trust in impersonal and impartial divine justice. Purgatory, he imagined, was a vast prison in which one was abandoned, cut off from the help and influence of patrons, family, and friends. It was therefore an act of great piety to pray for such souls:

> Often say masses for the souls of your dead ones and also for the abandoned souls that have passed out of this life. Imagine that you were in prison and were abandoned by relatives and friends, and no one ever came to visit you—how would you feel if someone you did not know came to visit you and free you from prison—how would you feel? Thus it is for abandoned souls.[15]

Paolo da Certaldo and his contemporaries conceived of heaven, on the other hand, as a celestial court of paradise, peopled by patron saints, called advocates (*avvocati*), who acted as divine intermediaries. These celestial lawyers advanced the interests of their earthly clients at the divine court of justice.

In order to reap the benefits of divine patronage, the members of the confraternities placed themselves under the protection of one or more saints (and in this the *laudesi* were not unique). The prologue to the 1333 statutes of Orsanmichele is typical in its description of the company, founded

> in the name of God the Father, the Son, and the Holy Ghost, amen. Out of honor and reverence for our Lord Jesus Christ, and His most Holy Mother, St. Mary, ever

13. *Ibid.*, p. 139.
14. *Ibid.*, pp. 222-223.
15. *Ibid.*, pp. 101-102.

virginal, and the blessed Archangel St. Michael, and the Blessed St. Laurence, and the whole Court of Paradise.[16]

The *laudesi* sought to procure the assistance of their protectors by singing the praises (*laude*) of the saints, by honoring the saints with feasts and processions, by maintaining altars dedicated to the saints, and by sponsoring masses at these altars. The men of San Zanobi, founded in 1281, sang hymns to the Virgin every evening,[17] as did members of the company of Sant' Agnese. They went on procession to the altar of the cathedral every Sunday following mass. Orsanmichele, the *laudesi* company of Santa Maria Novella, and San Zanobi, all ran schools to teach the *laude* to children. The governors of Orsanmichele arranged for the instruction of children and for singing of *laude* every evening in front of the company's painting of the Virgin.[18] Special hymns and candles were offered by this company for the vigils of all Marian feasts, the feast of Saint Michael, Christmas, Ascension, Pentecost, John the Baptist, Saint Reparata, the Twelve Apostles, Saint Zanobi, Saint Laurence, and All Saints.[19]

By maintaining altars and sponsoring masses, these confraternities sought protection for the living and the dead. Orsanmichele held masses every Wednesday,

> for all the living members of the confraternity so that Jesus Christ and his mother and Messer St. Michael, and all the Angels of Paradise will guard us from the tribulations of soul and body, and so that they will allow us to live in God's service, and so that they will allow us to die well.[20]

Dying well nor not, a member of a *laudesi* confraternity was buried by his *fratelli* with a full complement of torches and mourners, as the body, wrapped in a company shroud and carried on a company stretcher, was brought to its final resting place. Once the body was buried, the members of the confraternity said regular masses for his soul, in particular, and general masses for the souls of all dead *fratelli*.[21] The principal activities of the *laudesi* were directed at repairing, through good clientage, the relations between man and God, using the saints, especially Mary, as protectors and

---

16. L. del Prete, ed., *Capitoli della Compagnia della Madonna d'Orsanmichele dei secoli XIII e XIV* (Lucca, 1859), p. 19 (1333) (hereafter cited as Del Prete).

17. Monti, 1:162-164.

18. Del Prete, p. 19.

19. Del Prete, p. 3 (1294 statutes).

20. *Ibid.*, pp. 4-5.

21. *Ibid.*, pp. 2-4.

mediators. The *laudesi* also tried to heal relations between man and man by offering regular masses for civic peace.[22]

The *laudesi* confraternities stressed the exaltation of God and the saints. A second type of confraternity, the *disciplinati,* also originated in the thirteenth century. The *disciplinati* stressed not only the exaltation of divinity but also the penitential denigration of humanity. Members of *disciplinati* companies practiced the imitation of Christ's humility and suffering. Through flagellation (*disciplina* means "whip"), this form of fraternal piety emphasized personal conversion and penance.[23]

Flagellation had long been a form of Christian self-mortification. Both Benedict and Peter Damian recommended it to the clergy as an excellent means of conquering the flesh.[24] The widespread adoption of "the discipline" by organized groups of laymen dates from approximately 1260. At the time of the disastrous rout of the largely Florentine Guelph armies at the battle of Montaperti in 1260,[25] one Friar Raniero[26] organized a procession of laymen in Perugia, a procession characterized by mass self-flagellation. The processional movement organized by Friar Raniero quickly spread throughout northern Italy. Wherever the flagellants appeared, contemporaries recorded similar sights: members of all age groups and social classes whipping themselves, followed by numerous acts of peacemaking, and forgiving of old injuries, and the repaying of moneys obtained through usury. The first wave of processions bypassed Florence, but later processional movements in the fourteenth century reached the Arno republic. By 1376 at least 25 flagellant confraternities had been founded in the city.[27]

Social pacification was a central theme in every series of flagellant processions.[28] Those of 1335 began in Prato when a Dominican preacher,

22. *Ibid.,* p. 4; Meersseman, 2:932.

23. On the *disciplinati* movement, see Raffaello Morghen, "Ranieri Fasani e il movimento dei Disciplinati del 1260," in *Il movimento,* pp. 29-42; Morghen, "Le confraternite di disciplinati e gli aspetti della religiosità laica nell' età moderna," in *Risultati,* pp. 317-326; Giuseppe Alberigo, "Contributi alla storia delle confraternite dei disciplinati e della spiritualità laicale nei secoli XV e XVI," in *Il movimento,* pp. 156-214; Meersseman, 1:458ff.; Monti, 1:254-264; John Henderson, "The Flagellant Movement and Flagellant Confraternities in Central Italy, 1260-1400," *Studies in Church History* 15 (1978): 147-160; Norman Cohn, *The Pursuit of the Millenium* (New York: Harper & Row, 1961), pp. 124-148; Ida Magli, *Gli uomini della penitenza* (Milan: Garzanti, 1977), pp. 80-89.

24. Jean Leclercq, "La flagellazione volontaria nella tradizione spirituale dell'occidente," in *Il movimento,* pp. 73-83; Monti, 1:197-202.

25. On the problem of dating the outbreak of the mass flagellation of 1260, see Emilio Ardu, "La data d'inizio del movimento dei disciplinati," in *Il movimento,* pp. 368-370.

26. On the identity of Friar Raniero, see Emilio Ardu, "Frater Raynerius Faxanus de Perusio," in *Il movimento,* pp. 84-92.

27. Henderson, "Flagellant Movement," p. 157.

28. *Ibid.,* p. 156.

Venturino da Bergamo, organized a pilgrimage to diminish social and political faction in northern Italy. Each pilgrim wore a robe tied with a cord that had been knotted seven times. At each church visited along the march the pilgram whipped himself, crying "Mercy, Peace!"[29]

The company of the Crucifix of the *Bianchi,* founded in 1399, recalled in its statute books the turbulent period immediately preceding its foundation:

> During the year of the Lord 1399 there were many wars and disputes among the princes of the world and for these reasons our Italy was devastated, and all the people suffered great affliction, and in our own city the great belligerence of Galeazzo, Duke of Milan, was the cause of great anguish and expense, on account of the long and hard wars. Many sins triumphed in that time, for which God justly afflicted the people with His divine scourges. But He did not neglect to do so with His just and merciful hand. Through revelation . . . and through the celestial work of the Divine Spirit a great devotion was infused in the minds of men. That is, men everywhere, in Scotland, England, France, and Spain, began to dress in humble white linen robes that reached their feet, robes that were closed and hid one's face and head, leaving open a finger of light for one's eyes. They marched in a great processional throng, fasting, whipping themselves, and singing hymns, following the standard of our Lord Jesus Christ, which preceded the multitude. The crowd sang hymns and psalms in popular meter and in Latin verse, frequently repeating the phrases composed by Pope S. Gregory, "*Stabat mater dolorosa, iusta Crucem lagrimosa, dum pendebat filius,*" etc., and along with other pleas they shouted these words in vernacular: "*Misericordia eterno Dio, pace, pace, Signore pio*" ["Grant us mercy, eternal God, peace, pious Lord, give us peace"], and other similar prayers. . . . And in our city, more devoutly and less disorderly than elsewhere, such solemnity was celebrated with many prayers and pious acts of charity. Every sort of man and woman, including clerics and the bishop of Florence himself dressed like the others . . . whipping and chanting prayers of supplication, all of which lasted nine days in Florence. It was a divine work that in those days all the wars were suspended. And an infinite number of peace agreements were made between factions, and there was a general forgiveness of old hatreds, of injuries of every sort, even murders and wounds, and within many cities and castles friendships were made that would have been impossible to make by any other means.[30]

---

29. Meersseman, 2:604ff.; Papi, "Le associazione laiche," p. 242.

30. *Capitoli,* 537, *Statuti della compagnia del Crocefisso di Santa Maria Maddalena dei Bianchi,* prologue. This description dates from the sixteenth century but conforms to contemporary descriptions (see, for example, *Cronica volgare di anonimo fiorentino,* in *Rerum Italicarum Scriptores,* vol. 27, pt. 2, pp. 241-242.) Another description of this procession and the foundation or participation of four confraternities is found in the statutes of the company of the Blessed Sacrament meeting in Santa Lucia sul Prato, Archivio di Stato, Florence, Compagnie Religiose Soppresse (hereafter cited as CRS), 1769 (S 8, vol. 1), unpaginated. The four Bianchi companies were the Compagnia de' Bianchi, in San Piero del Murrone, the Compagnia del Crocefisso in Santo Spirito, the Compagnia di San Lorenzino, near Santissima Annunziata, and the Compagnia di Santa Lucia, near Santa Lucia sul Prato.

On the *Bianchi* movement, see Monti, 1:289-295; Arsenio Frugoni, "La devozione dei Bianchi del

The confraternal history of the procession of 1399, from which the preceding passage is taken, describes a temporary suspension of normal social relations, resulting in a transformation from hate and faction to forgiveness and brotherhood. Such are the features of what has been called "liminal" ritual action. Periods spent outside of the normal structure of social relations have been interpreted by Arnold Van Gennep as being one stage in a movement from an old status to a new one.[31] This movement has the same general form for all status transformations: separation, liminality, incorporation. In the first stage (separation) an individual undergoes a process of detachment, physically and mentally, from his accustomed status. In the liminal stage, the individual remains cut off from his old position in the social order but has not yet adopted his new status or role. He inhabits an indeterminate state. During this time, frequently a time of tension, uncertainty, and ambiguity, he learns to reject his previous status and is taught the responsibilities of his new position. It is this intermediate, transitional, liminal "moment" that provides the emotional and cultural preparation for the successful, willing adoption of his new role. The final stage incorporates the individual, now transformed, into his new place in the social structure. Max Gluckman's analysis of rites of passage, using Van Gennep's tripartite scheme as a frame of reference, placed this form of ritual action within a particular social context. Small-scale societies, societies whose roles and relations frequently overlapped, used rites of passage as vehicles for regularly sorting out basic obligations and for resolving social conflicts and tensions.[32]

Extending the analysis of Van Gennep and Gluckman, Victor Turner, in a series of studies, provided links between the social context of rites of passage and the actual symbols manipulated in the course of performing rituals.[33] It is the symbols present in rituals that give them meaning for

---

1399," in *L'attesa dell'età nuova nella spiritualità della fine del medioevo: Convegni III del Centro di Studi sulla spiritualità medievale* (Todi, 1962), pp. 232-248; Diana M. Webb, "Penitence and Peace Making in City and Contado: The Bianchi of 1399," *Studies in Church History* 16 (1979): 243-256. The most important primary sources are referenced in Bernard Toscani, ed., *Le laude dei Bianchi* (Florence: Libreria Editrice Fiorentina, 1979).

31. Arnold Van Gennep, *The Rites of Passage* (Chicago: University of Chicago Press, 1960), p. 10ff.

32. Max Gluckman, "Les Rites de Passage," in *The Ritual of Social Relations,* ed. Max Gluckman (Manchester: Manchester University Press, 1962), pp. 26-43.

33. Victor Turner, *The Ritual Process: Structure and Anti-Structure* (Ithaca, N.Y.: Cornell University Press, 1966), chaps. 3-5; *Dramas, Fields, and Metaphors: Symbolic Action in Human Society* (Ithaca, N.Y.: Cornell University Press, 1976). Turner's concepts of liminality and *communitas* are useful interpretations of the meaning and effects of symbols that appear in certain forms of ritual. *Communitas* and liminality should be understood as being possible modes of interpreting certain rituals, not as

those who perform and observe them. The manipulation of symbols during a ritual is what mobilizes the sentiments of the celebrants. Turner identified the liminal stage of rites of passage, the state of being "betwixt and between," as typically containing symbols of death and transfiguration. It is these symbols that allow a rite of passage to achieve its social transformation. During liminal states the celebrant is stripped of those objects that are symbolic of his ties to his customary jural, familial, economic, and social status. These symbols are replaced by other symbols, symbols of group allegiance or harmonious behavior. The liminal state allows the attainment of a sense of *communitas,* the experience of a suspension of normal bonds and obligations. *Communitas* is the sensation of belonging to an undifferentiated humanity, a sensation that may permit spontaneous, unstructured human relations to develop, relations temporarily purged of the complex ties and obligations of the social order.

The processional movement that engulfed Florence, and all of Italy, in 1399, can be said to have provided its participants with a liminal ritual experience and the heightened sensation of community that may be derived from it.[34] Members of both sexes and all social classes, dressed alike in humble garb, rallied behind a common symbol of death and rebirth, the crucifix, Christ's standard, chanting *laude* that frequently confessed men's failure to live together in harmony:

> *The more you are part of the world*
> *the more you create faction and hate,*
> *and you fail to love each other.*
> *All betray each other.*

---

universal phenomena. Turner's insights, while extremely useful, are often expressed in Jungian metaphors. I share neither Turner's fascination with Jungian poetics nor the structuralist-idealist sympathies of such language. For one criticism of Turnerian poetics, see Raymond Firth, *Symbols: Public and Private* (Ithaca, N.Y.: Cornell University Press, 1973), pp. 189-195.

More useful, I think, is the formulation of Terence Turner. Turner, agreeing with Gluckman that ritual is a form of "social action" about social relationships, and with Victor Turner that ritual is a "symbolic structure," views ritual through its symbolic content. For T. Turner that content is not universal, as it is for V. Turner. The symbolic content of ritual is, for T. Turner, "the most direct expression of, and thus, the most reliable guide to" the specific features of social relations that are transformed by the ritual process. See Terence Turner, "Transformation, Hierarchy, and Transcendence: A Reformulation of Van Gennep's Model of the Structure of Rites de Passage," in *Secular Ritual,* ed. Sally F. Moore and Barbara G. Myerhoff (Amsterdam: Van Gorcum & Co., 1977), pp. 53-70.

34. On the liminal quality of processions, see Victor Turner, "Pilgrimages as Social Processes," in *Dramas, Fields, and Metaphors,* pp. 166-230; and Victor Turner and Edith Turner, *Image and Pilgrimage in Christian Culture* (New York: Columbia University Press, 1978), pp. 1-39. On the ritual quality of processions in Italy, see Paolo Toschi, *Le origini del teatro Italiano* (Turin, 1955), pp. 25-27.

If you would be united together
you would not have such factions.
O, my sweet and prosperous sons,
For you I bear such great suffering. [35]

Through ritual self-abasement—the recitation of penitential psalms, the ritual enactment of Christ's crucifixion, the adoption of garments symbolic of poverty and low status—and through psychic disorientation produced by mass flagellation, singing and wailing, the participants underwent a liminal experience that suspended the traditional social order and produced a spirit of concord and unity. A later section of this chapter will examine certain rituals practiced within the confraternities that incorporated a similar pattern of separation, liminality, and resultant renewal of community.

One Florentine contemporary of the processions of 1399 left the following description of the organization of the processions in his city and the peaceable benefits that accrued to the citizenry:

Everyone confessed, took communion, and resolved to go on a nine day procession . . . The Priors arranged things for the best, and in order that things should go well, the Bishop of Florence went on procession together with all the women, girls, and boys, and with all the men who might want to go. And in order that they should not go very far from the city, [the Priors] ordered that every morning they should begin within the city and they should go out only a short distance from the city and every evening they should return to their homes within the city. And then they selected procession monitors and determined how each religious order and neighborhood [*contrada*] should march. . . . There were, on the first day, and on each subsequent day, at least forty thousand persons. The people were so well-disposed and so penitent for their sins that it seemed to be God's work. In the city they made many peace agreements and truces, and all persons of good affection embraced and kissed one another, and all sang the *lauda* that begins: "Grant us mercy, eternal God, peace, pious Lord, give us peace! Overlook our error." And thus almost all of them sang lauds to God, asking for peace, and they had in front of them the Crucifix, as

35. Toscani, *Le laude,* lauda 5, p. 98, lines 44-51:

> Quanto più nel mondo state,
> briga e odio sempre fate,
> e insieme non vi amate;
> e l'uno all'altro è traditore.
>
> Se voi fussi insieme uniti
> non saresti a ta' partiti;
> figliuo' mie' dolci e fioriti,
> di voi porto gran dolore.

See also *lauda* 4, pp. 93-95, lines 76-102.

well as in the middle of the procession and in many other places. . . . Out of every
gate of the city poured many persons in a well-ordered manner. And wherever they
went they made peace and concord with great devotion; then having completed the
nine days, they all returned to their homes, and the city, on account of all this,
remained in great concord.[36]

In addition to the neighborhood groups of men, women, and children that
marched round the walls of the city, each of the four quarters of the city
assembled a processional company of men to undertake a longer march.
Niccolò del Buono Busini recorded his participation:

On August 28 [1399], the *Bianchi* of Florence marched and formed companies
according to the quarters of the city: the quarter of Santo Spirito went to Val d'Elsa,
and the quarters of Santa Croce and Santa Maria Novella went on the same day
through the Val d'Arno all the way to Arezzo, and I, Niccolò, went with them. The
quarter of San Giovanni went through the Val di Siena to Valombrosa and to
Arezzo, and then, each [company] returned to Florence.[37]

The observed results of the processions such as those of 1399 gripped the
imagination of contemporaries as much as did the processions themselves.
In the background of the procession was war and social chaos. At the center
of the processional movement came the reverberating cry of "peace,
peace!" and at the end of the procession came social pacification, truces,
and mutual forgiveness. In the wake of these mass movements, townsmen
formed confraternities, wishing to preserve what they perceived to be the
spontaneous brotherhood that had characterized those processions. During
moments of communal disorder, flagellant confraternities often served as
symbols of and vehicles for promoting civic peace. In Bologna, for example,
during outbreaks of public disturbance in the thirteenth century, the city's
flagellant company gathered Guelphs and Ghibellines together in one body,
and as a united group the company pacified the town.[38] In Florence,
whether the crisis was that of a papal interdict (1377) or an attempt to
settle foreign conflict (1427), the flagellant companies were apt to go forth

---

36. *Cronica volgare di anonimo fiorentino*, pp. 241-242.

37. ASF, *Carte Strozziane*, 4, 563, *Ricordanze di Niccolò del Buono Busini*, 8or:

Ricordanza che a dì 28 d'aghosto andarono i bianchi in Firenze e fecesi le brigate a quartiere. Il quartiere
di Sancto Spirito andò nel parti di Val d'Elsa, il quartiere di Sancta Croce et il quartiere di Sancta Maria
Novella andarono per Val d'Arno, dì sopra, in fino d'Arezo e io Nicolo andaj colloro. Il quartiere di
Sancto Giovanni andò per val di Siena a Valombrosa e ad Arezo e di poi ognuno tornò a Firenze.

I would like to thank Professor James Banker for sharing this citation with me.

38. Meersseman, 1:469-470.

in procession, symbolizing unity and concord and seeking divine aid to remedy the defects of the human social order.[39]

Pacification and reconciliation were not required solely in times of extraordinary urban discord. The social world of the Italian town, with its tight bonds, could use ceremonies of reconciliation of a more intimate nature as well, based on admissions of guilt leading to repentance and forgiveness between a man and his friends. One fifteenth-century Florentine patrician, Giovanni Ciai, described his penitential practices in poetic form:

> *I remember how, having unjustly suffered many injurious*
> *words and villainous deeds,*
> *I myself have confronted, with furious words*
> *my enemy, and have sent him arrows and darts so poisonous*
> *that I have destroyed his name and worldly fame.*
> *And so, in my heart, because of my hate for him,*
> *I have already wounded and killed him,*
> *just by trying to perform my vendetta.*
> *But because I act outside of the Law,*
> *I restrain my blows, which, turned away, are useless,*
> *and my weapon lies twisted on the ground.*
> *If ever my tongue or hand*
> *has made false testimony against others,*
> *on behalf of myself, my friend, or my neighbor,*
> *God, pardon me, and him*
> *whom I offended, let him pardon me*
> *because it pains me that I was so wicked.*
> *In my heart I repent that I am so filled*
> *with carnal sin. And so, with*
> *a whip I often strike my flanks,*
> *from which, spilling forth, pooling around*
> *me while I kneel on the ground, my blood mixes with my tears.*
> *I, who am such a vile worm, have unleashed pride*
> *against God and my neighbor,*
> *for which I deserve death.*[40]

39. On the flagellant processions of 1377, see Richard Trexler, *The Spiritual Power: Florence under Interdict* (Leiden: E. J. Brill, 1974), p. 131. On the processions of 1427, see Bartolommeo di Michele del Corazza, "Diario Fiorentino, 1405-1438," *ASI*, 5th ser. 14 (1894): 280-281.

40. *Lirici Toscani del '400* Antonio Lanza, ed., (Rome: Bulzoni, 1973), p. 387, lines 43-69:

> Ricordomi, per molte inguriose
> parole e villanie sofferte a torto,

Ciai's poem contains all the major motifs of flagellant piety: self-denigration, admission of sin, Christ-like scourging, and searching for repentance and forgiveness. Church historians often assume that the meaning of a rite is to be found in its formal theology, forgetting that participants in rituals bestow their own meanings upon their own ceremonial acts. Ciai's poetry reveals the traditional themes associated with the *disciplinati,* but it does more. Ciai expounded upon the nature of his sinfulness and, in so doing, placed flagellation within a particular set of socially derived meanings. His sins are sins against his neighbors, the sins of hatred and enmity, the sins of pride and envy, of violence and vendetta.

Giovanni Ciai's poetry is similar in its themes to the *laude* that were composed by the *disciplinati.* Flagellant *laude,* in contrast to *laudesi* hymns of praise, explored man's sins, tribulations, and death. These poems were often based on the penitential psalms (Psalms 33, 37, 51, 102, 130, 143). They were recited during flagellant processions, divine services, feast day celebrations, funerals, and the rites of Holy Thursday and Good Friday.[41] Originally simple in form, the penitential *lauda* of the *disciplinati* evolved first into long dramatic poems and finally into the mystery plays, the *sacre rappresentazioni* of the late fourteenth and fifteenth centuries.

---

d'essermi con parole furiose
rivolto al mio nimico, onde gli ho porto
sì velenoso strale e la saetta
che 'l nome di sua fama al mondo ho morto.
Indi la sua persona a me dispetta ho già
nel mio disir ferita e morta,
cercando di fornir la mia vendetta.
Ma perché nulla legge mel comporta,
mi son ritratto e volti i colpi invano,
e l' offendibil arm' è a terra torta.
E se mai la mia lingua o la mia mano
falsa testimonianz' ha contro altrui,
per me o per amico o prossimano
Dio mel perdoni, e piaccia anche a colui
che fu l'ofeso rendermi perdono,
ché mi dolgo che sì malvagio fui.
Io mi pento di cor, ché scorso sono
nel peccato carnal; però con una
disciplina mie' fianchi spesso sprono
onde, versando, 'l sangue si rauna
dintorno a mie ginocchia poste 'n terra,
e con molte mie lagrime s'aduna.
Da me, che son vil vermo, si disserra
contra Dio e contra 'l prossimo superbia,
la qual meritamente mi sotterra.

41. Terruggia, "In quale momento," pp. 441-442.

Distinctions between *laudesi* and *disciplinati* companies, the former practicing pious reverence for the saints, and the latter, personal repentance,
should be drawn, but not too sharply. Some companies are, in fact, often
hard to classify.[42] In Florence, some *laudesi* companies spawned fraternities
of flagellants.[43] One company, San Gilio, had two sets of officers, one for its
flagellants, the other for the *laudesi*.[44] By the middle of the fourteenth
century, the styles of piety (apart from actual flagellation) practiced by both
groups had become commingled. A collection of *laude* belonging to one
confraternity contained *laude* of divine exaltation sung by the *laudesi* and
the penitential *laude* of the *disciplinati*.[45] The lauds sung by the flagellant
companies of Florence during processions in 1377 were typical of the
laudesi, honoring God, the Virgin, and the saints in paradise,[46] whereas the
laudesi company of Saint Sebastian emphasized the recitation of the penitential psalms, typical of flagellant piety.[47] Both types of confraternities elected
divine patrons and buried the dead. Both groups sought to repair relations
between man and God and between man and man.[48]

The Ritual Republic:
Confraternal Organization and Membership

In describing the similarity between guild organization and the structure
of the Florentine republic, Lauro Martines suggested that the "milieu of the
guild was in its way an education in statecraft, a preparation for politics."[49]
The confraternities of Florence, similarly, provided members with an education in republican civic procedure and culture. In organizational structure

42. On the difficulty of distinguishing *laudesi* and *disciplinati* groups, see Monti, 1:87; Papi, "Le
associazione laiche," p. 240.

43. Papi, "Le associazione laiche," p. 240.

44. Monti, 1:255-257; Biblioteca Nazionale Centrale, Florence (hereafter cited as BNF), *Banco
Rari*, 336 *Capitoli della Compagnia di San Gilio*, 1278-1284.

45. De Bartholomaeis, *Origini*, p. 388.

46. *Diario d' Anonimo*, in *Cronache dei secoli XIII e XIV* (Florence, 1876), p. 331.

47. *Capitoli*, 6, *Capitoli della Compagnia delle laude della Vergine Maria e di Sancto Philippo e di Sancto
Gherardo e di Sancto Sebastiano*, 1451.

48. By the end of the fifteenth century, the confraternity was so familiar to Florentines that
social clubs composed statutes that parodied fraternity statute books. For two examples of the
statutes of these *compagnie di piacere* (companies of pleasure), see I. del Badia, "La Compagnia della
Gazza: i suoi capitoli e le sue tramutazioni," *Miscellanea fiorentina di erudizione e storia* (Florence, 1902),
2:92-109; and Machiavelli, *Capitoli per una compagnia di piacere*, in *Tutte le Opere*, pp. 930-932.

49. Lauro Martines, *Lawyers and Statecraft in Renaissance Florence* (Princeton, N.J.: Princeton
University Press, 1968), p. 53.

2. FROM TRAITOR TO BROTHER

the typical late medieval Florentine confraternity was a miniature commune. The city's religious brotherhoods employed, in essentials, the methods of election and governance of the commune of Florence, including extensive rotation of offices, and temporary disqualification of individuals in order to diminish the possibility of monopolization of office by cliques. As in communal government, tenure of office within the confraternity was brief—4 months for most of the offices. Selection of officers followed the communal procedures of scrutiny (*squittino*), insertion (*imborsazione*) and extraction (*tratte*).

The electoral procedures followed by the company of the Annunciation were typical of those followed by other Florentine groups during the republican period.[50] Once every 5 years, the names of all members of the confraternity were placed in a pouch. As each name was withdrawn, all members present were allowed to vote on the suitability of that member for each public office in the confraternity. A favorable vote by three-fourths of the membership was required to become eligible for office.[51] This *squittino,* the scrutiny of the membership, was a moment of potentially intense conflict. For this reason, some companies (such as San Frediano) performed the scrutiny in secret, permitting only special election supervisors to perform the scrutiny and the *imborsazione,* the insertion of approved names into the office pouches.[52] The captains of the company of Santa Maria delle Laudi were instructed to perform a general scrutiny by themselves in order to "lessen the possibility of the occurrence of those scandals that often take place in the selection of officials of similar organizations."[53]

The statutes of the company of San Domenico ruled out participation by the governors:

> None of the three governors shall be able to carry out the *imborsazione,* but with careful consideration let them always elect and delegate that responsibility to kind men of the company who have divested themselves of any partiality, and above all let them take care not to give such authority needlessly, nor at such a time that the

50. The description that follows is taken from *Capitoli,* 314, *Capitoli della Compagnia della Santissima Annunziata,* 1495, chap. 2. For another example of electoral procedures see the 1477 statutes of the company of San Domenico, in Meersseman, 2:723-728.

51. The scrutiny records of 1440 for the company of San Zanobi have been preserved: *CRS,* 2177 (Z 1, vol. 17), *Partiti,* 1440-1447. The scrutiny records for the company of San Frediano for October 21, 1442, are found in the meeting records of that company: ASF, *Archivi delle Compagnie Soppresse* (archive 5, vol. 4), 37r-v.

52. *Archivi delle Compagnie Soppresse,* (archive 5, vol. 2), 19vff.

53. *Capitoli,* 53, *Capitoli della Compagnia di Santa Maria delle Laudi,* "acciò che si obuii agl'scandali che spesso interuengano nelle creationi degli ufficiali di simile luoghi, ordiniamo che i presenti capitani debbino . . . fare un squittino generale di tucti i fratelli di nostra compagnia."

company would generate scandal, and let them follow these procedures as much as they value the health of their own souls.[54]

"To keep the company at peace" and "to remove scandals," the fraternity of San Frediano, beginning in 1435, asked the archbishop to supervise the scrutiny. The archbishop agreed to intervene and required the company to submit its election records to curial officals for periodic review.[55]

After the completion of the scrutiny, SS. Annunziata, like other groups, locked their office pouches in special compartments. In order to reopen the pouches, it was necessary to have access to three different keys, held separately by the governor, the eldest councillor, and the company priest. Officers were selected by lot from the pouches every 4 months in a procedure known as the *tratta* (extraction, or drawing). The *tratte* were held on the first or second Sunday in December, April, and August, after the normal Sunday service. The governor of the company first read aloud the company statute describing those forbidden to hold confraternal office. Members in debt to the company, novices, or persons recently selected for office were considered ineligible (*divieti*) for the current term of office. Also considered ineligible were the family members of current or recent officers.[56] "And furthermore, we order," the members of the company of Saint Sebastian were instructed,

> for the good peace and concord of all the brothers of this company, that there shall be certain restrictions on those eligible for office, as is indicated below: there cannot be at any given time more than one member of the same family, or kinship alliance [*consorteria*], or partner, or employee of a family.[57]

After issuing the reminder that debtors were excluded from office, all members inscribed in the debt records of the company (those placed *aspecchio*) were given the chance to repay their financial obligations. The actual selection of names from the bags was itself a quasi-sacred experience,

54. *Capitoli della Compagnia di San Domenico*, in Meersseman, 2:727-728.

55. *Archivi delle Compagnie Soppresse* (archive 5, vol. 4), 59r, meeting record of September 17, 1447.

56. For examples of *divieti*, see *Capitoli*, 635, *Capitoli della Compagnia di San Benedetto de' Camaldoli*, 16r; *Capitoli*, 314, *Capitoli della Compagnia della Santissima Annunziata*, 1495, chap. 4; *Capitoli della Compagnia di San Domenico*, in Meersseman, 2:722; *Capitoli della Fraternita ovvero Compagnia della Misericordia*, 1490, in *Documenti inediti o poco noti per la storia della Misericordia di Firenze*, (1240-1525) (Florence, 1940), p. 68; *Capitoli*, 194, *Capitoli della Compagnia della Santa Concordia*, 1437, chap. 1.

57. *Capitoli*, 6, Saint Sebastian, capitolo 20: "Anchora vogliamo et ordiniamo per buona pace et concordia di tutti i fratelli di detta compagnia che gli ufficiali abbino certo diuieto come disotto si dirà: Non possa essere più che uno per uolta d'una medesima famiglia o consorteria o compagno o factore."

often taking place during or after the company chanted the Hymn of the Holy Spirit,[58] or, as in the company of the Annunciation, the Te Deum:

> And then the governor shall recite the Paternoster and the Ave Maria in order that God should give us the grace to draw good officials. The friar shall open the bag containing the choices for governor and he shall draw names from this pouch until he has found one who is neither a debtor nor is ineligible . . . and having performed the *tratta* the Te Deum Laudamus will be chanted.[59]

Exactly 1 month following each *tratta*, (i.e., the first or second Sunday in January, May, and September), the company installed its new officers. Here is one account of an installation:

> Having performed our devotions, the outgoing governors shall correct their officials for whatever deficiencies that have occurred during their terms of office. The new officers shall then be made to go in the middle of the room and they shall take our statute books, and the keys to the meeting chamber, and the old officers shall say a few words to them about the offices that they are about to receive. The old officers shall make them promise to observe our statutes, and to make our brothers observe our statutes, and to maintain the company in peace. They shall then exchange the sign of peace. The officers shall be made to sit in their appointed places and the new governors shall each go to the altar and make an offering of 2 *soldi* for that office. And then the old governors shall accuse themselves in public of failings during their own terms of office. The new governors shall correct them according to the nature of the transgressions committed, with love and charity. They shall then sit in their appointed places, and the new governors shall call their fellow officials and make each of them pay one *soldo* to our treasurer.[60]

---

58. *Capitoli della Compagnia di San Domenico,* 1477, Meersseman, 2:724.

59. *Capitoli,* 314, capitolo 2:

E di poi al governatore dicha el pater nostro e l'ave maria aciò che idio ci dia gratia di trarre buoni uficiali. El frate apre la borsa del governatore scelto e di quella se ne chaui uno che non abi divieto e non sia aspecchio e avendo divieto se ne tragha tanti s'abatino a chi possa essere. E choi se fusse aspechio sia stracciato e traghi tanti che s' abatino a chi possa essere. . . . E fatto la tratta si chianti *Te Deum laudamus.*

See also *Capitoli,* 6, capitolo 22.

60. *Capitoli,* 314, capitolo 2:

Fatto le nostre divotione che governatore vecchi coreghino il loro uficiali de' manchamenti avessino fatti nel loro ufficio, e di poi facino andare nel mezzo e nuovi governatori e loro toghino e libri de' nostri capitoli e le chiavi del luogho e dichino loro al quante parole del uficio anno a pigliare e fare promettere loro d'osservare e fare osservare e nostre capitoli a nostri frategli e di mantenere el luogho in pacie e di poi dieno la pace l'uno al altro. E di poi gli mandino a sedere a luoghi loro diputati e nuovi Governatori uadino al altare e facino l'oferta loro di soldi 2 per uno per detto uficio e di poi e governatori vechi s'achusino de' falli che loro anno chomessi nel loro ufficio. E governatori nuovi gli coreghino secondo e falli anno comessi chon amore e carità. E di poi uadino a sedere a luoghi loro. E di poi e governatori nuovi chiamino e loro uficiali e faccino paghare loro soldo uno per uno al nostra camarlingho.

The installation might include certain sacred ceremonies, perhaps in part to encourage the proper performance of official duties. Many companies required officers to confess and take communion immediately before their installation and at the end of their terms of office. Some companies included in their installation rites the handling of relics or other cult objects venerated by the membership.[61] The concluding act of the installation ceremony was customarily the general exchange of the kiss of peace.[62]

The most popular form of fraternal government combined executive and legislative authority in one group of officials, variously called priors (*priori*), governors (*governatori*), councillors (*consiglieri*), rulers (*reggitori*), or captains (*capitani*). These officials served their organizations in the same capacity that the priors and captains of the commune served the republic and *capitani* served the guilds and Parte Guelpha. The companies often elected 4 or 8 such senior officers, 1 or 2 from each quarter of the city. Changes in the administration of the commune were reflected in the administration of confraternities. For example, the Compagnia Maggiore della Vergine Maria, "del Bigallo", was directed, in the thirteenth century, by 12 captains, 2 chosen from each of the six districts of the city. When the city was repartitioned into quarters in 1343, the confraternity reduced the number of captains from 12 to 8, keeping the ratio of captains to neighborhoods at 2:1. Similarly, the 1326 statutes of San Zanobi, written before the city was repartitioned 2 decades later, describe an organization headed by 6 *reggitori*.[63] The 1294 statutes of Orsanmichele dictated that the company should be governed by 6 captains.[64] By the middle of the fourteenth century, after the repartition, Orsanmichele had replaced its chief officers, the 6 captains, with 4 councillors.[65] The company of Santa Maria della Croce al Tempio chose 2 captains from each quarter and 3 from the quarter in which the company met.[66]

The parallel between microcosm and macrocosm, between confraternity and city, is hinted at throughout the statutes of the company of San Domenico (1477). Chapter 4, on the selection of the governors, begins:

61. See, for example, *Capitoli*, 719, *Capitoli della Compagnia de' Sancti Martiri Innocenti*, 1487, 8v-9r.

62. See *Ibid.*, 606, *Capitoli della Compagnia di Santa Maria della Neve*, 1445: after the oath of office was administered, "si dieno la pace l'uno all'altro in segnio di buona et perfetto amore et carità."

63. *CRS*, 2170 (Z 1, vol. 1), *Capitoli della Compagnia delle Laudi della Vergine Maria e San Zanobi*, 1326, 1r.

64. Del Prete, *Capitoli della Compagnia della Madonna d'Orsanmichele*, 1294, chap. 1, p. 2.

65. *Ibid.*, fourteenth-century statutes, chap. 1, p. 36.

66. G. Corazzini, ed., *Ricordanze di Bartolomeo Masi calderaio fiorentino, dal 1478 al 1526* (Florence, Sansoni, 1906), p. 283.

If the Lord will not have guarded the city," says the prophetic Spirit, "he who guards the city will have labored in vain." If we will not have him who according to God and these statutes should guard our company, devoted brothers, we will have written these constitutions and built this place in vain.[67]

Commune-confraternity parallelism occurs in a subsequent chapter on the authority of confraternity officials.

"Let the mountains sustain peace and the hills, justice." The Prophet signifies by "mountains" the governors of the republics, and uses "hills" to signify the people governed, and so the Prophet is saying that, full of the Holy Spirit, the mountains will have peace and the hills will be justly governed. We mean by this, devoted brothers, that the first obligation of our superiors shall be to have concord together, to do nothing outside the jurisdiction of these statutes and to be present, as best as they are able, at all our meetings.[68]

In addition to sharing similar procedures of governance with the commune, the confraternity frequently retained within its meeting place visible reminders of the bridges that existed between company and commune. San Zanobi's meeting place in the cathedral, for example, was adorned with large shields depicting the arms of the church, the Florentine *popolo,* the commune, the confraternity, the Parte Guelpha, and Liberty.[69] The very urn in which the members of the company cast their votes was decorated with the arms of the Florentine republic.[70] By such associations, the confraternities, as Marvin Becker has written, "interlaced . . . religion and civic veneration."[71]

In a city as prone to factional violence as Florence, the Signoria viewed with great suspicion any organization capable of being used as a political pressure group or behaving in a potentially divisive or socially disruptive manner. Guildsmen were forbidden to join or form confraternities without the approval of their guilds. The potential for partisan organization troubled the commune, and the priors repeatedly attempted to forbid politically active Florentines, or socially dangerous groups such as the *sottoposti* from participating in confraternities.[72] The confraternity of San Marco was sup-

67. *Capitoli della Compagnia di San Domenico,* in Meersseman, 2:723.

68. *Ibid.,* 2:728.

69. CRS, 2170 (Z 1, vol. 4), Compagnia delle Laudi della Vergine Maria e San Zanobi, Libro de' Testamenti, 23r, from inventory of 1394.

70. *Ibid.*

71. Marvin Becker, "Aspects of Lay Piety in Early Renaissance Florence," in *The Pursuit of Holiness in Late Medieval and Renaissance Religion,* ed. Charles Trinkaus (Leiden: E. J. Brill, 1974), p. 195.

72. On the prohibition of the use of confraternities as surrogate guilds for the *sottoposti,* see

pressed by the Signoria in 1317 because its recruitment pattern changed. In that year it was on the verge of becoming an unofficial guild of *sottoposti* wool workers.[73]

The Florentine republic did, on occasion, permit some craft and *sottoposti* confraternities to be established. Two of the oldest were the companies of cobblers, SS. Giovanni Battista e Crespino, and goldsmiths, S. Eligio, both founded in the Trecento.[74] The painters founded San Luca in 1350,[75] the smiths founded the company of San Lorenzo in Santa Maria Novella in 1358,[76] and silk weavers from Lucca had been meeting in San Marco since the middle of the thirteenth century.[77] Florentine silk weavers organized at

---

Victor Rutenberg, *Popolo e movimenti popolari nell' Italia del '300 e '400* (Bologna: Il Mulino, 1971), pp. 60-61; and Monti, 1:181. Trexler (*Public Life,* pp. 378, 396, 410) has stressed the importance of fifteenth-century legislation barring political eligibles (*veduti*) from confraternal membership and has suggested that fifteenth-century companies of adolescents may have served as means whereby families whose adults were prohitibted from congregating could use their under-aged children to preserve political alliances. Although any Florentine whose name, or whose father's, son's, or grandfather's name, had been drawn from communal electoral pouches to fill one of the three major public offices was, theoretically, forbidden from joining a confraternity or remaining a member, such legislation rarely had lasting effects, and in practice does not seem to have kept the political class (the *veduti*) out of Florentine fraternities especially during the second half of the fifteenth century. See pp. 117, 169-173.

Furthermore, the prohibition of 1455 lowered the age at which the *veduti* had to leave religious companies from 24 to 20 and would have affected the boys' companies, whose members, in theory, had to leave an adolescents' company at the age of 24. The distinction that Trexler makes between companies of boys and companies of men should not be drawn too sharply. Members of adult companies were, not infrequently, as young as 18 years of age. For the entire fifteenth century, two-thirds of the members of the company of San Paolo joined between the ages of 18 and 24. Just as age 24 did not serve as a lower limit defining the membership of adult companies, age 24 did not serve as a true upper limit for membership in the boys' companies. Bartolomeo Masi joined San Giovanni Evangelista at the age of 10, 3 years younger than the statutory minimum, and did not formally leave the company until he was 27, in 1507, 3 years after the mandatory date of departure. *Ricordanze di Bartolomeo Masi,* pp. 15, 81. Even formal withdrawal from an adolescent company did not necessarily mean that one's participation had ceased. The meeting records of the company of the Purification of the Virgin Mary and Saint Zanobi *CRS,* 1646 (P 30, vol. 8) reveal that almost every major feast celebrated by the company was attended by at least a few members who had already resigned upon reaching the maximum age limit. Whereas the evidence presented by Masi and by the company of the Purification is from the late republic (early sixteenth century), no existing evidence suggests that age limitations were enforced with any greater rigor in the later fifteenth century.

73. Robert Davidsohn, *Storia di Firenze* (Florence: Sansoni, 1973), 6:213.

74. Papi, "Confraternite ed ordini mendicanti," pp. 726-727, n. 8. The cobblers marched in the procession for the feast of John the Baptist in 1454. For a description of the procession, see the transcription of Matteo Palmieri's *Cronaca* in A. D'Ancona, *Origini del teatro italiano* (Turin, 1891), 1:228. On S. Eligio degli Orafi, see *Capitoli, 595.*

75. This company met in Santa Maria Nuova. Its records are contained in the *Accademia del disegno* collection of the Florentine State Archives.

76. Papi, "Per un censimento," p. 120.

77. Papi, "Confraternite ed ordini mendicanti," pp. 726-727, n. 8.

the beginning of the fifteenth century, perhaps as early as 1405.[78] Washers
and carders of wool formed the company of Sant' Andrea in 1451.[79] The
company of San Iacopo de' Cimatori (wool shearers), which marched in the
procession for the feast of John the Baptist in 1454, was disbanded in 1508
for illegal guild activity and was reconstituted in 1510.[80] Another *sottoposti*
group, the cloth beaters, founded their company, Santa Maria degli Angeli,
in 1488.[81] A number of working-class groups also founded hospitals. The
dyers established a hospital for members of their craft in 1339.[82] Other
groups founding hospitals included haulers,[83] smiths,[84] tailors,[85] wool
washers,[86] and silk weavers.[87]

These craft associations were not confraternities in the traditional sense
of being voluntary religious associations. The confraternity of Sant'
Andrea de' Purgatori serves as a typical example of craft fraternal organization. This company, according to its 1466 statutes,[88] was controlled by the
consuls of the *Lana* (wool) guild, to which wool washers and carders were
sottoposti. The *Lana* guild held the company account books, and all members
of the company were inscribed in these accounts. Furthermore, any wool
carder or wool washer exercising this craft in Florence was required to join
Sant' Andrea and pay dues, and each member was entitled to medical and
burial benefits. The control of the confraternity by the guild was extensive.
The statutes speak of the consuls of the *Lana* guild as "Our protectors and
Lords, the Consuls of the Arte della Lana of the city of Florence," and the
company begged the consuls to look upon the members of the confraternity
as "figliuoli e servidori" (sons and servants). Guild-sponsored confrater-

78. *Capitoli*, 190, *Santa Croce de' Tessitori, Torcitori, Filatolai di seta, Capitoli*, 1574 reforms. These
statutes state that the company was founded in 1405. The earliest surviving documents from this
company date from 1511: CRS, 673 (C 68, vol. 1, pt. B), *Interesse Diverse*, 1511-1779. See also Trexler,
Public Life, p. 411.

79. *Capitoli*, 870, Sant' Andrea de' Purgatori, *Capitoli*, 1451.

80. On the 1454 procession see D'Ancona, *Origini del teatro italiano*, 1:228. The suppression and
refoundation of this company is mentioned by Trexler (*Public Life*, p. 414), who states that the
cimatori founded their company in 1494 (p. 412). This 1494 action was most probably a request for
formal approval by the guild or an approval of new statutes since the company had been in existence
for at least 40 years.

81. BNF, Ms. Magliabecchiano, XXV, 418, Leopoldo del Migliore, *Zibaldone*, 54r-v (hereafter
cited as del Migliore); Trexler, *Public Life*, p. 411.

82. Trexler, *Public Life*, p. 404, n. 175.

83. *Ibid.*, p. 404, p. 176.

84. *Ibid.*

85. Del Migliore, 31r-v.

86. *Capitoli*, 854, *Capitoli della Compagnia di Sant' Andrea de' Purgatori*, 1466.

87. Trexler, *Public Life*, p. 411, n. 206.

88. *Capitoli*, 854.

nities of *sottoposti* offered, if carefully monitored, as Sant' Andrea was, little threat to the regime and provided members of the working classes with a modicum of social insurance. Nevertheless, the major development of working-class confraternities was a sixteenth-century phenomenon, post-dating the fall of the republic.[89]

Only rarely were companies formed on the basis of ties as narrow as that of the parish. The company of San Frediano was founded in the fourteenth century in one of the poorest neighborhoods in the city, the *gonfalone* of the Green Dragon in the quarter of Santo Spirito, whose boundaries essentially duplicated the boundaries of the parish of San Frediano. Despite its ties to this parish church, the company enrolled members from throughout the quarter of Santo Spirito, including the poor of San Frediano, as well as many of the quarter's patrician families. The charitable activities of the company, however, were limited to the parish of San Frediano and the *gonfalone* of Drago.[90] Another parish confraternity, Santa Maria della Neve, was founded in 1445 in the parish of Sant' Ambrogio. This parish, like San Frediano, had been a locus of working-class political organization in the fourteenth century[91] and was the site of a festive brigade, the Grand Monarchy of the Red City.[92] The foundation of a parish confraternity in Sant' Ambrogio in 1445 was, therefore, almost certainly a formal incorporation of neighborhood working-class festive activity that had been present, in some rudimentary way, for quite some time. Apart from San Frediano, Sant' Ambrogio, and the neighborhood ties of several festive societies,[93] Florentine confraternal organization in the fourteenth and fifteenth cen-

---

89. See pp. 163-164, n. 1; 201-204.

90. In practice, the company limited its activities to the *gonfalone* of Drago and the parish of San Frediano. See, for example, the meeting record of July 13, 1455, *Archivi delle Compagnie Soppresse* (archive 5, vol. 4), 75r-v:

> Diliberarono e chapitani a dì 13 di luglio 1455 per quatro fave nere e ij asente . . . che cierte limosine s'anno addare a fanciulle per l'amore di dio non si posono dare fuori del nostro popolo o ghonfalone del Dragho di Santo Spirito. . . . Diliberarono i chapitani sopradicti e chonsiglieri e chamarlinghi per dodici fave nere e una asente . . . a di 25 di luglio [1455] che lla limosina de' danari per maritate le fanciulle lasciato per Michele di Simone bottaio per suo testamento non si posano dare alchuna fanciulla povera la quale non si è abitante in detto popolo di San Friano o de ziendio nel Ghonfalone del Dragho di Santo Spirito in niuno modo.

91. See p. 20.

92. The 1445 statutes of Santa Maria della Neve are *Capitoli, 606*. Unlike sixteenth-century parish confraternities, this group had no specific parish duties other than organizing the parish's procession to Santa Maria Impruneta. (21v-24r, lists the agreement between the rector of the parish and the men of the parish. For the identification of this confraternity as the Grand Monarchy of the Red City, See Trexler, *Public Life, p. 400.*

93. On these festive societies, see Trexler, *Public Life, passim.*

turies centered around social units larger than the neighborhood. The general transformation of citywide, socially heterogeneous companies into socially homogeneous parish organizations was, like the widespread growth of craft confraternities, a sixteenth-century phenomenon.[94]

Craft and neighborhood *compagnie* tended to reinforce preexisting social ties. But most of the more than 75 Florentine confraternities founded during the republic were more heterogeneous than other Florentine social groups such as clans, guilds, or neighborhoods. Although the membership of certain confraternities overrepresented nearby neighborhoods, even these confraternities, as a rule, drew their members from throughout the city. Unlike the parish confraternities founded in the sixteenth century, even the few neighborhood confraternities whose origins predate the fall of the republic only occasionally had parish obligations. Just as the confraternities of republican Florence tended to be geographically heterogeneous, so too were they socially heterogeneous, bringing together members of the patriciate, the major and minor guilds, and wealthier members of *sottoposti* groups. These heterogeneous confraternities of fourteenth- and fifteenth-century Florence might and could, therefore, offer their members a broader social group than their kinship-, occupation-, and neighborhood-centered culture, with its particularistic demands and obligations.[95] Although confraternities recruited members from different occupations, classes, clans, and neighborhoods, the extent of geographic and social heterogeneity of the membership of individual confraternities varied according to their functions. *Laudesi* confraternities, whose primary functions were to maintain altars, bury the dead, and secure the blessings of the saints through spiritual clientage, appear to have attracted a membership composed primarily of artisans and middle-class guildsmen who lived in or near the quarter housing the church in which the confraternity met. These churches were all major focuses of civic devotion. A document dated 1329 pertaining to the *laudesi* companies lists these organizations by their place of meeting. No church in which such a company met was strictly a parish church; all were centers of communal, mendicant, or penitential devotion: Santo Spirito, Santa Maria del Carmine, Santissima Annunziata, Santa Reparata (the cathedral), San Lorenzo, San Egidio, and San Marco. The document describes the members of each of these companies as "quasi tutti i buoni uomini della città e del suo dominio," a description that also pertains to the Misericordia and the Compagnia Maggiore della Vergine Maria.[96]

94. See pp. 163-164, n. 1.
95. See Chapter 1.
96. Davidsohn, *Storia di Firenze,* 7:183-184.

The document clearly suggests that the membership of these confraternities, composed primarily of respectable middle-class citizens, was geographically broadly based rather than centered in particular parish neighborhoods.

The records of the company of San Zanobi permit a more detailed analysis of a *laudesi* company's membership. A sample of 279 individuals who joined this company in the early 1330s reveals the relatively heterogeneous nature of *laudesi* membership. Of the members in the listing, 40% had family names. A number of persons so described came from such illustrious Florentine families as the Alberti, Pieri, Pucci, and Parenti. Of the members, 25% appear to have been persons of lower social status, since no family name or occupation was listed for them. Of the 31% (86) who were listed by occupation, approximately 5% were *sottoposti* laborers, 27% were independent contractors or middlemen in the production of cloth (relatively independent *sottoposti*), 12% were barbers, moneylenders or other providers of local services, 25% were local tradesmen or sellers of foodstuffs, 20% sold luxury items or traded in fine arts, 4% were bankers, professionals, or major guildsmen, and 5% were members of the clergy. Although weighted heavily in favor of the central city area near the cathedral where the company met, the members of San Zanobi came from every *sesto* of the city and from at least 43 of the 57 parishes of Florence.[97] In the early fifteenth century the membership of San Zanobi continued to be largely concentrated in the quarter of San Giovanni, although about 30% of the

---

97. CRS, 2176 (Z 1, vol. 12), *Libro dei Fratelli*. These statistics are drawn from years 1334-1336. I aggregated the raw data by parish, grouped the parishes by *gonfaloni,* and grouped the *gonfaloni* by respective *sesti*. Parishes that did not send residents to San Zanobi are not included. San Zanobi included 18 members from Sesto di Oltrarno; *gonfalone* comprising San Niccolò, 1, Santa Lucia de' Magnoli, 1, San Giorgio, 1; *gonfalone* comprising Santa Felicità, 1, San Iacopo Sopr'Arno, 1; *gonfalone* comprising San Felice in Piazza, 7; *gonfalone* comprising San Frediano, 5, Santa Maria in Verzaia, 1. From Sesto di San Piero in Scheraggio there were 25 members: *gonfalone* comprising San Piero in Scheraggio, 2, Orsanmichele, 2, San Romolo, 2; *gonfalone* comprising San Firenze, 4, Sant' Apollinare, 3, San Simone, 8; *gonfalone* comprising San Iacopo tra le Fossi, 2, San Romeo, 2. There were 10 members from Sesto di Borgo: *gonfalone* comprising Santa Maria Sopra Porta, 0, Santissimi Apostoli, 0; *gonfalone* comprising Santa Trinità, 6; *gonfalone* comprising Santa Lucia d'Ognissanti, 4. San Zanobi included 80 members from Sesto di Porta San Piero: *gonfalone* comprising San Piero Maggiore, 13, Sant' Ambrogio, 2; *gonfalone* comprising Sant' Andrea, 1; *gonfalone* comprising San Michele Visdomini, 30, San Piero Celorum, 7, Santa Maria degli Alberghi, 4, Santa Maria in Campo, 17, San Michele in Palco, 1, Santa Maria Nipotecosa, 1, San Benedetto, 4. There were 26 members from Sesto di San Pancrazio: *gonfalone* comprising Santa Maria degli Ughi, 1, San Piero Buonconsiglio, 2, San Donato, 3, San Pancrazio, 2; *gonfalone* comprising San Paolo, 5, San Michele Berteldi, 5, Santa Maria Novella, 8. Sesto di Porta Duomo included 119 members: *gonfalone* comprising San Lorenzo, 47; *gonfalone* comprising Santa Maria Maggiore, 8; *gonfalone* comprising Santa Reparata, 54, San Cristofano, 3, San Salvatore, 2, San Ruffillo, 1, San Leo, 2, San Tommaso, 2 (unknown, 1).

membership continued to come from the other three quarters of the city. Table 2.1 shows the quarter, *gonfalone,* and parish of residence for each of 78 members of San Zanobi who joined the company between 1419 and 1424.[98] The *sesti* of Florence were not redivided into quarters until 1343. To facilitate comparison of geographic units, I have aggregated the parishes listed in the 1334-1336 sample according to the quarter to which they were assigned in 1343. In this way the 1334-1336 figures can be compared to those of 1419-1424. The differences in the distribution among the quarters of the city between the fourteenth and the fifteenth centuries are miniscule. They are so slight that there is less than a 5% chance that the differences noted are due to anything other than random variation.[99] If one compares the distribution of entrants into San Zanobi in 1419-1424 with the distribution by quarter of all Florentines according to the 1427 *Catasto,* the extent of clustering in the quarter of San Giovanni is quite striking. In the company of San Zanobi the quarter of Santo Spirito was underrepresented by 73%, the quarter of Santa Croce was underrepresented by 63%, the quarter of Santa Maria Novella was underrepresented by 28%, and San Giovanni was overrepresented by 112%, that is, the company drew more than twice as many members from this quarter as it should have if its representation of each quarter had been proportional to the distribution of the population of the city as a whole. The *laudesi* company of San Zanobi, then, was citywide in its membership, clustering, however, in the quarter surrounding Santa Reparata, the cathedral. The origins of testamentary bequests to this company are consistent with this membership pattern.[100]

Other evidence corroborates the tendency of members of *laudesi* companies to cluster in, although not to recruit exclusively from, the district in which the company met. The *laudesi* company of Sant' Agnese, meeting in Santa Maria del Carmine, listed its entrants according to the *terziere* (third) of the *gonfalone* of San Frediano in which they lived, although the company was neither founded as a neighborhood group, nor did it become one, officially, until the sixteenth century. Members who did not live in one of

---

98. *CRS,* 2170 (Z 1, vol. 5, pt. K), *Libri Antichi,* 1419-1508, 8rff. Several *gonfaloni* are listed here as "?." This indicates that the *gonfalone* was associated with a parish whose *gonfalone* could not be determined because the parish was divided between two *gonfaloni.* San Zanobi's records, listing only parish and quarter, give no further indication of *gonfalone* of residence.

99. Chi-square equals .25 with 3 degrees of freedom. The probability that the differences noted are due to random error is greater than .95.

100. *CRS,* 2170 (Z 1, vol. 4), *Libro de' Testamenti.* The wills from 1313 to 1441 have the following distribution: San Frediano, 1; San Lorenzo, 3; Santa Maria Maggiore, 1; Santa Maria Novella, 1; Santa Reparata, 6; Santa Maria degli Alberghi, 1; Sant' Andrea, 1: Santo Stefano a Ponte, 1; San Michele Visdomini, 1; San Piero, 1; Santa Maria degli Angeli, 1.

Table 2.1
Company of San Zanobi: Parishes of Residence of Entrants

Quarter	Gonfalone	Parish	N	Total 1419-1424	%	Total 1334-1336	%
Santo Spirito	?	Santa Felicità	1				
	Nicchio	San Iacopo Sopr'Arno	1				
	Ferza	San Felice in Piazza	1				
	Scala	San Giorgio sulla Costa	1				
		San Niccolò	1				
		Santa Maria Sopr'Arno	1	Quarter = 6	7.9	18	6.5
Santa Croce	Caro	Orsanmichele	1				
		Santo Stefano al Ponte	1				
	Bue	Sant' Apollinare	1				
	Leon Nero	San Romeo	1				
	Ruote	Santo Stefano alla Badia	1	Quarter = 5	6.6	25	9.0
Santa Maria Novella	Leon Bianco	San Michele Berteldi	2				
		Santa Maria Novella	3				
		San Donato de' Vecchietti	1				

	unicorno	Santa Trinita	3			
		Santa Lucia sul Prato	1			
San Giovanni	Vipera	Santa Maria Sopra Porta	1	Quarter = 11	14.5	37	13.3
	?	Santa Reparata	18			
	?	San Michele (?)	1			
	?	San Marco	3			
	?	San Bartolommeo al Corso	1			
	?	Santa Maria Nipotecosa	4			
	?	Santo Stefano	1			
	?	San Tommaso	1			
	Leon d'Oro	San Lorenzo	5			
	Chiavi	Sant' Ambrogio	1			
		San Piero Maggiore	1			
	Drago	San Cristofano	1			
		San Salvatore	1			
	Vaio	Santa Maria in Campo	4			
		Santa Maria Maggiore	7			
		San Michele Visdomini	3			
		Santa Maria degli Alberghi	2			
				Quarter = 54	71.0	198	71.2
				City = 76	100.0	278	100.0

the three neighborhoods comprising this *gonfalone* were assigned to one of these three districts, for the officers of the company were selected by *terziere*.[101]

The largest confraternities of all types (San Zanobi, Orsanmichele, the Bigallo, San Sebastiano) were in some measure citywide and kept separate membership registers for each quarter or sixth of the city.[102]

Even more than the *laudesi,* the penitential and flagellant companies were truly citywide in their membership. One such confraternity was the Compagnia della Purificazione della Maria Vergine, whose surviving death register provides information about the composition of an early penitential brotherhood. It is probable that the first 40 names on this fifteenth-century list represent the original nucleus of late thirteenth-century and early fourteenth-century members.[103] Of these members, 8 are identified in the listing by Florentine geography. Only one location (Santa Croce) occurs twice; all others occur only once. No geographical clustering is apparent, for the seven locations are scattered throughout the city (San Simone, Ognissanti, Santa Croce, San Romolo, [Santa Maria in] Verzaia, San Giorgio, Sant' Andrea) and four of these (Ognissanti, Santa Croce, Verzaia, San Giorgio) are located at the far ends of the city. In addition to nine priests, monks, and friars, the members of the company included six artisans, four immigrants or persons of otherwise unidentifiable status, and 21 members of the patriciate, loosely defined (persons with the honorific titles Ser or Messer, persons bearing names of noble Florentine families, members of the major guilds). The occupations represented in the company include two silk merchants, two druggists, one wool merchant (*Lana* guildsman), a painter, a tailor, a goldsmith, a wool dyer, a linen manufacturer, a fur dealer, a

---

101. *Archivi delle Compagnie Soppresse* (archive 1, vol. 4), Sant' Agnese, *Libro di Partiti,* 1483-1509. See, for example, the meeting record of July 17, 1485 (7r):

> Item a dì 17 di luglio 1485 e prefati capitani per loro solenne partito a fave nere et bianche . . . ottennonno et uinsono che Fruosino di Francesco di Simone Renzi che ua pel terziere della cuculia d'età d'anni 31 et Agnolo d'Agnolo pettinagnolo che ua pel terziere dell'ermo d'età d'anni 36 siano et esser debbino de' nostri frategli, pagorono ognuno di loro soldi cinque.

On the selection of officers by *terziere,* see 3v. The *terzieri* of the *gonfalone* of Drago were Cuculia, San Frediano, and Ermo, that is, the areas surrounding the via Cuculia, the church of San Frediano, and the church of Santa Maria del Carmine.

102. For San Zanobi, see *CRS,* 2170 (Z 1, vol. 4), 22r, from inventory of 1394: "Et quattro libri segniati pe' quattro quartieri di Firenze cho la doue sono scritti gli uomini della compagnia et quegli che ui enterranno secondo el quartiere di che sono." For Orsanmichele, *Capitoli della Madonna d'Orsanmichele,* 1297, capitolo 8, in del Prete, p. 13; for the Bigallo, see Monti,1:150-153; for San Sebastian, see *Capitoli,* 6, 1451, capitolo 15. The burial registers of San Sebastian, *CRS,* 1872 (S 163, vol. 14), *Fratelli Defunti,* contain occasional mention of parishes of burial; these, too, are citywide.

103. *CRS* (P 31, vol. 1).

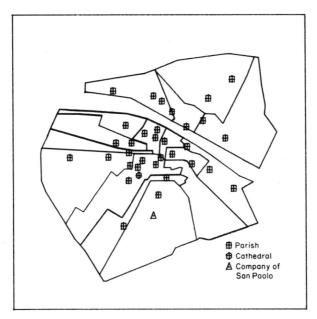

Figure 2.1. Company of San Paolo: Parishes of residence.

shoemaker, and a pursemaker. Six other members bear the honorific titles of Ser or Messer, indicating university education and the probable practice of notarial arts. Those with no listed occupations divide evenly between those with family names (high status) and those with geographical identification (probable low status). The membership of the Compagnia della Purificazione, then, was composed mainly of the middle and upper classes but extended throughout the guild community to include minor guildsmen and some individuals of negligible rank or status.

Figure 2.1 is a map of the parish residences of the members of the company of San Paolo in 1480. It reveals the citywide membership pattern typical of flagellant confraternities.[104] The membership of the flagellant company of Gesù Pellegrino was similarly drawn from throughout the entire city. Its fifteenth-century membership list contains significant representation from every *gonfalone* in Florence.[105] The only exceptions to the citywide nature of penitential or flagellant companies were the four *Bianchi* companies founded during the public processions of 1399. Following the return of the parties of men who marched in procession from each quar-

104. On the membership of the company of San Paolo, see chapter 3.

105. The membership records of this company were copied by Domenico Pollini and are contained in his memoirs: BNF ms. Magliabecchiano, VIII, 1282.

ter,[106] four flagellant confraternities were founded in Florence, each devoting particular reverence to the crucifix carried by the men of that quarter of the city. None of these confraternities identified itself in its surviving documents as a company "belonging" to one quarter. Still, a number of factors suggest that each of these four flagellant companies was formed in and by a *quartiere* of the city: the foundation of the companies immediately following the separate processions of each quarter in 1399; the reverence given by each company to the crucifix carried by the men of that quarter; and the fact that each of the four companies was founded in a different quarter (San Giovanni, in the church of San Piero del Murrone; Santo Spirito, in the church bearing the same name; Santa Croce, in San Lorenzino, near Santissima Annuziata; and Santa Maria Novella, near the church of Santa Lucia sul Prato).

The contrast between *laudesi* and *disciplinati* membership is detailed in Table 2.2, which compares the social composition of the *laudesi* company of San Zanobi and the flagellant company of San Paolo. Thirty-eight men of San Zanobi signed the statutes of the company when they were reformed in 1480. Of these, 30 were laymen, 17 of whom were located in the 1480 *Catasto.* The company of San Paolo had 206 members in 1480. Of these, 110 could be located in the *Catasto* of that year.[107] Although the samples use were small, they reveal significant differences between *laudesi* and flagellant membership.

The members of the flagellant company of San Paolo were much younger and almost three times as wealthy as the members of the *laudesi* company of San Zanobi, who were primarily shopkeepers and artisans. Because they were older, the members of San Zanobi were married, parents, and heads of households. Whereas 95% of them were married or widowers, less than half of the members of San Paolo had ever been married, and only half were heads of households.

What do the differences in membership characteristics suggest about the appeal of the *laudesi* as opposed to that of the *disciplinati* companies of Florence? *Laudesi* piety maintained the cultic rites of the community as performed in the central theaters of public devotion, the most important churches in each quarter of the city. Glorifying the saints and commemorating the dead, *laudesi* practices appealed to those groups of citizens whose networks were most concentrated at the local level of Florentine society:

---

106. See pp. 51-56.

107. The list of members of San Zanobi is contained in *CRS,* 2170 (Z 1, vol. 1), *Capitoli,* 1480, 28v. For the records of San Paolo, see p. 108, n. 1.

Table 2.2
Membership Characteristics: Confraternities of San Paolo and
San Zanobi in 1480

Characteristic	San Paolo		San Zanobi	
Marriage status				
Unmarried	58%		5%	
Married	42%		77%	
Widowed	0		18%	
Children present				
Parent	40%		65%	
Childless	60%		35%	
Position in household				
Head	46%		88%	
Brothers	12%		6%	
Son	42%		6%	
Average age of members	37.1		53.8	
Standard deviation	9.3		18.8	
Median wealth (florins)	605		228	
Occupation	(N)	(%)	(N)	(%)
Merchants	62	30	3	10
Arts, luxuries	5	17	2	7
Local trades	36	17	13	43
Sottoposti	5	2	1	3
Unknown	68	33	11	37
Total	206	99	30	100

shopkeepers and local tradesmen. Advanced in age, married or widowed, fathers of children, and heads of households, these men of moderate wealth viewed themselves as the lay guardians of the traditional piety and morality of the city. The local church in their quarter of the city was the focus of their own religious practice, and the social world of the quarter was, for them, broader than their day-to-day experience of neighborhood life. Eventual election to confraternal office in one of the city's major *laudesi* societies was certainly among the most prestigious positions to which members of the local elite of shopkeepers could aspire.

Flagellant piety, with its emphasis on social pacification, self-abnegation, and mendicant-like renunciation of local particularism, was truly citywide in its appeal and tended to attract, in significant numbers, members of the patriciate, as well as some tradesmen. Members of these organizations tended to be much younger than members of *laudesi* groups, and, as the next chapter will demonstrate, members of *disciplinati* confraternities tended to join these societies at that point in their lives when they made the transition from dependent members of families and residents of particular neighborhoods to heads of families and citizens of Florence. In the same way that the quarters of Florence were larger units of social interaction than the typical neighborhood of the *laudesi* shopkeeper, so, too, it may be hypothesized that the citywide society provided some members of the major guilds and the patriciate with a larger social world than that of the family quarter that was, at least until early manhood, the center of one's social life. Members of *laudesi* companies formed a local elite, maintaining the altars at traditional centers of devotion. Members of *disciplinati* companies formed a citywide elite and through rituals of status degradation and the ritual celebration of peace safeguarded the spiritual peace of the larger community. The *laudesi* companies, the guardians of the community of saints and the community of the dead, attracted the household heads of the artisan community of Florence, during that period in their family and personal life when they were most vulnerable to the crises of death and disease. The flagellant companies, on the other hand, younger members, men concerned with different life cycle crises—the crises of personal integration into larger social worlds.

Although complete demographic profiles of other companies are difficult to reconstruct for the fifteenth century, owing to a lack of account books, it appears that San Paolo more closely resembled other flagellant confraternities than it resembled San Zanobi and that San Zanobi more closely resembled other *laudesi* companies than it resembled San Paolo. Table 2.3 presents the distribution of occupations of members who joined the *laudesi* company of Sant' Agnese between 1485 and 1493.[108] The membership of this company was drawn primarily from the large *gonfalone* in which the company met. Like the company of San Zanobi, Sant' Agnese was composed primarily of shopkeepers and artisans, along with some *sottoposti* and a sprinkling of the patriciate (members of the Cegia, Giocondo, Canigiani, Frescobaldi, Serragli, and Salvetti clans, among others, including Bartolomeo Scala, chancellor of Florence, and Giulio and Giuliano de' Medici). Like San Zanobi, the members of this *laudesi* company were significantly older than the members of flagellant companies.[109]

The confraternity, like other medieval corporations a form of voluntary association, was not an organization in which any Florentine citizen or resident could freely enroll. Members of a corporation shared the benefits

---

108. *Archivi delle Compagnie Soppresse* (archive 1, vol. 4), Sant' Agnese, Partiti, 1483-1509.

109. On the age structure of flagellant companies and the ages at entrance of members of Sant' Agnese, see pp. 145-147, 216-217.

Table 2.3
Occupations of Members Joining Sant' Agnese, 1485-1493

Occupations occurring once		
Chandler	Cobbler	Stationer
Thread maker	Baker	Carpenter
Barber	Goldsmith	Wool washer
Embroiderer	Lantern maker	Wine seller
Cutter	Leather dealer	Tailor
Maker of weights and measures		Kiln operator

Occupations occurring twice or more		
Comb maker 2	Druggist 2	Grave digger 2
Saddler 3	Cloth beater 3	Painter 3
Silk guildsman 2		Weaver 8

Members listed by	N
Occupation	42
Last name	27
First name	6
Geography	1
Total	76

of membership, as well as a common sense of shame at corporate disgrace. Reward for meritorious activity helped to build a treasury of spiritual merit; shameful action was thought, in a similar vein, to stain the entire corporation. Corporate contamination could result in divine disfavor and loss of divine patronage or suppression by communal authorities. Fear of such misfortune, combined with a culturally induced suspicion of strangers, resulted in the creation of a specific set of enrollment procedures. Candidates for membership were not only investigated and approved by the officers and general membership of a confraternity but also, as in the guilds, had to be sponsored by present members in good standing. As one statute explained:

> Since in bringing a new member into our company there is a great danger that he might be a person of ill-repute [*persona scandalosa*] and since we wish to proceed cautiously, we hereby order that this procedure should be followed: if any of our brothers should know of any person who seems capable of following our good customs, mention him to the Governor or, if there is no Governor, to the Councillors. The Governor will announce his name in front of the whole company and he will direct the Masters of Novices to investigate his life and condition.[110]

110. Biblioteca Riccardiana, Florence (hereafter cited as Riccardiana) ms. Riccardiano 2382, *Capitoli della Compagnia di Santa Maria, in Santa Maria Sopr'Arno:*

The confraternity was neither a wholly private body nor a wholly civic one. It fostered in its rituals a sense of broader community, at the same time that its enrollment practices demanded personal sponsorship common to other Florentine corporations. Its membership cut across existing class, kin, and neighborhood bonds, providing a grouping broader than the traditional social units of Florence, but it could develop its own intense loyalties among its members, fostering a feeling that the confraternity was a special place, a "Garden of Eden,"[111] as one company thought of itself, to be protected from defilement and pollution, the most dreadful form of which, in the Florentine cosmology, was dishonor, shame, and loss of reputation. In order to preserve the sanctity of the company and, undoubtedly, to exclude those whom the members wished to exclude, Florentines did not extend the privilege of membership to whomever might desire it. An examination of membership lists reveals the presence of clusters of fellow family members, neighbors, and guildsmen. Fathers sponsored their sons, neighbors sponsored neighbors, patrons sponsored their clients.[112] Providing a ritual space for the temporary suspension of the dense networks of Florentine roles and relations, the confraternity, at the same time, depended upon existing social networks for its membership recruitment. Figure 2.2 illustrates the distribution of parishes of burial for the members of the company of Santa Brigida, a company of young men. The structure of membership reveals both a citywide orientation and geographical clustering of members into two neighborhood groups: one centered in the parish of San Piero Gatto-

---

Però che mettere uno di nuovo nella compagnia è grande pericolo che non fusse persona schandalosa, et però volendo cautamente in ciò provedere ordiniamo che si procedi in questa forma, ciò è: che se alcuno de' nostri fratelli conoscesse alcuna persona che gli paresse atto a seguitare e nostri buoni costumi il manifesti al governatore, et se non v' è, a consiglieri. El governatore lo nomini in corpo di compagnia et mandi e maestri de novitij a informarsi della sua uita et conditione.

For an almost identical rationale for closed membership and recommendations, see the statutes of the company of Saint Anthony of Padua, 1466: *CRS*, 137 (A 132, vol. 1). For similar provisions see *Capitoli*, 314, capitolo 10; *Capitoli*, 719, 17r; ms. Magliabecchiano; VIII, 1500, no. 6, 9r; *CRS*, 107 (A 98, vol. 1), 26r.

The company of San Paolo has left detailed records of actual selection procedures (aside, unfortunately, from information on sponsors.) The week after the candidate was proposed for membership by a current member, he was investigated by the governor and councillors of the company. If the officers approved the candidate, his membership was put to a vote of the entire membership the following week. If the membership approved him, the novice entered the company 1 week later. The screening procedures culminating in admissions lasted for an entire month. *CRS*, 1582 (P 1, vol. 6).

111. *Archivi delle Compagnie Soppresse* (archive 5, vol. 4, 18v-19r, from meeting records of October 30, 1440.

112. See Chapter 3.

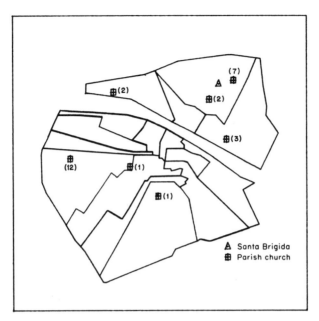

A Santa Brigida
⊞ Parish church

Figure 2.2. Parishes of burial of members of company of Santa Brigida, 1477-1498.

lini, near the church where the company met, and the other, across town, in the parish of Sant' Ambrogio, where parish confraternal activity (Santa Maria della Neve) was present.[113]

The citywide confraternity offered Florentines the chance to escape, weekly or biweekly, into a community of single-stranded, low density social relations, where roles and status might not overlap and where, therefore, true brotherhood might be practiced without fear of guilt or duplicity. The citywide confraternity offered more pragmatic rewards as well. Florentine family structure, favoring patrilocal residence, and neighborhood endogamy, provided only a limited amount of neighborhood circulation of

113. *CRS,* 285 (B 12, vol. 35), Santa Brigida, *Fratelli defunti.* The figures next to parish churches indicate the number of members residing in the parish. The only indication of parish affiliation is given in the death register of the company. Approximately one-third of those who died between 1477 and 1498 were assigned a parish of residence or burial in the register. In all cases in which both parishes of burial and parishes of residence were listed, the locations were identical. For this reason, I am assuming that parishes of burial given for persons of unknown parishes of residence were in fact parishes of residence as well. This map excludes four members buried in churches nearby but outside of the walls of Florence: San Lionardo, San Miniato al Monte, and San Salvi. On the location of Santa Brigida, see Walter and Elisabeth Poatz, *Die Kirchen von Florenz,* 6 vols. (Frankfurt am Main, 1952-1955), 1: 406-407.

males. In a society where patronage, recommendation, and personal ties were of primary importance, the confraternity was a vehicle for expanding personal networks and gaining access to patronage chains throughout the city and, thus, for exercising patronage and organizing factions on a citywide, rather than on a neighborhood, basis.

Since members entered the confraternity through existing social networks, the confraternity fostered particularist structures, as well as communal ones. Nevertheless, the principle of citywide participation provided Florentine confraternal members with a set of brothers many of whose personal and business relationships did not overlap outside of the confraternity. This in turn made possible the creation of a geographic as well as a ritual space for the suspension of those structures of conflicting and competitive personal obligation and alliance that made the management of one's commitments outside the confraternity such a dangerous enterprise.

A citywide confraternity, then, was composed on the one hand of a number of small clusters of members who knew one another relatively well; those clusters existed, on the other hand, within the context of a larger organization that brought together men who were, by and large, strangers: members of divergent factions, lineages, occupations, patronage chains, and neighborhoods. Table 2.4 summarizes patterns of sponsorship for the company of San Zanobi. Between 1419 and 1424 seven members sponsored more than one new entrant each. In every case except that of the sponsor Niccolò di Benintendo, most entrants sponsored by a particular member came from the same quarter of the city and from the same or neighboring parishes as the other entrants sponsored by that member. Furthermore, the geographical density of these networks of sponsorship was compounded by the multiplicity of relations between the same individuals: not only did the entrants sponsored by the same individual share a common neighborhood origin, frequently they shared common occupational and kinship ties as well. Although these members together formed a confraternity, a third of whose members came from throughout the city, the individual networks of sponsorship were considerably more dense and richly textured than the network comprising the confraternity as a whole.[114]

Symbolic Fraternity

The citywide confraternity could offer a certain escape from the demands of day-to-day friendships and feuds, in their neighborhood or class

114. CRS, 2170 (Z 1, vol. 5, pt. K), *Libri Antichi*, 1419-1508, 8rff.

Table 2.4

San Zanobi: Sponsors of More Than One Member, 1419–1424

Sponsor	Entrant's quarter	Entrant's parish	Relationship: sponsor > new member
Bartolommeo di Miniato	Santo Spirito	San Iacopo	? > goldsmith
	Santo Spirito	Santa Felicità	? > ?
	Santo Spirito	San Giorgio	? > cobbler
	San Giovanni	San Bartolommeo	? > goldsmith
	San Giovanni	San Marco	? > barber
Bendetto di Marco	Santa Maria Novella	Santa Trinità	Brother; druggist > druggist
	Santa Maria Novella	Santa Trinità	Brother; druggist > druggist
	Santa Maria Novella	Santa Trinità	Brother; druggist > druggist
	Santa Croce	Santo Stefano alla Badia	druggist > town crier
Dino di Tingho	San Giovanni	Santa Reparata	Goldsmith > silk guild
	San Giovanni	Santa Reparata	Goldsmith > saddler
Giovanni del Capella	San Giovanni	San Marco	Goldsmith > soap maker
	San Giovanni	San Marco	Goldsmith > soap maker
Niccolò di Benintendo	Santa Croce	Orsanmichele	Brothers; chandler > chandler
	San Giovanni	San Lorenzo	Chandler > linen dealer
	Santo Spirito	San Felice in Piazza	Chandler > ?
Pagolo barbiere	San Giovanni	San Michele Berteldi	Barber > ?
	San Giovanni	San Michele Berteldi	Barber > maestro
	San Giovanni	Santa Maria Maggiore	Barber > linen dealer
	San Giovanni	Santa Maria Maggiore	Barber > carpenter
	San Giovanni	Santa Reparata	Barber > ?
	San Giovanni	San Michele Visdomini	Barber > ?
Piero di Puccio	San Giovanni	San Tommaso	Silk guild > arms maker
	San Giovanni	Santa Reparata	Silk guild > arms maker
	San Giovanni	Santa Maria degli Alberghi	Silk guild > druggist
	San Giovanni	Santa Maria Nipotecosa	Silk guild > arms maker
	San Giovanni	San Lorenzo	Silk guild > ?
	San Giovanni	Santo Stefano	Silk guild > ?
	Santa Croce	Sant' Apollinare	Silk guild > locksmith

contexts, in two different ways. First, by grouping together in one relatively
loose structure a number of individually dense but collectively less dense
personal networks, the confraternity provided the member with a certain
anonymity that was seldom found in society at large. Second, the individual
networks that did tie together some members outside of the confraternity
provided members with real friends, kinsmen, and neighbors, but carefully
chosen ones, in front of whom and with whom one could share liminal
rituals of forgiveness and reconciliation. Indeed, that liminal escape was a
necessary component of the brothers' pursuit of community with God and
with one another. In the interest of that pursuit and in order that the
organization might continue and flourish, the confraternity also had to
foster a sense of solidarity and mutual commitment, as well as an ethic and
piety of brotherhood. The confraternity, like the mendicant order, stressed
mutual obligations. Members became debtors to the confraternity if they
failed to attend meetings or funerals or to contribute to the spiritual and
financial capital of the company. Rapid rotation of officers, including *infermieri,* who visited sick confraternity members; *limosinieri,* who dispensed
confraternity charity; and *sagrestani,* who prepared and, under the guidance
of a priest, helped to conduct weekly liturgical activities, circulated members and increased social contacts among them. Confraternity memoirs and
statutes emphasized the unifying symbols of the confraternity: its patron
saint, meeting place, emblems, relics and cult objects, dress conventions,
and commissioned art. The confraternity attempted to promote feelings of
shared intimacy by enforcing codes of secrecy, creating a "special knowledge" that separated members from nonmembers. The ritual activity of the
company also stressed common particpation: The mass was often sung or
chanted by the whole body of the company and was frequently
supplemented by vernacular hymns. Other liturgical activity reinforced the
company's perception of itself as a community; frequent processions and
feasts provided clear lines demarcating the social space of the confraternity.

Each confraternity had its distinctive dress and insignia, often worn on
the shoulder, cap, or sleeve of vestments. Members of the flagellant company of Jesus were required to wear

> white sackcloth with a vermillion crucifix on the left shoulder, belted with a cord of
> hemp. And when they go outside they go barefooted with their faces hidden,
> striking themselves with whips of white leather. Within the meeting hall they whip
> themselves with rope whips in order to dampen the noise and sound.[115]

115. Ms. Magliabecchiano, VIII, 1500, vol. 6, *Capitoli della Compagnia del Gesù,* 1332, 3 r-v:

Ed il loro vestimento è di sacco rinfranato bianco con una crocellina uermiglia in sulla spalla ritta, cinti

The garments of the flagellant companies were slit open at the back from the shoulder to the waist, and for this reason, the brothers of Jesus were admonished to "wear the garment in such a manner that one is uncovered modestly, without appearing nude.[116] The company of the Annunciation wore similar white robes, hemp belts, and carried rope whips. Their caps bore the emblem of the angel of the Annunciation and the dove of the Holy Spirit. As an additional insignia, the company decorated its precious objects with one of the emblems symbolic of Florence itself, the lily.[117] The robes of the *laudesi* company of Saint Mary were adorned with yellow crosses on a red field.[118] The linen vestments of San Domenico carried the image of that saint on the left sleeve.[119] The statutes of the company of San Girolamo informed its members that "your sign shall be the Holy Cross, which, being in front of your hearts always shall keep you warm and inflamed."[120] The members of the company of Saint Sebastian wore a more elaborate decoration: a crucifix suspended under a martyr's crown, with the crown itself bearing the symbol of the saint's martyrdom—a hand pierced by an arrow.[121] A white and red cross worn on the right shoulder identified the bearer as a member of the company of the Bigallo.[122] The brothers of the Compagnia de' Neri wore black robes appropriate to their burial activities. The company of San Zanobi explained the meaning of its emblem, a gold cross on a circular black field, as follows:

This glorious and holy sign is not without meaning and significance . . . and the significance of the symbol is this: the completely round circle signifies the perfect union and glorious faith that we ought to bear toward God our creator, whose power has neither beginning nor end, and the union that all members of our company ought to bear toward each other, and toward our neighbor, serving without sin in perfect charity continuously by the grace of God. And the black field signifies the memory of death that we should all bear in our hearts and souls, so that we prevent ourselves from contravening the will of God. And the still more precious sign of the Cross signifies that the heart and soul of each of us should be

---

con corda di canape annodata. Et quando escono fuori vanno scalzi colla faccia turata disciplinandosi con disciplina di quoio bianco, ma dentro fanno con disciplina di corda per fuggire strepito e romore.

116. *Ibid.*, 6r: "Ciascuno prenda la veste sua espoglisi honestamente sanza apparire ignudo."

117. *Capitoli*, 314, *Capitoli della Compagnia della Santissima Annunziata*, 1495.

118. *Capitoli*, 53, *Capitoli della Compagnia di Santa Maria delle Laudi*, in Santa Croce.

119. Meersseman, 2:698.

120. *Capitoli*, 195, *Capitoli della Compagnia di San Girolamo*, 1441, "E sia il vostro segno la Santa Croce, la quale avendola voi avanti sempre per ogetto ne' vostri cuori, in quella di nuovo riscaldati e infiammati."

121. *Capitoli*, 6, prologue.

122. Monti, 1:9.

continuously reminded of the most glorious passion of Jesus Christ, the source of our salvation and our souls' redemption. The cross is gold because gold is superior to all other metals and is the most precious. And so our souls ought to love our creator always, Who is above every other love, because the love of God comes before everything else.[123]

Some companies marched in procession on the feast day of John the Baptist and other major holidays. During these periodic public displays of pageantry, the members marched as a group behind elaborate standards. The *laudesi* company of Santa Croce carried a banner bearing a large star surrounded by an image of the Virgin Mary.[124] The members of San Domenico marched beneath the image of Jesus crucified, with a red star on a green field on the other side.[125] The company of Jesus marched behind a crucifix during its processions.[126] The four *Bianchi* companies founded during the mass processions of 1399 paraded thereafter behind the crucifixes that they carried that year and made those crosses objects of elaborate veneration.[127] The men of San Zanobi carried a painting of the Virgin as well as a standard depicting the Annunciation on one side and the majesty of God on the other. This standard was supported by a wooden tabernacle decorated with wooden crosses.[128] This equipment was carried on all major processions, and the statutes of this and of other companies described at great length the reverence, honor, and respect owed such vestments, emblems, and standards.[129]

123. *CRS*, 2170 (Z 1, vol. 1), *Capitoli della Compagnia di San Zanobi*, 1427, 4v-5r, describes the company sign:

> Campo nero e croce d'oro. Et questo glorioso et sancto segno non sanza grande cagione et significatione come detto. . . . Ella significatione di detto segno e che il cerchio tondo uuole significare la perfecta unione et fede gloriosa che dobbiamo auere in uerso il nostro creatore idio il quale non ebbe principio et nonna fine la sua potentia. Et così noi in uerso l'uno l'altro di tutta nostra compagnia. Et ancora in uerso ogni nostro proximo. Con seruare sanza peccato con perfecta Karità per continuo per la gratia di dio. E il campo nero significa la memoria della morte che noi avere dobbiamo ne' nostri cuori et anime. Acciò checci guardiamo di non fare contra alla uoluntà di Dio. Et più ancora il pretioso segno della croce significa che'l animo di ciascheduno di noi e nelli nostri cuori dobbiamo avere per continua memoria la gloriosa passione di Iesù Christo nella quale fu la nostra salute e redemptione delle nostre anime. Essendo d'oro significa che come l'oro è sopra a ogni metallo e più pretioso. Così le nostre anime debbono per continuo amare il nostro creatore. Il quale è sopra a ogni altro amore et ogni cosa uiene meno fuori che l'amore di dio.

124. Monti, 1:164-165.

125. Meersseman, 2:698.

126. Ms. Magliabecchiano, VIII, 1500, vol. 6, *Capitoli della Compagnia del Gesù*, 1332, 15v.

127. On the *Bianchi* companies of 1399, see pp. 51-56.

128. *CRS*, 2170 (Z 1, vol. 4), San Zanobi, *Libro de' Testamenti*, 20r, from inventory of 1354; Monti, 1:162-164.

129. *CRS*, 2170 (Z 1, vol. 1), *Capitoli della Compagnia di San Zanobi*, 1335 reforms, 7r-8v. See also

Whatever the brother's level of education or literacy, he could be expected to be familiar with the statutes of the company. The statute book was a compendium of organizational rules, procedures, and standards of behavior amply sprinkled with quotations from the church fathers and the scriptures.[130] For many confraternity members, the statute book was undoubtedly the most familiar of all religious documents. These statutes were read to the members periodically. Some companies, such as Orsanmichele, read the statutes aloud every month.[131] The officers of other companies, such as San Zanobi, San Domenico, and San Benedetto, were required to read their statutes publicly at least once during their term of office, that is, at least once every 3-4 months.[132] Other companies read selected chapters, most commonly those dealing with the morals of members.[133]

The piety of the proper confraternity member, as defined by the statute books, was an active piety cast in terms of behavioral prescriptions and proscriptions. This prologue, concerning the attainment of grace and salvation, is common to numerous fifteenth- and sixteenth-century *capitoli:*

> The Holy Spirit speaks through the mouth of the Prophet Malachai and says, "Flee evil and do good." Those words contain the two parts of justice necessary for salvation, without which the glorious prize of eternal life cannot be attained. However, doing good but failing to flee evil will not bring one to the gate of salvation. Accordingly, some devout and spirited persons of this company, inspired by God to live according to the two parts of justice, for the honor of God and the salvation of their souls, desirous of as much divine grace as is possible for persons placed in secular life and wishing to arrive at eternal life, decided to adopt a form of life which is founded in three most excellent grades, confirmed by divine Scriptures and praised by the doctrines of the Holy Doctors. The first grade is the contemplative life, which consists in elevating the mind to God through prayer, and meditation. The second grade is the active life, which consists in satisfying one's neighbor's needs with pure intention. The third grade is the moral life, which consists in ordering oneself with honest life and virtuous and holy conversation.[134]

Capitoli, 152, San Giovanni Battista, 1455, 12v-14r; *Capitoli della Compagnia della Madonna d'Orsanmichele,* 1294, capitolo 13, in del Prete, p. 7, and the 1297 statutes, capitolo 9, *ibid.,* pp. 13-14.

130. On the general character of confraternity statues, see Lodovico Scaramuggi, "Considerazioni su statuti e matricole di confraternite di disciplinati," in *Risultati,* pp. 134-194.

131. *Capitoli della Madonna d'Orsanmichele,* fourteenth century, in del Prete, p. 38, capitolo 11.

132. *CRS,* 2170, (Z 1, vol. 1), *Capitoli della Compagnia di San Zanobi,* 1326, 6v; *Capitoli della Compagnia di San Domenico,* 1477, in Meersseman, 2:728; *Capitoli,* 635, *Capitoli della Compagnia di San Benedetto de' Camaldoli,* 1385, 11v.

133. *Capitoli,* 606, *Capitoli della Compagnia di Santa Maria della Neve,* 1445.

134. This particular version is from *Capitoli,* 201, *Capitoli della Compagnia del Santissimo Sacramento in Santa Felicità,* 1571, 3r-v. For other examples of versions that are more or less identical, or close paraphrases, see the following fifteenth- and sixteenth-century statutes: *CRS,* 2170 (Z 1, vol. 1), *Capitoli*

The admonition to "do good and avoid evil" was a familiar *topos* in fifteenth-century Florentine popular spirituality. Both Sant' Antonino and San Bernardino used this motif as the basis for describing the religious obligations of laymen.[135] The concrete realization of the commandment to flee evil and do good consisted in performing three obligations: worship, charity toward one's neighbor, and leading a moral life.

Simple Christian theology was communicated to the members of confraternities through easy-to-learn formulas and familiar catechetical devices. The duties of the captains of the company of Saint Sebastian, for example, included instructing members in:

> the true Catholic faith, that is, the Ten Commandments of the Law, the Ten Articles of the Faith, the Seven Works of Spiritual and Corporeal Mercy, the Seven Gifts of the Holy Spirit, the Seven Sacraments of the Holy Church, the Five Senses of the Body, and in all other things that every faithful Christian ought to know.[136]

The company of Saint Francis set aside one regular period monthly for this rudimentary religious training:

> He who wishes to reach eternal life observes the divine commandments. And since each Christian is obliged by divine law to observe these commandments, we declare that their observance shall be efficaciously embraced with devotion. And in order that ignorance should never be the reason for falling into error or failure to observe these commandments, we desire that on the first Sunday of every month they be read in front of all our brothers in a manner that will ensure that each one understands them. And similarly, one should do the same thing with the Articles of the Faith.[137]

The "imitation of Christ" has long been considered to be one of the central motifs of pre-Reformation piety. Examining the spirituality of the late Middle Ages from Martin Luther's perspective, some historians have advanced the thesis that medieval piety placed an intolerable burden on

---

della Compagnia di San Zanobi, 1427; ASF, *Conventi Soppressi*, 92, vol. 390, *Capitoli della Compagnia di San Francesco*, 1427; *Capitoli*, 606, *Capitoli della Compagnia di Santa Maria della Neve*, 1445: *Capitoli*, 6, *Capitoli della Compagnia delle Laudi della Vergine Maria e di Sancto Philippo e di Sancto Sebastiano e di Sancto Gherardo*, 1451; *Capitoli*, 314, *Capitali della Compagnia della Santissima Annunziata*, 1495; *Capitoli*, 152, *Capitoli della Compagnia di San Giovanni Battista*, 1499; *Capitoli*, 608, *Capitoli della Compagnia di Santa Maria del Chiodo*, 1566; *Capitoli*, 3, *Capitoli della Compagnia di San Bernardino*, 1569; *Capitoli*, 623, *Capitoli della Compagnia di Sant' Antonio de' Macellari*, 1577; *Capitoli*, 649, *Capitoli della Compagnia del Santissimo Sacramento in Santa Trinità*, 1594; *Capitoli*, 5, Capitoli della Compagnia di San Leo, 1595.

135. Sant' Antonino, *Opera a ben vivere* (Florence, 1923), p. 7; San Bernardino da Siena, *Le prediche volgari*, ed. Piero Bargellini (Milan, 1936), sermon 4, p. 99ff.

136. *Capitoli*, 6, chap. 1.

137. *Conventi Soppressi*, 92, vol. 390, *Capitoli della Compagnia di San Francesco*, 1427.

fourteenth- and fifteenth-century sinners, forcing them to undertake a ceaseless imitation of Christ, to fast, make devotions and pilgrimages in a never-ending quest for perfection.[138] Confraternal piety, rather than exacerbating guilt about devotions yet unperformed, placed bounds around the devotional life by setting forth quite precisely what was required of a man seeking salvation. Rather than to prescribe unlimited devotions, confraternities required members to perform specific, limited, manageable tasks. These tasks were stated simply in the statutes of the company and, together with elementary theology, provided the confraternity member with a sense of religion and religious obligation that was within his ability to grasp and to fulfill. For the members of San Domenico, one of the central motifs of flagellant piety, the "imitation of Christ," was simply defined as "the observance of the Holy Commandments of God and His Church."[139]

Apart from variations in devotional practices (the relative importance of flagellation or singing of lauds) and specific forms of charity practiced toward the outside community, the obligations of confraternity members were similar from brotherhood to brotherhood. Brothers were obliged to recite daily prayers (customarily ranging from 5 to 15 Hail Marys and Our Fathers), to fast 1 day each week, to confess three times each year and take communion at least twice, to attend the regularly scheduled meetings of the company (weekly, fortnightly, or monthly), and to attend all major feasts (usually including Christmas, All Saints' Day, the four Marian feasts, all feasts of the Apostles, Holy Week, and the feast of the particular patron of the company). Members were also required to mourn the dead, whether simply by reciting the Ave Maria and Paternoster or by attending more elaborate memorial masses. The required period of mourning lasted from 3 days to 1 month. Members so delegated were required to visit ill brothers and to attend funerals. Finally, all members, except those who were too poor, were obligated to pay confraternity dues (ranging from several *soldi* to several *lire*) and all additional fiscal levies.[140]

138. Steven Ozment, *The Reformation in the Cities* (New Haven: Yale University Press, 1975), p. 22ff.

139. *Capitoli della Compagnia di San Domenico,* 1477, in Meersseman, 2:719:

Prenda ciascheduno la sua crocie, dicie il Salvatore, et seguiti me. Benché portando lui sì intollerabile crocie per gli altrui peccati, salendo alla sua gloria a noi per li nostri medesimi, volendo acquistare la gloria altrui, fussi dovuta molto maggiore penitentia, niente dimeno riguardando la debolezza delle nostre spalle et sperando nella sua misericordia, ce obligheremo solo a questo, che la prima nostri observantia et obligo sia de' sancti comandamenti d'Iddio e di sua Chiesa.

140. These obligations could be stated as simply as those of the company of San Domenico, *Capitoli,* 1477, in Meersseman, 2:720-721, or as elaborately as those of the company of Santa Brigida, whose exposition ran to more than 100 pages of text. Laurenziana, *Ashburnham,* 460, *Capitoli della Compagnia di Santa Brigida.*

Members of a number of companies took on additional obligations to the Florentine community. These companies administered special forms of beneficence, being, in this regard, quasi-public institutions. Orsanmichele distributed communal charity to the poor. The Misericordia buried the poor, especially in time of plague or famine. The Compagnia de' Neri administered the last rites to those executed by the commune. The company of San Martino provided assistance to impoverished patricians.[141]

The obligation to "abstain from evil" manifested itself in a confraternal code of ethics intended to suppress those sins that weakened the community.[142] Confraternity statute books singled out for punishment any member who

> commits the unspeakable sin of [sodomy], anyone who, out of maleficent disdain, disobeys the governors, anyone who makes public the name of any brother or any secret of the company, anyone who precipitates factions or foments discord, anyone who solicits written or oral votes for any office, anyone who misleads brothers, anyone who counterfeits or falsifies any decision, order, or document of the company . . . anyone who plays games of dice or cards, or who makes illegal contracts, or who keeps concubines, or blasphemes or curses God or the Saints, or regularly frequents taverns.[143]

The statute books proscribed particularly those acts that could create shame and cause violence: gambling, sodomy, the frequenting of taverns and prostitutes. One must not ruin one's own reputation, for that would stain the reputation of the brotherhood. Confraternities even forbade their members, by statute, to quarrel among themselves. Some companies proscribed the swearing of oaths to factional groups.[144] Others prohibited their members from participating in the street battles (*pugne*) of neighborhood youth gangs that accompanied the celebration of certain holidays.[145] Members were forbidden to treat their confraternal brothers as strangers or "others," and the claims of ritual brotherhood thus barred *fratelli* from taking each other to court or practicing usury.

141. L. Passerini, *Storia degli Stabilimenti di Beneficenza e d'Istruzione Elementare Gratuita della Città di Firenze* (Florence, 1853), *passim* (hereafter cited as Passerini); Trexler, "Charity and the Defense of Urban Elites," *passim*.

142. A similar stress on sins that weaken the social fabric of the community has been observed by Richard Trexler in *Synodal Law in Florence and Fiesole, 1306-1518* (Rome, 1971), pp. 134-135.

143. Statutes of the company of San Domenico, in Meersseman, 2:721.

144. P. Sisto da Pisa, O. Capp., "Gli statuti fondamentali del Terz' Ordine," in VII *centenario del Terz' Ordine Francescano: 1221-1921, Studi Francescani* (special issue, 1921): 27-28.

145. BNF *Banco Rari,* 336, *Statuti della Compagnia di San Gilio,* 1278.

Confraternal regulations identified pious behavior with the correct performance of the mutual obligations that bound the community together and kept it at peace. Without peace, the fraternity would dissolve and members would lose the social and spiritual benefits associated with active membership. Conversely, the fulfillment of membership obligations was thought to be conducive to peace and social harmony, for the fulfillment of such obligations would promote the social bonds upon which peace is based. Only in a spirit of peace could confraternal activity take place, and "therefore we order," read the statutes of the company of the Annunciation, "that we anchor ourselves in holy peace and good brotherhood and concord so that we may be able to serve God more devotedly and to cultivate worthy fruits of penance."[146] The statutes of the company of San Gilio were written in 1278 (and modified in 1296), "to the honor of God and to the good and peaceful state of the company."[147] This confraternity obliged its members to maintain benevolent relations with their *confratelli* not only for the good of the company but also so that they might serve as a model of social relations in the faction-ridden city:

> We hereby order that all members of this confraternity, whether young or old, comport themselves honestly, and that they love one another. And when we are found together we should honor and aid each other in a spirit of friendship so that other persons observing us will make a good example of us.[148]

The officers of the company were required to pacify quarreling members:

> To keep our company free from scandal we order that . . . if there should be any villainous exchange between members, the captains are obliged to pacify them within five days, and together with the friar [chaplain of the company], they should reason discreetly with the men who are angered with one another. And if any person or persons are not willing to be reconciled, the captains and the friar shall expel from the company whoever such persons may be. If any member strikes another member in anger, the captains and friar shall be obliged to expel him from the company.[149]

Members of Orsanmichele were expected to bring accusations to bear against themselves if they found themselves hating other members. If such

---

146. *Capitoli*, 314, *Capitoli della Compagnia della Santissima Annunziata*, 1495, chap. 2: "Et però ordiniamo aciò che noi ci fondiamo in sancta pace et buona fratellanza et concordia aciò che più divotamente possiamo servire addio et fare degni frutti di penitentia."

147. *Ibid.*

148. *Ibid.*

149. *Ibid.* See also *Capitoli*, 719, Sancti Martiri Innocenti, *Capitoli*, 1487, 23r.

accusations were brought by other members, the governors imposed double penance upon the malefactors.[150] Many companies, following the republic's practice of creating official peacemakers during periods of civil strife, elected *paciali* (peacemakers).[151] Usually the penalty for fomenting discord was severe, most companies "expelling immediately anyone who attempts to create factions, division, or who instigates disturbances or disturbs fraternal union and peace.[152]

For the members of the company of San Paolo, peace and reconciliation were fundamental to the fulfillment of confraternal obligations, to the nature of the holy life, and to the imitation of Christ. The statutes of San Paolo invite the members to follow the wishes of Saint Paul:

> I beseech all of you, my sons . . . that you proceed worthily along the path to which you have been called, with every humility and meekness, each of you supporting the other patiently, in charity, diligent to conserve the union of the spirit in the bond of peace, since you have all been called in one and the same hope of your vocation . . . . Together be benign and merciful, pardoning each other as God in the passion of Christ pardoned you, giving Him as the price for your sins. . . . Seek peace with everyone and seek saintliness, without which no one ever beholds God.[153]

The Rites of Community

I have described several facets of the Florentine confraternity in the thirteenth through fifteenth centuries, its citywide rather than parish or neighborhood orientation, its emphasis on civic, communal models, collective worship, shared symbols, and mutual assistance. These elements of

---

150. *Capitoli della Compagnia della Madonna d'Orsanmichele,* fourteenth century, chap. 10, in del Prete, p. 38.

151. *Capitoli,* 314 *Capitoli della Compagnia della Santissima Annunziata,* 1495, capitolo 17; *Capitoli,* 606, *Capitoli della Compagnia di Santa Maria della Neve,* 1445; *Capitoli della Compagnia di San Domenico,* 1477, in Meersseman, 2:725, 731.

152. *CRS,* 107 (A 98, vol. 1), *Capitoli della Compagnia di Sant' Antonio Abate,* chap. 15: "Subito s'intenda raso, chi temptassi setta, divisione, o fussi seminatore di schandali, o turbassi l'unione et pace fraterna." Any member of the company of Holy Concord who had not made peace with his brothers was forbidden from attending meetings. *Capitoli,* 194, 1437 statutes.

153. *Capitoli,* 29, San Paolo in Via dell' Acqua, *Capitoli,* 16v:

> Voi tucti figliuoli miei, priego io, pregione del signore che uoi chiaminati degnamente per la uia che uoi siate suti chiamati, con ogni humilità et mansuetudine, con patientia sopportando l'uno l'altro in carità, diligenti a conseruarui l'unione dello spirito nel uincolo della pace, si chome siate chiamati tutti in una medesima speranza della uocatione uostra. . . . Siate insieme benigni, misericordiosi perdonando l'uno l'altro, chome dio nella passione di Christo perdono a uoi, dandolo in prezo de' peccati uostri. . . . Che uoi seguitate la pace con tucti et la sanctimonia, sanza la quale nessuno mai uedra idio.

confraternity life should not be understood in isolation from one another. All contributed to the formation of a ritual space to which the member might repair weekly or biweekly, where he could dissolve tension and animosity, practice peace, and promote community loyalty. Outside the walls of the confraternity, the city dweller's competitive, overlapping, often conflicting personal obligations and alliances could make the management of his commitments an anxious and hazardous enterprise. Within the confraternity, where a man's association with his "brothers" was characterized by much less overlapping and competition, he could assuage a conscience made guilty by the conflicting demands of Florentine social relations.

Some of the late medieval confraternities, it appears, were founded in an atmosphere of social upheaval, during periods of political and social chaos; all developed against the background of the day-to-day tensions that the structure of Florentine social relations produced. Social pacification remained the central theme underlying much confraternal activity throughout the period of the Florentine republic. From the moment that a Florentine joined a brotherhood he was exposed continuously to celebrations of peace. During fraternal initiation ceremonies the novice was given the kiss of peace by the officers or by the entire membership of the company.[154] A number of Florentine confraternities sponsored a Mass of Peace for the entire community, so that, as one company hoped, "God should conserve and maintain in true peace and unity our city and the members of our company."[155] The 1431 statutes of the flagellant company of Santa Maria del Carmine suggest the range of peacemaking in Florentine confraternities. The company was founded, its statutes remind the membership, in the name of the "salvation and peace of our city and of every citizen."[156] At the beginning of each service the company chaplain intoned, "Omnipotent God, grant us peace."[157] At the beginning of each term of office the officers of the company celebrated "a devout Mass for the peace and good state of our city and countryside."[158] The central moment of the

154. Conventi Soppressi, 92, vol. 390, Capitoli della Compagnia di San Francesco, 1427, chap. 21, "Et allora i Guardiani si bacino col detto novitio in segnio di pace." See also Capitoli, 439, Capitoli della Compagnia della Disciplina in Santa Maria del Carmine, 1431, capitolo 3: "Sia riceuuto nella nostra compagnia e la sera che entra si canti Veni Creator Spiritus e dichasi l'oratione dello Spirito e'l novitio uada umilmente dando la pacie prima al correttore e dipoi a tutti gli altri frategli."

155. Both the Bigallo (Monti, 1:153-156) and Orsanmichele (del Prete, Capitoli, 1294, chap. 5, p. 4) held peace masses every Thursday.

156. Capitoli, 439, prologue.

157. Ibid., chap. 14: "Pacis conciedat nobis omnipotens Dominus."

158. Ibid., chap. 12: "Ordiniamo cogni camarlingho nel prencipio del suo uficio sia tenuto di fare dire una diuota messa per la pacie e per lo buono stato della nostra cittade e contado."

rites of initiation was the exchange of the sign of peace between novices and the membership.[159] Members were required to pray each day, reciting:

> five Paternosters and Ave Marias, kneeling, out of reverence for the five sighs of our Lord Jesus Christ, for the peace and good state of our city and countryside, and three Paternosters with Ave Marias, in honor of the Holy Trinity, for the preservation and peace of our company.[160]

Florentine confraternity rituals provided lay Florentines with a symbolic means of repairing and renewing their communal bonds. We are fortunate to have, in the statute books of the flagellant company of Sant' Antonio, a fairly detailed account of the rituals performed at each regular meeting of the company.[161] Immediately upon entering the confraternity, the member was reminded of its sacred character, marked off, as it was, by ritual. At

159. *Ibid.,* chap. 3.
160. *Ibid.,* chap. 7:

> Ogni dì ne dicha cinque pater nostri e cinque aue marie ginochioni a riverenza delle cinque piaghe del nostra Signore giesù christo, per la pace e buon stato della nostra città e contado, e tre paternostri coll'ave marie a onore e riverenza della Sancta Trinità per conservamento e pacie della nostra compagnia.

For examples of confraternal prayers for peace, see *Capitoli,* 606, *Capitoli della Compagnia di Santa Maria della Neve,* 1495; *Capitoli,* 194, Santa Concordia, 1437, chap. 15.

161. *CRS,* 107 (A 98, vol. 1), *Capitoli della Compagnia di Sant' Antonio Abate,* 1485, 17v-22r.

Descriptions of confraternity rituals were seldom provided in detail. A similar version of this ritual, in abbreviated form, is contained in the statutes of the company of Sant' Antonio da Padova, *CRS,* 137 (a 132, vol. 1):

> E ciascuno quando entra dentro annunctij la pace dicendo la pace di dio sia con noi overo in questa chasa. E poi si ponghi ginochioni e dicha un Paternostro choll' Ave Maria e poi torni alla porta e scanbi o quello che ve è tanto ui stia che uenga un altro. E uno de fratelli quale prima giunge leggha qualche buono exemplo tanto chella champanella sia sonata. E in chontante che sia sonato il terzo segno ciaschuno si rasegni nell' oratorio e il ghovernatore dello ufficio chominci et dicha, "Sit nomen domini benedictum." E i frategli rispondino, "Et hoc nunc et usquem in seculum." E poi dica, "adiutorium nostrum in nomine domini." Rispondino et dichino tutti, "Pater noster." Et di chi lo secreto et finito dica il ghovernatore prima o ueramente cho' lui che farà l'ufficio, "Confitear domino omnipotenti." E i fratelli rispondino il modo usato. E fatta la chonfessione si dichi il matutino o i salmi o quello paresse a ghovernatori chome detto di sopra nella entrata degli ufficiali. E diesi la pace. Et doppo le dette chose si spenghano i lumi et faccisi disciplina. Et uno de' fratelli si facci una rachomandigia generale. Et per essere exaudito si dicha cinque Paternostri, e cinque Ave Marie. E poi si dicha per l'anime che sono nel purgatorio, "De profundis clamavi," e ll'oratione, cioè, "Fidelium deus." Et di poi si rivestino i fratelli. E chomincisi a chantare una Lauda fino chessieno rivestiti e di poi r'acesso illume si faccia la sperge di poi il sacrestano inchominci il Miserere mei deo et finito questo si dicha l'oratione de' peccati. E di poi quando sia sonata la chanpana alla voluntà o allora deputata sieno licenziati.

Other extant versions of this ritual, roughly equivalent, are found in the following sets of statutes: *Capitoli,* 81, San Hieronymo, 1491, chap. 10; *Capitoli,* 152, San Giovanni Battista, 1499, 10v-11r; *Capitoli,* 29, San Paolo, 29rff.; *CRS,* 3 (A8, vol. 1), Sant' Agostino, 27v-28r; *Capitoli,* 314, Santissima Annunziata, 1495, chap. 13.

the doors of the confraternity the bond between members was reaffirmed. A member entering the confraternity was welcomed into the oratory with the greeting "go in peace" by the member who had arrived most recently. Having welcomed the new arrival, the member proceeded into the oratory of the confraternity, leaving the last man to offer the same greeting to the member who would next arrive. This unbroken chain of greeting, a rite of incorporation, highlighted the solidarity of the group. Upon entering the oratory, the confraternity member approached the altar and recited an Ave Maria and a Paternoster, remaining silent except when performing official duties or ceremonies. Leaving the sanctuary, he then entered the sleeping chamber (*dormentorio*), where members retired after flagellation. The spatial movement was accompanied by a ritual transition. In the sleeping chamber the member left behind the outward signs of his place in the social structure. He changed into the hooded robes, open at the back, worn by his ritual brothers. Now dressed like the others, he was indistinguishable from the rest of the company. Having suspended his normal status, he was now a brother, brotherhood being that purest bond of equality between persons sharing personal ties. In the confraternity even fathers and sons shared a bond of ritual brotherhood; status, rank, and role were replaced by mutual obligations shared equally by all. The wearing of hooded robes and the use of dim lighting fostered a sense of anonymity that helped to remove the inhibitions of those who participated in self-deprecating and emotionally charged rites in front of their kinsmen and friends. The *fratello* left the *dormentorio* and having undergone a preliminary transformation, reentered the sanctuary. As he reentered he occupied the first available seat, without regard for the identity of those who sat around him. This procedure, like the entry rite, affirmed the unbroken unity of the membership as all gathered within the sanctuary.

At the entrance of the governor, all members kneeled. Each member confessed his sins to the governor and was absolved by the chaplain of the company. The governor was also empowered to give correction in public, as the statutes of San Domenico illustrate: "to impose a penance in money, not to exceed one florin, or a pilgrimage, not to exceed one day's journey. And he shall require each member to beg forgiveness of the other."[162] Sant' Antonio excluded the imposition of pilgrimages as penance, "in order that our failings should not be known [outside of the company], and to insure that the corrections imposed have been performed." The governor of Sant' Antonio was, however, empowered to order flagellation as penance. And

---

162. *Capitoli della Compagnia di San Domenico*, 1477, in Meersseman, 2:728.

although penance was not to be displayed to the outside world, it was to be visible to the other members. The correction was "public, that it may be seen by everyone, if only to serve as an example to the others."[163] Fraternal confession of sin was clearly on occasion not a private, secret act but rather a public unburdening leading to public reconciliation. For the members of Orsanmichele, confraternal confession was a "remedy" for sins against one's neighbor.[164] The revelation of secrets, especially those sins against one's intimates, was a moment of hazard and extreme vulnerability for the Florentine, normally loathe to reveal anything to anyone. The selection of trustworthy confessors must have been a most delicate matter. Confraternities maintained lists of all members who entered the clergy in order that, in the words prefacing one such list, "our brothers should know where they can go in security to seek counsel, fraternally, for soul and body."[165] Public confession of sin provided additional bonds between members. Often, private sins became secrets common to the membership. For this reason the obligation to maintain secrecy about company affairs was mandatory, "so

163. *CRS,* 107 (A 98, vol. 1), Sant' Antonio Abate:

E tutte le correptione che dal Ghovernatore inposta saranno si satisfaccino nel luogho et non altrove, per che non vogliamo siano di peretrinaggio accioché e nostri defecti suoi del luogho non si manifestino, et a che per essere certi che tale i correptione si mettino a effecto, in adoratione col la veste et discipline in mezzo uestato o nudo, più o meno secondo la sua conscientia. . . . Non larechi il correpto coperta, ma publica, che da ciascuno sia veduta, solo per exemplo degli altri.

On public confession, see also *Capitoli,* 452, *Capitoli della Compagnia della Purificazione di Maria Vergine,* 1389:

I capitani facciano fare di due mesi una uolta correctione in questo modo, Cioè che in prima si leggha questo capitolo dinanzi alla compagnia, poi con ogni mansuetudine ciascuno, et principalmente i capitani e camarlinghi e consiglieri, eschano fuori del usato luogho a uno a uno. Et accusati palesemente per gli altri della compagnia ritornino dentro et inginocchiati dell' offese commesse contro alla compagnia secondo i capitoli humilmente s'acchusino dinanzi al correctore et a tutta la compagnia, el correctore secondo il fallo il correggha et ciascuno diuotamente facci quello chegli sia ingiunto in penitenzia.

On the practice of assigning flagellation as a form of penance, see *Capitoli,* 606.

164. *Capitoli della Compagnia della Madonna d'Orsanmichele,* 1294, capitolo 15 in del Prete, pp. 7-8:

Anche, cun ciò sia cosa che 'l nimico del'umana generatione non cessi continuamente di tentare li uomi e le femine, e di farli discorrere ne' peccati e ne' li ofendimenti di Dio e del prossimo, e per prendere lo rimedio che Dio nostro Segnore ci à conceduto, ordiniamo che ciascuno de la nostra Conpagnia, il quale serà in etade da ciò, si confessi e confessare si debia due volte l'anno o più, o 'l meno una, generalmente di tutti i suoi peccati.

CRS, 1594 (P 1, vol. 42), Compagnia di San Paolo, *Fratelli Morti,* 26r:

Qui apresso farò richordi di tutti quelli fussino andati alla religione che fussino stati dalla innanzi detta chompagnia di Messer Sancto Paolo Apostolo . . . . perchè e fratelli sappiano dove eppossono andare sicchuramente effraterneuolemente addomandare consigli e delle anime e del chorpo.

that no one should lose the secrets of his conscience."[166] Members caught gossiping outside the brotherhood were expelled immediately.[167]

Following confession, the company recited opening prayers and sang a hymn of peace. Then all of the lights, except one illuminating the image of Saint Anthony, were extinguished. By plunging the chamber into darkness, a sense of disorientation, a suspension of customary spatial, temporal, and visual order was produced. The illuminated image of Saint Anthony, the patron and mediator of the confraternal community and its principal symbol of unity, provided the only focused contact with the sensory world. Leather whips were then distributed, and after the governor exhorted the *fratelli* to practice true penance, a penance of lamentation and tears, the remaining light in the chamber was put out. The members, now cut off totally from the social structure and the normal structure of perception, offered silent prayers. Flagellation began, accompanied by a responsive liturgy of humiliation and debasement, focused on the Passion of Christ, death, and the evil and brevity of earthly life, drawn from the penitential psalms. Having temporarily dissociated themselves from the social structure, the members, at that moment, were able to see themselves as part of larger, all-inclusive communities and offered prayers on behalf of such communities: the church, Christianity, dead souls. The members washed their wounds. Having scourged, humiliated, and debased themselves, the brothers now underwent the symbolic death of sleep. They returned to the dormitory and slept on simple mats, covered with threadbare "vile" coverlets.

Early the next morning, the brothers were awakened by a bell; they rose and began the final rites of incorporation. Chanting, they marched out of the sleeping chamber together. Symbolically they reentered the world: The lights in the oratory, extinguished when the liminal rites of flagellation began, were now rekindled. Reassembled as a purified body, they recited the Credo, the affirmation of those beliefs that Christians shared in common. Following a prayer for peace, the company sang the gradual psalms (119-134), which celebrate the unity of Jerusalem, peace, harmony, and brotherhood. After a final Ave Maria, recited together (balancing the first, which had been recited individually the night before upon entrance), the company was dismissed.

166. *Capitoli*, 439, *Capitoli della Compagnia della Disciplina in Santa Maria del Carmine*, 1431, capitolo 8: "Ordiniamo che non sia alcuno il quale ardischa rivelare o manifestare alcuna cosa de' fatti della compagnia ne se ne altrui nel luogho nostro accio che non si perda il secreto della conscientia."

167. CRS, 2170 (Z 1, vol. 1), *Capitoli della Compagnia di San Zanobi*, 1427-1428, 17r; *Capitoli*, 6, Saint Sebastian, *Capitoli*, 1451, capitolo 4.

The induction of new members into the confraternity was also celebrated
with rites of incorporation. The induction ritual is described in the statutes
of the company of San Paolo for the year 1472:

> They [the novices] should be received into the speaking chamber [*parlatorio*] by the
> Masters of Novices themselves. The Governor should send one of his Councillors
> together with the Provisioner to read to them the second chapter of these statutes
> [on proscribed behavior]. At the time when the priest chants the *Miserere* at the
> altar, alternating verse by verse with the choir [the rest of the company], send the
> novices in. And the Sacristan having already placed robes on the altar and lighted
> the candles in the oratory, the novices shall be brought into the oratory at the
> recitation of the *Asperges Me* and they shall first kneel in the middle of the chamber,
> and then, having been signaled, shall rise and be guided to the altar, where the
> preliminary prayers shall have been recited by the priest. At the altar the novices
> shall be asked, "What is your desire?," and shall respond, "My salvation, the mercy
> of God, and the peace of this company." At the recitation of the *Induat Te Deus,*
> their cloaks shall be carried into the sacristy and they shall receive the vestments of
> the company. And, as the priest intones "*Veni Creator* [*Spiritus*], they shall turn,
> kneeling to the choir, and shall await the kiss of peace from the brethren. While the
> hymn is being sung, the Governor, Councillors, and, following them, the first choir
> [the company was divided into two choirs for antiphonal chanting] shall proceed to
> give the novices the kiss of peace. The Governor shall raise each novice up to a
> standing position from the position in which each novice had been kneeling, and
> they [the first choir and the officers] shall return with the others and the other
> choir shall do the same. The novices shall turn again to the altar, kneeling at the
> intonation of *Accende Lumen.* The priest shall give each one of them a lighted candle
> which they shall hold during the recitation of the next three prayers, the prayer of
> the Holy Spirit, the prayer of Our Advocate [Saint Paul], and the Hymn of Peace.
> The prayers having been completed, a brother designated by the Governor shall
> recite to the Novices the meaning, if this is why they entered, of the fruits of
> perseverance, and that they should do everything secretly, so that the birds in the
> air will not carry off the exposed seed.[168]

168. *Capitoli,* 29, statutes of the company of San Paolo, 1472, 27r-28rff.:

L'entrata loro, non potendo essere più che quattro per uolta, si faccia in questo modo che receuuti in
parlatorio da maestri d'epsi nouitij. Il gouernatore mandi uno de' suoi consiglieri chol proueditore a
leggergli al secondo di questi capitoli, et dimandarli se piace loro entrare con quelle obligationi. Se
dichano di non sieno acompagnati insino alla porta, licentiandogli; se dichano di sí, referito dentro, al
tempo si dicha il *Miserere* dal religioso all'altare un uerso lui, l'altro il choro. Et hauendo e sacrestani già
distesa la uesta in sulla predella et accese le falchole per lo oratorio sieno allo *Asperges Me,* condotti dentro
et inginocchiati prima immeza, siena leuati chol cenno, condotti allo altare doue dette le prime orationi
dal religioso et dimandati quello uoglino, risposto che "hanno el mio primo saluto, la misericordia di Dio,
et la pace di questa compagnia." Alla *Induat Te Deus* sieno portati il loro mantelli in sacrestia et epsi
riceuuta la uesta et intonato dal religioso *Veni Creator* sieno uolti ginocchioni al coro aspectando la pace da
fratelli. Mentre si canta l'ymno il gouernatore, consiglieri, et seguente, choro la uadino a dare loro
leuandogli il gouernatore per humanità d'inginocchioni et tornandosi in giù pel choro dentro chon gli

It is noteworthy that, at the outset, the novice was guided to the door of the confraternity by his kinsman or other sponsor. At that moment, however, he began rites that made him the "brother" of all members. As a ceremonial transition in status for the novice, the initiation rite was in some respects reminiscent of the ancient rites of baptism.[169] In front of the members of the company, the signs of the novice's previous status in the world were removed; he replaced his worldly garb with the garments of the confraternal community. Throughout the rite, the images of rebirth shaped the ceremony. At crucial moments he knelt, and was then "raised" up by the governor of the company. At other moments, he "turned" to receive the Holy Spirit. Lighted candles and prayers celebrating the symbolic meaning of light and flame were prominent during the ritual. By the end of the rite he had been embraced by his new brothers and taught the meaning of community.

The confraternity was a brotherhood, a corporate body, but it was not a sworn association. If a member swore an oath of loyalty or obedience to the confraternity and failed to follow all statutory obligations, he would fall into mortal sin for breaking his solemn oath. For this reason, almost all confraternities expressly forbade the swearing of oaths, so that, as the statutes of San Zanobi explained, "no one will be culpable" on account of infringements of confraternal rules.[170] The only oath that novices were accustomed to swear was one common among flagellant companies, to the effect that

---

altri al luogo suo. Chosí faccia l'altro coro. Et riuolti e nouitij ginocchioni all'altare allo *Accende Lumen.* Il religioso pongha loro una candela per uno in mano accesa le quali tenghino tanto sieno decte le tre orationi dello Spirito Sancto, Nostro Aduocato, et Pace. Le quali finite uno mandato dal gouernatore dicha loro il contento se è concepto di loro uenuta, del fructo della perseuerantia et che tutto operino secretamente. Acciò che gli uccelli dell'aria non se ne portino il seme iscoperto.

For similar ceremonies, see *Capitoli*, 6, Saint Sebastian, capitolo 24; *Capitoli*, 81, *Capitoli della Compagnia di San Girolamo*, 1491, chap. 9.

169. On the ancient rites and symbols of baptism in the early church, see Jean Danielou, *The Bible and the Liturgy* (Notre Dame: University of Notre Dame Press, 1966), chaps. 1–2.

170. CRS, 2170 (Z 1, vol. 1), *Capitoli della Compagnia di San Zanobi*, 1326, 6v; See also the 1454 statutes of Gesù Pellegrino included in the *Ricordanze* of Domenico Pollini, BNF, 8, 1282, 83r "come niuno per questi capitoli è obrigato a colpa d'anima ma a pene corporali." *Capitoli*, 314, *Capitoli della Compagnia della Santissima Annunziata*, 1495 reforms. See also the more extensive prohibitions against the swearing of oaths and vows in sixteenth-century statue books: *Capitoli*, 202, *Capitoli della Compagnia di Santa Maria della Croce al Tempio*, 1586: "Dichiarando per espresso che quando non fusse osservato né messo ad effecto tutte quelle cose si ordinerano in questi capitoli o parte di quelli non s'intenda alcuno cadere in peccato mortale né ueniale, eccetto chi non uolessi osservarli per dispregio, sia sopra della sua conscienzia et di questo ne lasciamo giudizio a Dio."; *Capitoli*, 608, *Capitoli della Compagnia di Santa Maria del Chiodo*, 1566; *Capitoli*, 649, *Capitoli della Compagnia del Santissimo Sacramento in Santa Trinità*, 1594, pp. 7–8. See also Meersseman, 1:29–34.

they were not members of other confraternities.[171] Brotherhoods in other places and times have made ceremonies like oath swearing or mingling of blood a sign of their bond. The members of Florentine confraternities made the sacrament of communion, the sacrifice and collective partaking of Christ's body, a sacrament of brotherhood. "Communion," in the words of one fraternal orator, "is the consummation and perfection of all the divine sacraments that collect and conjoin our lives, divided into so many parts, into one single perfect state, and it imparts to us and gives the confraternity unity through the Lord almighty."[172] For Cristoforo Landino, preaching before the company of the Magi, the sacrament of communion was not only a symbolic act of fraternal unity but also the act through which such unity was made possible, because communion cleansed man of social vices. Through communion, the brothers were "purged of the old condition of malice and iniquity," and became "new unleavened dough of sincerity and purity."[173]

---

171. See *CRS*, 1582 (P 1, vol. 6), San Paolo, meeting record of October 27, 1453:

Fu deliberato pel chorpo della chompagnia che pel avenire tutti i novizi . . . . prima di manifestino agl' altri frategli nela loro entrata, si deba dare loro ingiuramento primo religioso o primo de' frategli che detto novizio non sia in oltra compagnia di disciplina o simile che non posse entrare altrove se in prima non à rinunziata questa compagnia.

San Paolo's prohibition of multiple memberships followed a decree of Archbishop Antonio. (See *CRS*, 1582, meeting record of January 7, 1453). The decree was incorporated into the 1472 statute reforms accomplished during Lorenzo de' Medici's governorship. And Lorenzo, at that time, swore publicly that he had renounced all other companies ("Io . . . havendo prima publicamente rinuntiato a qualunque altra compagnia che pei capitoli nostri nuovi sia vietata") as the statutes required. His oath is contained in a letter to San Paolo published by M. Del Piazzo, "Gli autografi di Lorenzo de' Medici nell' Archivio di Stato di Firenze," *Rinascimento* 8 (1957):226-227. On the basis of this letter, R. Trexler has stated that Lorenzo resigned from all confraternities, and that he did so because he had reached the age (25) at which *veduti* had to resign from confraternities (*Public Life*, pp. 439-440). But he did not resign from San Paolo. Far from leaving San Paolo, Lorenzo states in his letter that, obeying the statutes that he had drafted, he renounced all other confraternities in order to *remain* in San Paolo. On his participation in San Paolo after 1472, see p. 117, this volume.

One company that did require its members to swear "*giuramento*" was the company of Saint Sebastian (*Capitoli*, 6, 1451, chap. 24).

172. Riccardiana, ms. Riccardiano 2204, anonymous, *Oratio ad comunionem:* "È adunque la comunione una consumatione et perfectione di tutti i sacramenti diuini che collega et congiunge le vite nostre in più parti divise in un solo unico et perfecto stato et comunicaci et dona la compagnia et individua unità del sommo iddio."

173. *Ibid., Sermone di Messere Christofano Landino fatto in commemoratione del corpo di Christo et recitato nella Compagnia de' Magi*, 178v.

For an extended treatment of communion in terms reminiscent of a rite of passage from a state of social impurity to social purity in fifteenth-century Florence, see Giovanni Dominici's sermon for Holy Saturday, edited by Maria Teresa Casella, "Una nuova predica del Dominici," *Miscellanea Gilles Gerard Meersseman, Italia Sacra* 15 (1970) 1:375ff.

The most solemn day of confraternal assembly and the day of greatest
attendance was the Thursday before Easter—Maundy Thursday. Easter was
a parish affair; Holy Thursday, however, was given elaborate celebration in
the Florentine confraternities. There, the brothers reenacted the arche-
typal Christian brotherhood of the Last Supper, and recalled the treason of
one confrère. To apprehend the connections between social relations
and ritual behavior, it is instructive to examine Holy Thursday in some
detail.[174]

The celebration of Holy Thursday solemnized three events: the incipient
treason of Judas, the Last Supper, and Christ's washing the feet of his
disciples. (*Disciplinati* companies dated the origin of flagellation rites to Holy
Thursday and celebrated this event as well.) The service began with a
reading of the scriptural and patristic accounts of Judas's betrayal of Christ,
summed up in one rich phrase—Christ's lament, "*Amicus meus osculo me
tradidit*" "My friend betrayed me with a kiss". The phrase is equally descriptive of what Judas once did to Christ and what Florentines regularly did to
one another. The narration of the events of Holy Thursday highlighted
throughout Christ's abandonment by his friends: "All my friends have
abandoned me and have deviously overcome me. He in whom I delighted,
betrayed me. And with terrible glances they have assaulted me with cruel
blows."[175] After the recitation of the liturgy came the performance of the

---

174. On the rites of Holy Thursday, see A. Malvy, "Lavement des pieds," *Dictionnaire de théologie
catholique*, 9, cols. 16-36; Thomas Schafer, *Die Fusswaschung im Monastischen Brauchtum und in der
Lateinischen Liturgie, Texte und Arbeiten* 47 (1956).

For the Florentine ritual, see *Capitoli*, 439, *Capitoli della Compagnia della Disciplina in Santa Maria del
Carmine*, 1431; *Capitoli*, 314, *Capitoli della Compagnia della Santissima Annunziata*, 1495, chap. 16; *Capitoli
della Compagnia di San Domenico*, 1477, in Meersseman, 2:736. The transformation in meaning and
practice of Holy Thursday is discussed in Chapter 5.

Holy Thursday rites celebrated elsewhere in fifteenth-century Italy emphasized rather different
values. For a description of Holy Thursday at the court of Ercole d'Este, see the unpublished
manuscript of Sherrill Cohen (Princeton University), "To See the Duke: Sovereign and Subjects in
Renaissance Ferrara."

175. *Capitoli*, 439: "Omnes amici mei derelinquerunt me et preualuerunt insidiantes michi
tradidit me quem diligebam et terribilibus oculis plagha crudeli percutiens aceto petabant me."

The emphasis on Judas' treason was common to many Italian Holy Thursday celebrations. See,
for example, the *lauda* recited in Assisi on that day:

> Venne cristo humiliato
> ai pie de giuda per lavere
> avea facto già quel mercato
> venduto lui trenta denare
> o cortese salvadore
> coy lavaste altradetore.

Quoted in Terruggia, "In quale momento," p. 444.

rite of the *mandatum,* or, in Italian, *la lavanda,* the washing of feet. According to the Gospel of John, Christ washed the feet of his disciples after celebrating the Last Supper. In monastic communities the abbot commemorated this event by washing the feet of the other monks. In Florentine confraternities, either the governor washed the feet of the other officers,[176] or all officers washed the feet of the other members.[177] Following the ceremony, the entire company sang the hymn *Ubi caritas est* ("Where charity resides") and partook of a meal together, a meal that could be a simple and solemn commemoration of the Last Supper or a more festive affair.[178] Afterwards, additional hymns were sung, and one of the lay brothers or an invited guest delivered a sermon in Italian explaining the significance of the events of the day to the membership.[179] The service concluded with prayers and a ceremony of reconciliation "beginning with the governor, kneeling and embracing, however God inspires him, begging forgiveness. And so too shall the other brothers be reconciled, each one following the other in turn."[180]

A number of the vernacular sermons delivered by confraternity members on Holy Thursday are extant. The sermons serve to convey the significance of the rites for fifteenth-century Florentines. In 1470 Alamanno Rinuccini began his sermon to the company of the Magi with: "We ought to consider this evening our Lord and Master Christ Jesus, first His holy and profound humility, and second, His unbounded and fervent charity." For Rinuccini, Holy Thursday was composed of two ceremonial elements:

176. Hatfield, "Magi," p. 126.

177. *Capitoli della Campagnia di San Domenico,* 1477, in Meersseman, 2:736.

178. *Capitoli,* 314.

179. The sermons composed by laymen and delivered in the adolescent and adult companies of Florence were not, of course, wholly original in content, filled, as they were, with classical, patristic, and scholastic citations. If one is interested in the originality of these sermons, this presents a problem. If, however, one views classical, patristic, and scholastic quotations as options open to lay preachers, then these sermons are quite revealing. Although much of the material is traditional, the specific choice of which "traditional" material to include in a sermon is still left to the lay preacher. And it is this lay preacher who selects those citations that best express his own sense of the meaning of ritual and religion. The identification of material as being the "traditional" stuff of sermons does not help explain why this or that citation is used. Rather than express meaning in their own words, lay preachers often chose the words of others but, nevertheless, expressed their own meanings by making the choices that they did. On these sermons, see Paul Oskar Kristeller, "Lay Religious Traditions and Florentine Platonism," in *Studies in Renaissance Thought and Letters* (Rome: Studi e Testi, 1956), p. 105.

Richard Trexler has remarked that these sermons would not have been understood by confraternity audiences because they were written in Latin ("Adolescence and Salvation," p. 220). This may inadvertently mislead. Although the sermons had Latin titles, and a sprinkling of brief Latin quotations, invariably repeated in translation, the sermons were written in Italian.

180. *Capitoli,* 439.

the rites of humility celebrated in the *lavanda* and the rites of charity celebrated by the confraternal banquet, the commemoration of the Last Supper. Rinuccini presented his listeners with a hierarchy of three grades of humility,

> the first of which consists in patiently enduring and placing ourselves under those whom, for whatever dignity or excellence, are our superiors, and not outdoing those who are our equals. And this is called sufficient [humility]. The second grade of this virtue consists in placing ourselves under those who are our equals and not placing our equals over or preferring them to those who are inferior to us, and this humility is called abundant. . . . The third and most perfect grade of this virtue, called superabundant, consists in bowing to and placing ourselves under those who are subject to us and who are inferior to us, out of love for God. . . . Whence we see clearly that this third grade of humility, most worthy and most excellent, was found in Christ Jesus, because none of those with whom He conversed was superior or equal to Him, but all were subject and inferior to Him by nature.[181]

Having given the scriptural and patristic citations supporting the virtues of humility, Rinuccini pointed to the *lavanda* and the Last Supper as the supreme examples of humility and charity, which members of the confraternity should try to imitate. Christ himself, said Rinuccini, chose to debase himself by feasting with and washing the feet of all his apostles with the intent of setting a profound example of brotherhood in the face of treason:

> O profound humility! O boundless clemency! O custom unheard of until that hour! What heart is so hardened, so harsh and unyielding, that it ought not humiliate and lower itself? Who is there, I ask, in whom there is so much excellence as to descend to such baseness as God who became man, who remained kneeling in front of His own disciples in order to wash the feet of His own servants, even that servant who would betray Him? Chrysostom says, "Our Lord washed the feet of the traitorous, thieving and sacrilegious Judas. And at the time of his treason, although He knew that his sin was unredeemable, He had him as a companion at His meal—and you, man, dare to inflate yourself with pride and march with your brow and head raised!" And so, each of us ought to wash the feet of the others, even the feet of our servants.[182]

For Rinuccini, active Florentine citizen and humanist, the essential meaning of the *lavanda* rite lay in the temporary reversal of the social order, a social order that he considered just. How was this reversal accomplished?

---

181. Alamanno Rinuccini, *Lettere ed Orazioni*, ed. Vito R. Giustiniani (Florence: Leo S. Olschki, 1953), pp. 149-150. See also Giustiniani, *Alamanno Rinuccini 1426-1499* (Köln, 1965), pp. 184ff.
182. *Ibid.*, pp. 154-155.

The status inversion was accomplished in several ways. Most obviously, the company officers, normally owed respect and reverence, were ritually degraded. They humiliated themselves by becoming the servants of the rest of the membership. The other members also suffered symbolic degradation by becoming ritually poor and inferior, playing the role of the poor disciples whom Christ served; these members meanwhile achieved status equality through common self-abasement. To the truly poor, or men of low to middling status, the rite had the potential of bringing certain satisfactions: For a moment all were equal, and for an even briefer moment the poor were served by their social superiors.

Giovanni Nesi delivered the Holy Thursday sermon to the company of adolescents, the Nativity, in 1476. Nesi, too, spoke of the rites of Holy Thursday as rites of humiliation, rites that both affirmed and renewed the justice of the social order. Nesi's sermon described humility as that virtue

> from which originates piety toward kinsmen, reverence toward elders, obedience toward those who rightly command you. [And humility] is the self-awareness of not besting others in anything, so that they should become one group in which the rich man befriends the poor man, the great befriends the lowly, the powerful befriends the powerless, and the lord befriends his servant. And having put aside honors and human dignities, let each (as is the precept of the Lord) not love his neighbor less than he loves himself. . . . Pythagoras certainly understood this when he said that friendship is one composed of many, and knowing that all things are held in common among friends. The rich distributors and possessors of riches should be magnificent and those of lesser endowment should become liberal. From which issues a concern not only not to offend one's neighbor, but, if possible, to defend him.[183]

What meanings did members draw from the Holy Thursday rites? What transformations were the rites intended to accomplish? The confraternity orators spoke with one voice in stressing the spirit of charity as a byproduct of the day's devotions:

> Consider that if you are all united in the bond of Holy Charity no adversity, either external or internal will be able to harm you at any time. This [charity] places perpetual tranquility in the mind and everlasting security in the soul. From her union and concord come forth. From her, finally, every goodness results. In her presence everything is possible, without her all is nothing. Through which, most beloved [brothers], let us turn to each other with hearts warmed by the virtue of charity and her companion, humility; let us forgive one another our injuries, let us

183. Cesare Vasoli, ed., *Johannis Nesi adolescentis oratio de humilitate habita in fraternitate natiuitatis die XI aprelis Mcccclxxvi,* "Giovanni Nesi tra Donato Acciaiuoli e Girolamo Savonarola: Testi editi e inediti," in *Umanesimo e teologia tra '400 e '500 (Memorie Domenicane,* n.s. 4 (1973): 142-143.

forget the hatreds that exist between us, let us do away with our mutual envies, let us lower our heads, imitating our Lord Jesus.[184]

We join, for a moment, a group of young men belonging to the brother-hood of the Nativity. It is Holy Thursday, 1476. The washing ritual has just ended, and the membership has finished singing the hymn to charity. The festive meal, a collective food-sharing among those who are rediscovering their brotherhood, has just ended. Giovanni Nesi's sermon is in progress:

> . . . What can any one of us say on our own behalf? . . . We do not want to relinquish our pomp, to leave behind our pride, put out our arrogance, pardon our injuries, forget things that have offended us, put a halt to our depraved desires, cast out our vices, flee our evil habits, and follow goodness.
>
> Venerable Fathers and most beloved Brothers, on account of this, having seen that the virtue of humility is as useful and salutary as the vice of pride is pernicious and pestiferous, our Lord Christ commanded the former with His words and deeds as much as He detested the latter. Therefore, you ought to desire as much as you can to humiliate yourselves and to follow His example. . . You should want to pardon him who has injured you, since as it is written, "forgive and you shall be forgiven." Desire to convert enmity into amity, hate and dissimulation into love and benevolence, pride into humility. Then search your conscience, recall the memory of your own crimes, and before the face of God remove them by confessing honestly to your crimes, by contrition and penance, through prayer, fasts, and flagellation; with grief, sighs, and tears cleanse your breast. . . . You shall be a temple of God, which, through His grace together with your good works you shall keep clean and purged.[185]

The structure of Holy Thursday's events reveals much about the context of ritual brotherhood in Renaissance Florence. At the beginning of the ceremonies the members were taught the meaning of Christ's humility and Judas's betrayal. The members were ritually separated from the normal structure of stratification and interpersonal rivalry. Made to feel guilty, the members then underwent acts of ritual of degradation and role-reversal, the temporary suspension of social categories, and during this period of sym-bolic inversion, when the world was turned upside down, the members learned the underlying meaning of social relations and experienced a mo-ment of liberation from them. This symbolic inversion allowed a temporary, carefully demarcated escape from the social order, at the same time that it taught the justice of that order. Neither Nesi nor Rinuccini challenged the fundamental correctness of the social order. Both commented on its "in-

---

184. Riccardiana, Ms. 2204, fol. 211v, anonymous Holy Thursday sermon, *Il Giovedì Santo.*
185. In Vasoli, "Giovanni Nesi," pp. 146-147.

herent" hierarchies, and the necessary obligations and structures of obedience found therein. In Nesi's analysis of humility kinsmen were owed piety, elders were owed reverence, and social superiors were owed obedience. It was through humility that all classes and groups maintained their proper relations with one another. It was through the periodic experience of humiliation that the justice of the social order was maintained. The common status degradation of Holy Thursday was just such a temporary humiliation that reminded the brothers of their general obligations and the requirement that these be performed in a spirit of humility. Thus Nesi exhorted all the members to undergo public humiliation on Holy Thursday, "so that they should become one group." He asked them to put aside temporarily their "honors and human dignities," in order that within the confraternity the powerful and the powerless, the rich and the poor, and a man and his neighbor could all experience unity.

After the foot washing ended, the brothers participated in rites of incorporation. By singing together the hymn of charity and unity, by sharing in a common meal, and by participating in acts of formal reconciliation and the forgiveness of mutual hatreds, the members emerged from the ritual process purified and united. They experienced the symbolic passage from traitor to brother.

In investigating the life of the confraternity and the meanings attached to its rituals of piety and community, it would, of course, be helpful to have before us extensive testimony from individual members, expressing their attitudes toward participation and their own sense of fraternity. Unfortunately, such private reflections are rarely available to us. But perhaps we may at least sense the reality of a man's bond with his *confratelli* when we read of the fulfillment of Bernardo the cloth dyer's wish to be buried in the confraternity following his death from the plague, which he contracted while tending poor plague victims.[186] Or, we may note Francesco the ironmonger's tearful appeal to all the members that they might grant him pardon and continue to recommend him in their prayers, although he had to resign his membership.[187] Or, we may listen to the account of one

---

186. *CRS,* 1594 (P 1, vol. 42), San Paolo, *Fratelli Morti,* 40v:

Bernardo di Iachopo tintore. Morí di morbo Mercholedì adì 14 di luglio [1479] a ore 12 1/2 el quale era uisso ottimamente et molto essercitatosi in servigio de' poveri uerghognosi. Et così da essi poveri e altri fu souenuto nella sua mallatia qualunche fusse di morbo senpre ebbe molti huomini et donne assuo ghoverno per modo gli durò più di dì otto. Morì sanctamente et volle per sua divozione essere sepulto nella nostra compagnia.

187. *Ibid.,* 31r:

Francesco di Domenicho ferrauecchio domando licienza in domenicha mattina addì xviiij d'aghosto 1453

member's farewell to his *confratelli* prior to leaving the company of San Paolo in order to enter the priesthood:

> Giovanni di Filippo del Buono entered the clergy on the 19th of November, 1452, in the Badia of Florence. And the night before that Sunday he had been in the company in a state of great devotion. Having finished the recitation of the divine office, he called all the brothers together in the choir, and with great humility he knelt. He asked everyone to forgive his acts of negligence and his failings, and he thanked God and the company because they were the reasons that made him come to his holy decision. He was embraced by everyone, with a multitude of tears and with great tenderness, and everyone gave him [the kiss of] holy peace. And this was a very great consolation to all who were there.[188]

---

inginocchiato nel meza del choro con molte lagrime domandando perdonanza a tutti diciendo per buona e giusta chagione non potere dall' otto inanzi venire più al luogho e cchess'avessi per racchomandato nell'orazioni ecchosi glui fu dato licienza.

188. *Ibid.*, 27r:

Giovanni di Filippo d'Antonio del Buono picchiando alla religione addì xviiij di novembre 1452 in Badia di Firenze. E detto dì 19 venne in domenicha ella notte innanzi era stato alla chompagnia con grande divozione. E finito tutto l'uffici fecie chiamare tutti i fratelli in choro e iui chon grande humilità s'inginocchio. E a tutti domando perdon delle nighrigienzie e falli chonmessi ecché ringraziaua iddio elluogho elloro ch'erano stati chagione difarli pigliare chosì sancto partito. . . . per tutti grande moltitudine di lagrime pertenereza e quasi dattutti fu abbraciato e datogli la sancta pacie. Effù grandissima chonsolazione achi uisi trouo.

Chapter THREE

Participation and Membership
THE COMPANY OF SAN PAOLO
IN THE FIFTEENTH CENTURY

The preceding chapter examined the structure and ritual of confraternities in the republican period of Florentine history. Confraternal organization followed the model of the commune of Florence, and fraternal ritual, emphasizing the transformative capacities of rites of passage, offered Florentines the possibility of ritually renewing in microcosm the civic aspirations of Florentine republican culture. The principal sources used in the reconstruction of fraternal organization and ritual behavior—sermons and statute books—were, to a large extent, sources descriptive of the normative standards that confraternities sought to promote in their members. Fraternity members did not record for posterity their intimate reflections on the nature of the confraternal experience. Fraternity officials did on occasion, however, record the membership histories of their *confratelli*. By examining these membership histories, one can approach certain questions about the nature of fraternal behavior and the fraternal setting. Did the confraternity succeed in suspending during its meetings traditional class, clan, occupational, and neighborhood networks? Who came to meetings? Did members attend meetings and partake of the sacraments with the frequency prescribed in confraternity statutes? By linking membership histories to the demographic profiles contained in the city's tax registers—the *Catasto*—the appeal of confraternal membership and participation for the different subpopulations of Florentine society can be compared. To whom did the confraternity appeal? If, as the preceding chapter suggested, the confraternity regularly enacted rites of passage, were these ritual passages related to any concurrent passages between social roles or life cycle events? If rituals are meaningful only in the sense that they are meaningful for real individuals who come to define and shape rituals for themselves, to *whom,* precisely, did confraternal activity appeal?

Records of membership participation that permit such reconstructions are scarce. Only one set of records containing both membership histories and attendance registers has been located for the fifteenth century—the registers of the company of San Paolo, founded in 1434.[1] Membership histories of individual members commenced in 1434 and ended in 1493. Attendance records begin in 1472 and continue in a spotty fashion to the end of the century and resume once more in a virtually unusable form (most pages are at least partially rotted), for the second half of the sixteenth century. The fifteenth-century registers of San Paolo are especially useful for several reasons. First, these registers, unlike those of the following century, are relatively complete and undamaged. Second, fifteenth-century methods of identifying members often included the identification of the occupations of members. Finally, the overlap of the attendance and membership records with the *Catasto* of 1480 allows an analysis of patterns of participation to be made meaningful by placing members in their appropriate sociodemographic contexts. This analysis is divided into three sections. After a brief description of the composition of the company in 1480, in order to compare it to the adult male population of Florence, the secular history of San Paolo over the course of the quattrocento will be outlined, detailing the company's pattern of growth and the major changes in its membership composition over time. Subsequent sections examine two indexes of participation: length of membership in confraternities, and patterns of attendance.

This analysis is limited to the fifteenth century. The *Catasto* was replaced thereafter by a simple property inventory, the *Decima,* lacking the demographic detail of the *Catasto.* The absence of demographic information for sixteenth-century Florentines renders the sixteenth-century confraternity registers a less productive source. San Paolo in the fifteenth century, then, is the focus of this chapter; what follows should be interpreted as presenting a series of clinical inferences, to use Clifford Geertz's phrase, rather than as an investigation using comparative methods to generate testable hypotheses. Those aspects of San Paolo's membership history that allow comparative treatment will be so treated. There is reason to believe, however, that

---

1. The sources used in this reconstruction of the membership of the company of San Paolo are its statutes, revised in 1472 (*Capitoli,* 29) and documents from the P 1 series of *CRS: Miscellaneous memoirs: CRS,* 1579 (P 1, no. 1), *Libro de' Fondatori;* 1579 (P 1, no. 2a), *Memorie Diverse;* 1591 (P 1, no. 34), *Libro de' Sette Membri,* 1472-1548. Meeting records: 1582 (P 1, nos. 6-8), *Partiti e Ricordi,* 1448-1502. Membership lists: 1592 (P 1, nos. 36-37), *Campione de' Fratelli,* 1447-1487; 1594 (P 1, no. 42), *Fratelli Morti,* 1452-1477.

the experience of the company of San Paolo was not unique. It had much in common with the other Florentine confraternities in the republican period. It was, first of all, a *compagnia di disciplina,* and its ritual practice conforms in all details to that outlined in the previous chapter. The membership of San Paolo was, like other *disciplinati* companies of the fifteenth century, composed of all segments of male Florentine society. Almost all occupational groups, age groups, and levels of wealth were found in the company, as is revealed by examining a sample of 110 members belonging to the company in 1480 who could be located in the *Catasto* of that year.[2]

Figure 3.1 compares two cumulative age distributions: the confraternity in 1480 and the entire male population of the city, aged 15 or older. The graph records the percentage of male Florentines and members of San Paolo at or below each age. The two distributions are virtually identical. The mean age of confraternity members was 37.1, and that of Florentines,

2. The 1480 *Catasto* included 110 members of San Paolo in 1480. The remaining 96 members could not be unambiguously traced in these tax registers. The sample of members found in the *Catasto* overrepresents members with surnames, for surnamed Florentines are easier to locate in the tax registers and once located are identified with less ambiguity. The sample is thus biased in favor of wealthier Florentines, but differences in wealth do not affect the principal variables examined in this study of confraternal association and behavior, attendance, and length of membership. Two-by-two breakdowns at the median, of length of membership by wealth, attendance by wealth, and total sacramental participation (combining yearly communion and confession) by wealth produced chi-square statistics that were not statistically significant: length of membership, 1.24, with 1 degree of freedom, $p > .25$; attendance, 1.34, with 1 degree of freedom, $p = .25$; and sacramental participation, .59 with 1 degree of freedom, $p > .25$.

Of the 206 members in 1480, 104 were active, that is, they attended at least one meeting during the year. As a further check on sampling bias, the mean figures for attendance and length of membership were compared for all 104 active members and the 53 active members located in the 1480 *Catasto:*

Membership of San Paolo in 1480: Comparison of All Active Members and *Catasto* Sample

Variable	Company mean	Company standard deviation	Sample mean	Sample standard deviation	Sample standard error	z	Significance (2-tailed test)
Days attended	19.6	16.1	18.2	16.2	2.2	.64	.52
Years of membership	10.4	8.3	10.1	8.4	1.1	.27	.79
		Total active membership	N 104				
		Catasto sample	N 53				

A one-sample z-test was performed, using the population standard deviation to calculate the standard error of the difference. (The sample standard deviation is provided for comparison but was not used in the calculation of z.) As the test indicates, the chance that the small difference noted between the sample and the population is due to random sampling is, for attendance, 52%, and, for length of membership, 79%. In terms of statistical significance, the population parameters and sample statistics are identical.

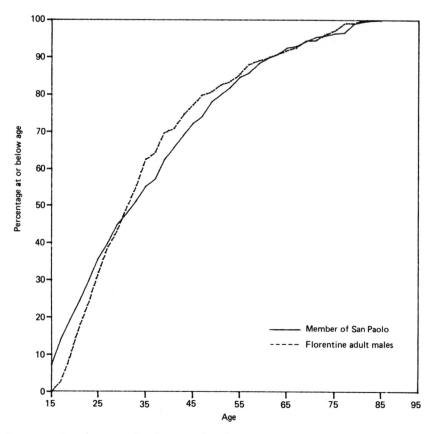

Figure 3.1. Cumulative age distributions of confraternity of San Paolo and Florentine adult males, 1480.

36.5. This difference is statistically insignificant at a .999 confidence level, indicating that there exists only one chance in a thousand that the differences observed in mean ages are the product of something other than randomness of observation. Of the members, 26% were over 44 years of age; 19% were between the ages of 35 and 44; 32% were between 25 and 34; and 24% were between the ages of 15 and 24.

Of all members of San Paolo sampled, 46% were heads of households; 12% lived in households of brothers (*fratellanze*); and the remainder, 42%, were sons of household heads, approximately 67% of whom lived in households headed by fathers. Unmarried members constituted 49% of the sample, and the remainder were married or remarried. Of sampled members, 32% lived in households in which their father was present. Members had, on average, 1.5 children each. The typical member had joined the company 14 years earlier, at age 23, and lived in a parish approximately .8

kilometer (.8 km) from the meeting place of San Paolo. Only 25% of the members of the company lived less than .4 km from San Paolo, another 25% lived within .8 km, and the remaining 50% lived more than .8 km from their confraternity. Members resided in almost every parish of the city. (See Figure 2.1.)

The median family net worth, 605 florins, of confraternity members was about 2.5 times that of the city, which was 235 florins. Although the distributions of confraternity and city familial wealth were different, San Paolo included among its members Florentines of all levels of wealth. Even the poorest Florentines were found in San Paolo, although not to the same extent that they were found in the general population. The poorest 35% of the city of Florence was represented by 10% of the members of San Paolo. The remaining gradations of wealth above the bottom 35% of Florentines are represented in proportions closer to their proportions in the general population.

Like other republican flagellant fraternities, the members of San Paolo did not cluster into a single age interval, residential location, or class. The occupational distribution of the company was, in a similar fashion, more representative of the city as a whole than of a single guild, trade, or segment of the economy. Table 3.1 summarizes the distribution of occupations found in San Paolo in 1480. The occupations that occurred most frequently were those of the professions and major guilds of the city. Occupations occurring almost as frequently, however, included local trades and one textile craft. Although members tended to come from the most prestigious occupational groups in Florence in 1480, the membership represented a rich assortment of trades drawn from throughout the community.

Cycles of Growth

The death registers of the company permit the examination of patterns of total membership from the year of the confraternity's creation (1434) through the end of the fifteenth century. Table 3.2 details the main membership events by year: the number of members joining for the first time, the number of members expelled for the first time, the total number of members who joined that year (the sum of the number of first admissions and the readmissions of those previously expelled), the total number of expulsions (first, second, and third expulsions), the number of members who left the company to join the clergy, the number of members who died, the total membership at the end of the year, and the rate of change of total membership over the previous year. For the entire period 1434-1493 (based on 3-year moving averages of the data in Table 3.2) 13.6 (8.5%) members

Table 3.1

Occupations of Members of Company of San Paolo (1480)

Occupations occurring once

Armorer	Baker	Barber
Bed maker	Bleacher	Cloak maker
Kiln maker	Sewer	Slipper maker
Saddler	Sculptor	Wine seller
Wool washer		Calimala guildsman (cloth seller)

Occupations occurring two to four times

Belt maker	Brass worker	Doublet maker
Carpenter	Cutler	Fur dealer
Peddler	Smith	Purse maker
Stationer	Tanner	Wool shearer

Occupations occurring five or more times

Banker	Goldsmith	Spice dealer
Notary	Shoemaker	Silk manufacturer
Student	Painter	Wool manufacturer
Linen dealer		

Major occupational categories

Occupation	N	%
Unknown	68	33
Sottoposti (textile)	5	2
Miscellaneous services	5	2
Local trades	12	6
Clothing articles	13	6
Textile middlemen	6	3
Fur, spices, leather	12	6
Construction	12	6
Arts	11	5
Notary, professional	24	12
Major merchants	38	18
Total	206	99

were admitted or readmitted each year, (first admissions = 12.8 members, or 7.9%). An average of 6.5 members (4.0%) were expelled annually (first expulsions = 6.2 members, or 3.8%). Every other year one member entered the clergy. The annual mortality rate was 1.6%, or 2.5 members.

Figures 3.2a and 3.2b graph the membership trends for the period 1434-1493. The average growth per year for the period was 3.25 members, or an average rate of growth of 1.9% per year. Was this growth rate constant for the entire period? To compare varying *rates* of growth, instead of varying *absolute amounts* of growth, it is necessary to transform absolute

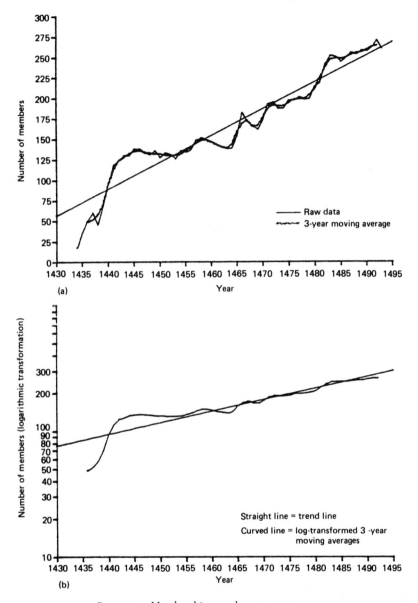

Figure 3.2. Membership trends, 1434-1493.

change into relative change, allowing comparisons to be made of proportional change from year to year. A logarithmic transformation is presented in Figure 3.2b. In a logarithmic plot the distance between 50 and 100 is the same relative distance (100% growth) as the distance between 100 and 200

Table 3.2
Company of San Paolo, Membership Events, 1434-1493

Year	Continuing members	Joined		Expelled		Total joined		Total expelled		Clerics		Deaths		Total members	Rate of change
		N	%	N	%	N	%	N	%	N	%	N	%	N	%
1434	0	18	—	0	—	18	—	—	—	0	—	0	—	18	—
1435	18	18	100.0	0	.0	18	100.0	0	.0	0	.0	0	.0	36	100.0
1436	36	18	50.0	3	8.3	19	52.8	3	8.3	1	2.8	1	2.8	50	38.9
1437	50	10	19.0	0	.0	11	22.0	0	.0	0	.0	1	2.0	60	20.0
1438	60	11	18.0	26	43.3	11	18.3	26	43.3	0	.0	0	.0	45	−25.0
1439	45	27	59.0	2	4.4	27	60.0	3	6.7	0	.0	0	.0	69	53.3
1440	69	30	43.0	0	.0	30	43.5	0	.0	1	1.4	1	1.4	97	40.6
1441	97	29	29.0	7	7.2	30	30.9	7	7.2	0	.0	1	1.0	119	22.7
1442	119	7	5.0	2	1.7	7	5.9	2	1.7	0	.0	0	.0	124	4.2
1443	124	6	4.0	0	.0	6	4.8	0	.0	0	.0	0	.0	130	4.8
1444	130	2	1.0	0	.0	2	1.5	0	.0	0	.0	2	1.5	130	.0
1445	130	10	7.0	0	.0	10	7.7	0	.0	0	.0	2	1.5	138	6.2
1446	138	11	7.0	8	5.8	11	8.0	8	5.8	0	.0	3	2.2	138	.0
1447	138	8	5.0	11	8.0	9	6.5	11	8.0	1	.7	2	1.4	133	−3.6
1448	133	10	7.0	11	8.3	10	7.5	11	8.3	0	.0	1	.8	131	−1.5
1449	131	9	6.0	0	.0	9	6.9	0	.0	0	.0	4	3.1	136	3.8
1450	136	4	2.0	7	5.1	4	2.9	7	5.1	0	.0	5	3.7	128	−5.9
1451	128	9	7.0	1	.8	10	7.8	1	.8	1	.8	3	2.3	133	3.9
1452	133	7	5.0	5	3.8	7	5.3	5	3.8	1	.8	3	2.3	131	−1.5
1453	131	15	11.0	20	15.3	16	12.2	20	15.3	0	.0	1	.8	126	−3.8
1454	126	12	9.0	1	.8	12	9.5	1	.8	0	.0	1	.8	136	7.9
1455	136	14	10.0	15	11.0	14	10.3	16	11.8	0	.0	0	.0	134	−1.5
1456	134	9	6.0	4	3.0	9	6.7	4	3.0	0	.0	2	1.5	137	2.2
1457	137	15	10.0	3	2.2	18	13.1	4	2.9	0	.0	2	1.5	149	8.8

Year															
1460	149	0	.0	0	.0	0	.0	0	.0	0	.0	3	2.0	1465	−2.0
1461	146	0	.0	0	.0	0	.0	0	.0	0	.0	3	2.1	143	−2.1
1462	143	0	.0	0	.0	0	.0	0	.0	0	.0	3	2.1	140	−2.1
1463	140	0	.0	0	.0	0	.0	0	.0	0	.0	2	1.4	138	−1.4
1464	138	1	.0	0	.0	1	.7	0	.0	0	.0	0	.0	139	.7
1465	139	32	23.0	17	12.2	32	23.0	17	12.2	0	.0	1	.7	153	10.1
1466	153	37	24.0	6	3.9	37	24.2	6	3.9	1	.7	1	.7	182	19.0
1467	182	11	6.0	21	11.5	17	9.3	22	12.1	2	1.1	4	2.2	171	−6.0
1468	171	13	7.0	16	9.4	13	7.6	16	9.4	0	.0	3	1.8	165	−3.5
1469	165	6	3.0	7	4.2	6	3.6	7	4.2	1	.0	3	1.8	161	−2.4
1470	161	17	10.0	2	1.2	17	10.6	2	1.2	0	.6	3	1.9	172	6.8
1471	172	11	6.0	3	1.7	28	16.3	4	2.3	2	.0	3	1.7	193	12.2
1472	193	12	6.0	4	2.1	13	6.7	5	2.6	0	1.0	4	2.1	195	1.0
1473	195	12	6.0	16	8.2	13	6.7	16	8.2	2	.0	5	2.6	187	−4.1
1474	187	14	7.0	8	4.3	14	7.5	12	6.4	0	.5	1	.5	187	.0
1475	187	22	11.0	9	4.8	22	11.8	10	5.3	1	.5	1	.5	197	5.3
1476	197	14	7.0	9	4.6	14	7.1	11	5.6	1	.0	3	1.5	197	.0
1477	197	16	8.0	7	3.6	16	8.1	8	4.1	0	1.0	2	1.0	201	2.0
1478	201	6	2.0	2	1.0	6	3.0	2	1.0	2	1.0	5	2.5	198	−1.5
1479	198	17	8.0	1	.5	19	9.6	1	.5	2	.5	16	8.1	199	.5
1480	199	19	9.0	4	2.0	24	12.1	4	2.0	1	.5	4	2.0	214	7.5
1481	214	19	8.0	9	4.2	19	8.9	11	5.1	1	.0	4	1.9	218	1.9
1482	218	34	15.0	6	2.8	34	15.6	6	2.8	0	.0	5	2.3	241	10.6
1483	241	28	11.0	14	5.8	28	11.6	15	6.2	0	.4	2	.8	251	4.1
1484	251	12	4.0	9	3.6	13	5.2	10	4.0	1	.4	3	1.2	250	−.4
1485	250	13	5.0	9	3.6	14	5.6	10	4.0	3	1.2	7	2.8	244	−2.4
1486	244	15	6.0	6	2.5	15	6.1	6	2.5	1	.4	3	1.2	249	2.0
1487	249	13	5.0	4	1.6	13	5.2	5	2.0	1	.4	1	.4	255	2.4
1488	255	21	8.0	20	7.8	22	8.6	20	7.8	2	.8	2	.8	253	−.8
1489	253	12	4.0	4	1.6	12	4.7	4	1.6	2	.8	1	.4	258	2.0
1490	258	6	2.0	3	1.2	6	2.3	3	1.2	0	.0	4	1.6	257	−.4
1491	257	6	2.0	1	.4	7	2.7	1	.4	0	.0	1	.4	262	1.9
1492	262	24	9.0	10	3.8	26	9.9	11	4.2	2	.8	5	1.9	270	3.1
1493	270	3	1.0	8	3.0	3	1.1	9	3.3	0	.0	4	1.5	260	−3.

(100% growth), although the absolute change from 100 to 200 (100) is twice as great as the absolute change from 50 to 100 (50). If the rate of change is stable from 1 year to the next, the plot ought to approximate a diagonal line, since the same amount of movement along the axis of time ought to produce the same *relative* increase along the axis of membership. To the extent that the data form a slope that is steeper than an imaginary diagonal of perfectly constant proportional growth, the rate of growth is increasing faster than a constant rate; to the extent that the data have a slope that is flatter than the diagonal, the company is growing, but at an ever decreasing rate. This graph reveals three distinct periods of membership growth: (*a*) 1434-1441, during which time the confraternity experienced a rapid increase; (*b*) 1441-1464, during which time the growth was marginal, and at times negative (indicated by a line sloping downward from left to right); and (*c*) 1464-1493, a period of slight positive growth.

Founded in 1434 and having attracted 18 members by the end of that year, the company experienced a rapid rate of growth—16% per year—during its first 8 years of existence, during which time it wrote its first set of statutes and purchased its own oratory. By the time the company had reached a membership of about 120 members, its growth began to stabilize. The rate of change from one year to the next (see Table 3.2) dropped sharply. Following this stabilization by approximately 1 year came a decree of the Signoria of Florence, which attempted to block the enrollment of politically active adults in religious confraternities. Those whose names had been drawn for the three highest offices of the republic (or whose fathers, brothers, or sons had been drawn) were forbidden, if they were over age 25, from joining confraternities. By 1447 the company of San Paolo had made contingency plans to ensure that the economic burden that this regulation imposed (a sudden lack of wealthier members able to support the financial obligations of the confraternity) would not require the sale of the company's meeting place, an oratory on the via dell' Acqua, formerly called Trinità Vecchia (Old Trinity Church). To safeguard their oratory, purchased for 300 florins, the members voted to allow the boys' company, San Giovanni Evangelista, to rent part of the oratory and, by so doing, helped to defray the cost of upkeep. This desperate move was eventually regretted. For the next 3 centuries the two companies would be involved in legal battles over the determination of which company was the rightful owner of the oratory.[3] The legislation of 1443 soon was moderated because of the

3. The documents describing this legal dispute are found in CRS, 1579 (P 1, vol. 2, pt. B). On the location of the oratory, see Walter and Elisabeth Paatz, *Die Kirchen von Florenz*, 2 vols. (Frankfurt am Main, 1952-1955), 5:397-398.

intervention of Archbishop Antonino. The company suffered another political setback in 1458 when all of the confraternities of the city were suppressed. The decline in the growth rate from 16% during the years 1434-1441 to 1% for the years 1441-1464 is explained by a combination of several factors: the process of stabilization after the initial foundation of the company, the restrictions on membership imposed by the commune, and the suppression, during which time the only cause of change in membership was the death of older members. The suppression was, however, relatively mild, lasting only 6 years. For the remainder of the century, the company was virtually untroubled by communal intervention and was, indeed, unofficially patronized by the leading family in the city.[4] Lorenzo de' Medici was the company's governor in 1472, 1473, 1475, and 1477, *limosiniere* in 1473, 1475, 1476, 1484, and 1487, and the principal author of its statute revisions in 1472. After 1464 the company enjoyed a relatively modest rate of growth, punctuated at the beginning of the period (1465-1467) by relatively large movements of members (see Table 3.2). Presumably, on the one hand, a backlog of potential recruits had accumulated, waiting for the suppression to end to enroll (the rate of entrance in 1465 was 23% and in 1466, 24%), and, on the other hand, those members who had allowed their active membership to lapse during the suppression and had failed to participate in the affairs of the company once it reopened were expelled (12.2% of the

---

4. The similarity between the dates of significant confraternity events and the fortunes of the Medici (the foundation of San Paolo in 1434, the return of Cosimo to Florence in 1434; the suppression from 1458 to 1464, the crisis of the summer of 1458; the suppression in 1494, the expulsion of the Medici in 1494) should not be interpreted as suggesting that San Paolo was nothing more than a political arm of the Medici. The suppressions of 1458 and 1494 closed all the companies of Florence, not just San Paolo. (See, e.g., the gap in the records of San Frediano from November 1, 1458, to May 2, 1465, ASF, *Archivi delle Compagnie Soppresse* (archive 5, vol. 4). San Zanobi's record of the suppression is contained in CRS, 2176 (Z 1, vol. 14), 11v-12v. On the 1494 suppression, see Chapter 4.

Lorenzo de' Medici was a member of a number of the most important brotherhoods in Florence, among them San Domenico, Sant' Agnese, the Magi, Gesù Pellegrino (Rab Hatfield, "The Compagnia de' Magi," *Journal of the Warburg and Courtauld Institutes* 33 (1970): 124, n. 73), and the Compagnia de' Neri, Santa Maria della Croce al Tempio, whose statutes he reformed in 1488 (Passerini, p. 484). Whatever San Paolo's links to Lorenzo, its records list in minute detail the extensive liturgical and cultic activities performed by the company on a weekly basis. If San Paolo operated as a political meeting place for the Medici faction (and no evidence of this has been uncovered in any meeting register), it is, nevertheless, undeniable that the company members performed an impressive array of ritual activities.

The original seven members who founded the company in 1434 were Piero di Bartolo chalzolaio, Mariotto di Zanobi tintore, Tomaso di Filippo Panichi, Frate Paolo di Giovanni Bellincioni, Filippo di Francesco Calandri, Benedetto di Bartolomeo chalzolaio, and Antonio di Ser Battista chorazaio. None of the individuals are mentioned as being among the Medici friends and partisans of 1434 identified by Dale Kent in *The Rise of the Medici: Faction in Florence, 1426-1434* (Oxford: Oxford University Press, 1978), pp. 352-354.

continuing members were expelled in 1465, and another 12% suffered the same fate in 1467). The 6-year suppression produced a real transformation in the membership of the confraternity. Based on expulsion and entrance statistics, it is estimated that approximately one-third of those who were members in 1458 failed to continue in San Paolo (excluding those who died in the interim) once it had reopened. Of the 165 members of San Paolo in 1468, 80, or 49%, were members who had joined in the 3.5 years since the company began to meet again.

One major change in membership composition occurred during the period as a whole between 1434 and 1493: a shift in the social composition of the company. Table 3.3 (column percentages) details the distribution of members of San Paolo by major occupational category and by the year in which members joined. For the entire period, 36% of the membership had no recorded occupation, 6% were dependent *sottoposti* (wage earners employed in the production of textiles), and an equal proportion of members, 7%, were engaged in intermediate stages of production of textiles as middlemen or small independent *sottoposti* contractors. Tailors and others selling or reselling finished cloth for local consumption made up 3% of the total membership of the company. Persons engaged in various service capacities, government employment, and transportation comprised another 3% of the membership. Local tradesmen and provisioners made up 6% of the membership; artists, masons, sculptors, metal workers, and others engaged in fine arts, decorative arts, and construction accounted for 8% of the membership of San Paolo. The last three categories in Table 3.3 describe the major guildsmen of the city, the chief manufacturers, bankers, merchants, and professionals whose services and markets encompassed the entire city and whose prestige was considerably greater than that of those occupations previously considered: dealers in fur, leather, and spices (including druggists), 4%; notaries, doctors of law and medicine, and other titled, university-trained professionals, 11%; and major merchants, 15%. Of 796 members who joined the confraternity, 24, or 3%, could not be assigned a date of entrance and were excluded from the calculation of this table.

All occupational categories were represented throughout the 60 years covered in this study; however, the varying proportions of occupations represented in San Paolo indicates a social transformation. The proportion of wool workers and wool craftsmen fell steeply, and the proportion of prestige occupations rose throughout the period. The first 12 years of the company's history witnessed the enrollment of 24% of its total membership for the fifteenth century. Of all textile workers and all textile craftsmen

Table 3.3
Occupations by Year in Which Member Joined (twelve-year-intervals)[a]

Occupation	1434-1445	1446-1457	1458-1469	1470-1481	1482-1493	Total
			Year joined			
			Observed values			
Occupation unknown	78	39	35	54	73	279
Dependent *sottoposti*	19	5	3	8	8	43
Independent *sottoposti*	21	11	7	8	6	53
Miscellaneous textile	1	9	5	8	3	26
Miscellaneous service	6	8	6	1	6	27
Food, trades	11	8	11	10	9	49
Arts, construction	12	5	7	26	12	62
Fur, spices	6	11	5	8	4	34
Notary, professional	13	10	11	20	28	82
Major merchants	15	16	12	36	38	117
Total	182	122	102	179	187	772
			Row percentages			
Occupation unknown	28	14	13	19	26	100
Dependent *sottoposti*	44	12	7	19	19	100
Independent *sottoposti*	40	21	13	15	11	100
Miscellaneous textile	4	35	19	31	12	101
Miscellaneous service	22	30	22	4	22	100
Food, trades	22	16	22	20	18	98
Arts, construction	19	8	11	42	19	99
Fur, spices	18	32	15	24	12	101
Notary, professional	16	12	13	24	34	99
Major merchants	13	14	10	31	32	100
Total	24	16	13	23	24	100
			Column percentages			
Occupation unknown	43	32	34	30	39	36
Dependent *sottoposti*	10	4	3	4	4	6
Independent *sottoposti*	12	9	7	4	3	7
Miscellaneous textile	1	7	5	4	2	3
Miscellaneous service	3	7	6	1	3	3
Food, trades	6	7	11	6	5	6
Art, construction	7	4	7	15	6	8
Fur, spices	3	9	5	4	2	4
Notary, professional	7	8	11	11	15	11
Major merchant	8	13	12	20	20	15
Total	100	100	101	99	99	99

[a] Chi-square = 94.82 with 36 degrees of freedom; $p < .001$.

who ever joined San Paolo in the fifteenth century, 44% and 40%, respectively, entered in these first 12 years. The last interval, 1482-1493, also accounted for the entrance of 24% of the entire membership. Professionals and major guild merchants accounted for 34% and 32% of the entering members in these years. As a percentage of entering members, the proportion of wool workers entering in the earlier period fell from 10% in 1434-1445 to 4% in 1446-1447 and remained at that rate thereafter; cloth craftsmen fell from a rate of 12% to 7% in the first 12 years and continued to fall to 3% of all entering members by 1482-1493. During the same period the proportion of notaries and professionals doubled, from 7% to 15% of entrants, and the percentage of major guildsmen more than doubled, rising from 8% to 20%.

Table 3.4 summarizes these trends, grouping wool workers, wool craftsmen, and sellers of clothing into one category, providers of local trades and services into another, artists, construction workers, and metal workers into a third, and major guildsmen and professionals into a fourth category. The overall proportion of persons in textile-related occupations (exclusive of major guildsmen, at the top of the chain of production and sale) fell from 23% at the beginning of the period to 9% at the end, whereas prestige professions and professionals doubled from 19% to 37%. Low- and high-status occupations moved in opposite directions as the company took on an increasingly elite character during the course of the century, which may be due, in part, to growing class segregation found throughout late quattrocento Florence.

Length of Membership

Theorizing about benefits and satisfactions of confraternal membership is of limited value without knowing the length of time that Florentines actually remained members of confraternities. Length of membership is perhaps the most telling index of membership loyalty, that is, the extent to which confraternal ritual and social activity were perceived as being beneficial enough to warrant continued association and investment of time and money.

The account books of San Paolo continue, sporadically, beyond 1495 and begin again in a detailed manner in the middle of the sixteenth century. The company's entrance and death registers, however, do not extend beyond the end of the fifteenth century. The subpopulation whose participation in San Paolo can best be reconstructed consists of those members who joined the company between 1434, the year of its foundation, and 1493, almost 2

Table 3.4
Occupations by Year in Which Member Joined (twelve-year-intervals)[a]

Occupation	Year joined					
	1434-1445	1446-1457	1458-1469	1470-1481	1482-1493	Total
	Observed values					
Occupation unknown	78	39	35	54	73	279
Textile work	41	25	15	24	17	122
Local trades	17	16	17	11	15	76
Arts, construction	12	5	7	26	12	62
Major merchants	34	37	28	64	70	233
Total	182	122	102	179	187	772
	Row percentages					
Occupation unknown	28	14	13	19	26	100
Textile work	34	20	12	20	14	100
Local trades	22	21	22	14	20	99
Arts, construction	19	8	11	42	19	99
Major merchants	15	16	12	27	30	100
Total	24	16	13	23	24.	100.
	Column percentages					
Occupation unknown	43	32	34	30	39	36
Textile work	23	20	15	13	9	16
Local trades	9	13	17	6	8	10
Arts, construction	7	4	7	15	6	8
Major merchants	19	30	27	36	37	30
Total	101	99	100	100	99	100

[a] Chi-square = 53.76 with 16 degrees of freedom; $p < .001$.

years before it was temporarily suppressed. No members joined between 1493 and 1495, although information is contained in these registers about other types of membership events occurring in 1494 and 1495.

In calculating the length of membership in San Paolo, the effects of a complicating factor must be dealt with. The termination of the registers, essentially in 1493, artificially truncates the observable membership histories of members who had not died or been expelled by 1495. Table 3.5 charts the effects of the 1495 register termination date on the observable length of membership of San Paolo *fratelli* (all possible causes of termination are considered).[5] Members are grouped according to the 6-year interval in

5. Excluded from this table are 52 members (6.5%) who could not be assigned dates of entrance or who terminated at an unknown date before 1495.

Table 3-5
Years of Membership by Year in Which Member Joined

Number of years member	Year joined									Total
	1434-1439	1440-1445	1446-1451	1452-1458	1464-1469	1470-1475	1476-1481	1482-1487	1488-1493	
	Observed values									
0	17	6	1	2	14	6	5	3	3	57
2	20	10	12	6	15	18	17	27	43	168
6	11	17	7	14	21	26	17	41	26	180
11	19	12	4	20	17	16	50	40	—	178
21	18	12	10	11	32	19	—	—	—	102
36	7	21	14	17	—	—	—	—	—	59
Total	92	78	48	70	99	85	89	111	72	744
	Cumulative column totals									
0	100	100	100	100	100	100	100	100	100	100
2	83	92	98	98	85	92	94	97	96	93
6	61	79	73	89	70	71	75	73	36	70
11	49	57	58	69	49	41	56	36	—	46
21	28	42	50	40	32	22	—	—	—	22
36	8	27	29	24	—	—	—	—	—	8

which they joined (an interval of 6 years was chosen because it allowed the 6-year suppression, 1458-1464, to be isolated), and the members joining during the same interval are treated as one cohort. If one examines the table of cumulative column totals from the bottom to the top, one observes the absence of cell entries for the final intervals (following 1464) caused by termination of the company records in 1495. If one reads across the table, however, one can note the similarity of attrition rates among the cohorts of members. Table 3.5 reveals a comparable pattern of attrition until one reaches an interval biased by the inevitable lack of entries after 1464. Thus members joining in all periods were exposed to the same risk of attrition 2 years after joining, but only those members who joined before 1490 could be exposed to an observable risk of attrition for 6 years following their dates of entrance. The proportion of members remaining in the company does fluctuate from cohort to cohort (across the table), but not according to any observable pattern, until one examines the last cell for which there is an entry, in the last column, 1488-1493, where the rapid rate of attrition is due almost exclusively to the structure of the data caused by the termination of registers, and not to any structural change in confraternity membership. Successive cohorts suffer an essentially similar pattern of attrition. Since comparative purposes will be better served by an examination of members sharing the same observable (i.e., period for which data exists) length of time at risk of attrition, this analysis of length of membership will be based on all members joining in the period 1434-1458, treated as a single cohort.

The members of San Paolo joining the company between 1434 and 1458 shared an observable period of risk of attrition of at least 37 years. (This is based on the period of risk of a member who joined at the last year of cohort construction, 1458. Beyond 37 years the periods of risk can be made comparable only through estimation procedures, since data is unavailable beyond 1495.) Table 3.6 presents the survival probabilities (or proportions of members surviving to each year of membership) for this cohort. The survival probabilities beyond 37 years are estimates, not actual observations of cohort activity.[6] These survival probabilities indicate that the confraternity was capable of generating a great degree of loyalty; for 15 years after a member joined San Paolo, there existed close to a 50% chance that he would still be a member of the company. Of the members, 25% survived to at least 31 years of membership.

6. The estimates of attrition rates beyond 37 years of membership were based on an analysis of the rate with which the attrition rates themselves changed.

How representative were these survival probabilities? The flood of 1557 destroyed most confraternity membership inventories, and many additional records were ruined by the flood of 1966. The membership records of the company of Sant' Antonio Abate, another flagellant fraternity, commenced in 1485, survived and contain listings of entrances, expulsions, clericalization, and deaths, similar to the records of San Paolo. Like other companies, for the first 50 years of the sixteenth century the affairs of Sant' Antonio were disrupted. However, unlike most, Sant' Antonio survived relatively intact, suffering less disruption and damage than other companies, although during the 1530s, its records were disrupted. A sample of 131 members who

Table 3.6
Proportion of Members of San Paolo Surviving to Year X

Surviving to year	Proportion surviving
0	1.000
1	.972
3	.865
5	.760
7	.708
9	.653
11	.573
13	.542
15	.479
17	.441
19	.413
21	.382
23	.337
25	.330
27	.323
29	.281
31	.247
33	.233
35	.215
37	.191
39	.156
41	.130
43	.112
45	.095
47	.078
49	.063
51	.048
53	.036
55	.026
57	.018
59	.000

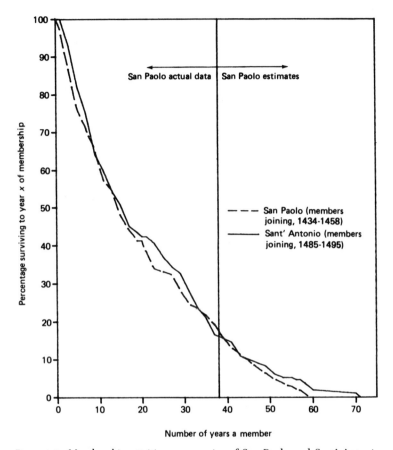

Figure 3.3. Membership attrition, companies of San Paolo and Sant' Antonio.

joined between 1485 and 1495 allows some comparisons of length of membership to be made, although the registers of Sant' Antonio are not as detailed as those of San Paolo and begin too late to permit analyses based on nominal record linkages with the *Catasto* surveys, as is done for San Paolo.[7] Figure 3.3 graphs the survival probabilities of members of San Paolo and Sant' Antonio.[8] The curves are virtually identical.[9] Similarly, the difference

7. *CRS,* 119 (A 98, vol. 34), Sant' Antonio Abate, *Entrature di Fratelli,* 1r-192v.

8. Excluded from this graph are 15 members of Sant' Antonio and 4 members of San Paolo who left to join the clergy. In both companies clerics continued to associate with their respective fraternities, although after 1472 clerics were forbidden from being full members of San Paolo.

9. The largest absolute difference in the two cumulative probability distributions was .063, which is less than the threshold statistic of .1197 required to validate the hypothesis that the two distributions are statistically significant at a weak confidence level of .8 (and a statistical significance of .2) for the Kolmogorov-Smirnov test applied here. The curves are statistically identical.

in average annual rates of attrition, 5.77% for San Paolo, and 5.00% for Sant' Antonio, are due primarily to random error.[10] In other words, both companies exhibited losses of membership that were roughly identical, about 5-6% per year. And, as we shall see, the tenure of members at the time they died, entered the clergy, or were expelled was also similar for the two companies.

On the average, members of San Paolo remained in the company for 20.3 years, and members of Sant' Antonio, for 19.4 years. Length of membership was a function of the two principal causes of membership termination: expulsion from the company and the death of members. Differences in the survival probability curves not attributable to random error were the product of different proportions of members dying and suffering expulsion in the two organizations. Because of frequent suppression, sixteenth-century companies tried at all costs to retain members and used powers of expulsion sparingly. Thus a higher proportion of members were expelled from San Paolo than from Sant' Antonio, but this difference results from different organizational policies adopted at different times, not from differences in members' own behavior. Table 3.7 describes the length of membership at which significant membership-cycle events took place in these two confraternities.[11] In each case, differences are statistically insignificant. Eight members of San Paolo who were expelled had rejoined the company following a previous expulsion. Those expelled from Sant' An-

---

10. Since repeated observations of members of the same cohort are not independent of each other (the number of members surviving at time $t + 1$ is a function of the number of members surviving to time t), the basic assumptions of simple linear regression (a lack of correlation in the error terms, independent observations) are violated and a least squares linear regression of the form $\log Y = a + bX$ is inappropriate, although it is a common technique used to calculate compound growth rates. The procedure used here to calculate these rates (slopes) was a randomized nonparametric technique suggested by L. Marascuilo and M. McSweeney, *Nonparametric and Distribution-Free Methods for the Social Sciences* (Monterey, Calif.: Brooks/Cole, 1977), pp. 293-295, 348-349. This method yields the following 95% confidence intervals for the estimated attrition rates:

$$\text{Sant' Antonio} = 4.65 < 5.00 < 6.61$$
$$\text{San Paolo} = 5.32 < 5.77 < 5.78$$

The large-sample approximation of the Wilcoxon test for differences between slopes of regression estimates produced a statistic, $z = 1.05$, that is statistically insignificant at even such a conservative level of significance as .15.

11. Only four members of the 1434-1458 cohort of San Paolo joined the clergy. The calculation of length of membership at time of entrance into religious orders employed a larger group of members—those 28 members who joined the clergy (and for whom full information exists) between 1434 and 1495. The average length of membership at the time of entrance into the clergy, 3.82 years, is so brief that the termination of records in 1495 does not really bias these statistics, because the termination date affects only a few members at risk of becoming clerics. No members entered the company between 1493 and the suppression in 1495, and, therefore, almost all of San Paolo's

Table 3.7
Mean Length of Membership at Date of Membership-Cycle Event, Companies of San Paolo and Sant' Antonio Abate

Event	N	Number of years member	Standard deviation	Standard error
Death[a]				
San Paolo	98	24.5	14.2	1.4
Sant' Antonio	90	22.3	17.0	1.8
All expulsions[b]				
San Paolo	158	10.4	9.3	.7
Sant' Antonio	26	9.4	8.9	1.7
First expulsions[c]				
San Paolo	150	9.3	7.6	.6
Sant' Antonio	26	9.4	8.9	1.7
Entered clergy[d]				
San Paolo	28	3.8	3.5	.7
Sant' Antonio	15	4.0	5.0	1.3

[a] $z = .537$; $.32 > p > .29$
[b] $z = .957$; $.17 > p > .16$
[c] $z = .027$; $.50 > p > .48$
[d] $z = .125$; $.46 > p > .44$

tonio had never been expelled before. Table 3.7 therefore presents two comparisons: first, of all San Paolo expulsions with those of Sant' Antonio, and second, of all first expulsions from San Paolo with those of Sant' Antonio. Neither comparison yields a difference that is statistically significant, however, the second comparison presents expulsion figures that are literally and statistically identical: 9.34 years for San Paolo, 9.39 years for Sant' Antonio. The striking similarity of these figures, drawn from two in-

members, except those joining in 1492 and 1493, had observable periods of risk of making clerical vows of at least 4 years, and most members had much longer observable periods of risk. Out of a total of 796 members at risk, 17 joined the clergy within their first 4 years of membership, 9 more joined within 9 years of membership, and 2 others joined within 15 years of entrance. Based on these observations, the probability of the 1495 suppression masking entrance into the clergy and, thus, of biasing these figures by overrepresentation or underrepresentation of brief or long periods of membership is quite small. According to the observed rates, the San Paolo figures probably underestimate a total of .67 members who joined within 15 years of entrance, 1.29 members who joined the clergy within 9 years, and .74 members who joined the clergy within 4 years. At most, this underestimation would raise the average length of membership at time of entrance into the clergy, currently calculated at 3.82 years, to a minimum length of membership of 3.94 years or a maximim of 4.29 years.

dependent groups of Florentines, suggests that the behavior of members of San Paolo was typical of members of Florentine flagellant groups more generally.

Why were members expelled? Table 3.8 lists the grounds for expulsion of members from San Paolo between 1434 and 1493. The single greatest number of expulsions occurred on one day of the year. Every spring, at the first meeting after Easter, the members of San Paolo held their spring membership scrutiny. At this meeting the records of members' attendance and their acts of confession and communion were reviewed. The statutes dictated that all persons who had not been in attendance for the previous 4 months or who had been negligent in partaking of the sacraments be expelled. Of all expulsions, 33% occurred during this spring membership review. An additional 27% of all expulsions reflected negligent attendance, confession, and communion at other times of the year. Altogether, infrequent attendance accounted, at minimum, for 60% of all expulsions from the brotherhood of St. Paul.

For a substantial number of members who were expelled, 23%, the membership registers did not give a reason for this action. However, the practice of regularly recording the reasons for expulsion did not begin until the mid-1450s. Of all expulsions lacking stated reasons, 87% occurred before 1458. There is no reason to assume that the causes of these expulsions differed significantly from those of the later period. This brings the total percentage of expulsions that are likely to be attributable to a member's own decision to cease participating in San Paolo to approximately 80%. Four out of five members who were expelled from San Paolo were expelled after they had themselves ceased participating in the affairs of the company.

Those expulsions not attributable to negligent attendance were caused by various infractions of the company's code of conduct. Members who joined other confraternities without renouncing membership in San Paolo violated company statutes and a decree of Archbishop Antonino against memberships in more than one confraternity.[12] These members accounted for 6.6% of all expulsions, or 10% of those expelled on grounds other than negligence. Members who violated the moral code of the company, including a group of three sodomites, all fellow used-clothes dealers, accounted for 3% of all expulsions. Another 3% of those expelled were so punished for revealing company secrets. And approximately 4% of those dismissed from the company failed to submit to forms of penance and correction assigned by the company.

12. See p. 98.

Table 3.8
Reasons for Expulsion, All Members Expelled, 1434-1493

Reason	N	%
No reason cited	84	23.0
Spring scrutiny	121	33.1
Negligent attendance, confession, or communion	100	27.3
Joined other company	24	6.6
Revealed secrets	12	3.3
Disobeyed officers or did not accept correction	14	3.8
Morals charge		
Sodomy	(3)	
Other sex crimes	(1)	
Kept concubine	(1)	
Apostasy	(1)	
Dishonesty or false contracts	(3)	
Condemned by communal authorities	(2)	
Total moral crimes	11	3.0
Total expulsions	366	100.1

Some members left the confraternity for a life of greater sanctity. On the average, members who resigned from these confraternities to join the clergy did so after 4 years of membership. Again, the similarity of the behavior of members of San Paolo and Sant' Antonio is striking.

It is a commonplace among historians of religion that the penitential piety of flagellant confraternity members was often practiced by the elderly. Old men, it is believed, sought to placate God by deathbed conversions; or they thought that burial in the penitential garb of organizations that they joined very late in life might smooth the way to heaven. The registers of San Paolo and Sant' Antonio tell a different story. Those who remained in these companies until their deaths had been members for an average of 22.3 to 24.5 years. Few Florentines joined flagellant confraternities late in life. On the basis of such evidence it is reasonable to conclude that Florentines did not join penitential confraternities immediately before their deaths as part of remorseful conversions. As the final section of this chapter demonstrates, Florentines joined flagellant confraternities, not as old men preparing to die well, but as young men embarking on the *vita activa*. [13]

13. See also pp. 144ff.

Participation

Nineteen officers, in office for 4 months, directed the affairs of San Paolo. These officers can be divided into three main categories: executive officers, service officers, and ceremonial officers.

The company was directed by its governor (*governatore*), whose duties were to "propose, correct, and absolve." The governor directed meetings, enforced the statutes of San Paolo, and determined which members needed punishment or correction. This officer also appointed temporary replacements for absent officers and approved the requests of members asking to be excused from flagellation. At the time of his assumption of office, the governor appointed 16 of the remaining 18 officials who held seven of the remaining eight offices of the company: two masters of novices, (*maestri de' novizi*), four visitors of the sick (*infermieri*), four distributors of charity (*limosinieri*), one provisioner (*proveditore*), one master of ceremonies (*cerimoniere*), two ministers (*ministri*), and two sacristans (*sagrestani*).

Assisting the governor were the remaining two officials elected by the membership, the councillors (*consiglieri*). Together with the governor, the councillors formed the advisory-legislative council that decided all day-to-day business of the company and handled all sensitive matters regarding the private affairs of the company and its members.

The masters of novices conducted investigations into the character of the membership candidates proposed by other members. These officials also prepared new members for their initiation into the company and formally "received" them when they arrived at the company under the guidance of their sponsors.

The company *infermieri* aided ill members. Accompanying the confraternity chaplains, these officers were charged with "treating the soul first, and then the body, recording confession and the other sacraments." Their this-worldly concerns included reporting hardship and insanity cases to the governor and assisting ill members in the management of their finances and personal affairs.

Each Saturday the company *limosinieri* distributed 50 1-pound loaves of bread. On feast days twice as many loaves were distributed. The loaves were destined

first, for needy brothers. Lacking these, [the loaves] should be given to nearby neighbors [*proximi vicini*], suffering true and honest poverty. Lacking recipients in the first and second groups, you should have regard for the shamed poor [normally impoverished members of the patriciate] who can do much with your small donation.[14]

Like the selection of members themselves, the charity account books record that recipients of charity were personally sponsored by confraternity members.[15] Thus the pooled resources of the company were distributed to the clients of individual members. Since any member could recommend a worthy object of charity and bring the individual to the door of the company on Saturday afternoon, the confraternity offered its poorer members the chance not only to receive patronage but also to distribute it to clients and offered its richer members the opportunity to expand further their network of clients.

The company provisioner stood at the heart of confraternal administration. Coordinating the diverse charitable services provided by San Paolo, the provisioner kept all records of company expenses, arranged funerals, and took inventory of all company possessions. He recorded membership activity of the members of the company, acted as recording secretary at company meetings, and functioned generally as a liaison between the governor and councillors and individual members charged with carrying out specific administrative duties.

Three types of officers directed the liturgical and ceremonial activity of the company. The *cerimoniere* helped to conduct liturgical services, led the company in its chants, and organized confession and communion. The *ministri* performed the function of custodians of the dormitory, keeping the blankets and mattresses in order, cleaning the dormitory, and lighting the fire in the chamber when the members entered to retire for the evening, after flagellation. The ministers covered the brothers with blankets after they retired and reported to the governor the breaking of silence in the dormitory. Sacristans performed the final office in the company. Their duties included keeping the keys to the oratory and arriving early to open the doors of the company and light the lights. The sacristan prepared the garments worn by novices, readied the accessory equipment used in burials, passed out the peace-board that was kissed by the members during the kiss of peace, and distributed the *discipline* (whips used in flagellation). Four

14. *Capitoli*, 29, 18r.

15. On the charity accounts of San Paolo, see *CRS*, 1592 (P 1, vol. 37), 1-100.

The practice of disbursing group funds through individual patrons was an established tradition in Florence. During famines guilds distributed grain to their members; the members, in turn, distributed this grain to their own employees and clients. See Giuliano Pinto, "Firenze e la carestia del 1346-1347," *ASI*, 130 (1972): 45.

priests (*correctori*) directed the actual celebration of the mass within the company. In keeping with the citywide nature of San Paolo, these priests represented the four sections of the city, coming from the Badia of Florence, San Marco, the Cestello, and Santa Croce.

Table 3.9 groups the officers of the company in the year 1480 by the length of time that each had been a member at the time of holding office. This distribution presents a rather clear picture of the *cursus honorum* operating in San Paolo. If one concentrates on the pattern of filled and empty cells, one can visualize a diagonal line running from the top left to the bottom right of the table. The first offices that a confraternity member was allowed to hold directed the performance of company rituals. Of the 10 offices held by members who had been in the company for less than 2 years, 7 were offices involving the performance of essentially custodial chores associated with ceremonial activity. This evidence implies that participation in and acquisition of knowledge of the ritual dimensions of confraternity life were necessary preliminaries to other confraternal responsibilities. The executive offices (governor, councillor)—those positions with the greatest power and prestige—were reserved for brothers who had been members for the longest time. Linking the ceremonial and the executive offices were the service positions: provisioner, visitor of the sick, and distributor of charity, offices open to all members, offices whose duties brought young and old members together.

Those members of San Paolo who were younger than age 55 were required to take communion four times each year, to confess at least once each month, and to fast every Saturday (presumably as an act of ritual purification in preparation for the company's meetings on Saturday evening). Each day, "in memory of Christ's passion," the *fratelli* were obliged to say seven Paternosters and seven Ave Marias and to repeat these prayers at mealtime. Members were obliged to recite the De Profundis every Monday in memory of the souls of those deceased brothers in purgatory. The statutes dictated that for 30 days following the death of a member, the brothers were to recite the Miserere. In addition to the payment of dues of one *soldo* annually, each member was to contribute one *staio* (bushel) of grain, out of which the company milled flour, baked bread, and organized the weekly distribution of loaves to the poor. Finally, members were obliged to attend at least one meeting every 4 months, or at least three times each year.

It is impossible to estimate the extent of private devotions practiced by the membership of San Paolo. The company officers, however, kept regular records of the members' monthly confession and communion and atten-

Table 3.9
Officers by Length of Membership at Time of Office Holding, January–December 1480

Years	Sagrestani	Ministri	Cerimonieri	Proveditori	Limosinieri	Infermieri	Maestri de' novizi	Consiglieri	Governatori	Total
0	4	3			3					10
2	1			1	4	3	1			10
5	1	3	2			3		1		10
11			1	2	3	3	3	2	2	16
21					2	3	2	3	1	11
Total	6	6	3	3	12	12	6	6	3	57

dance. During the 52 weeks of 1480 (January 1479-December 1480, Florentine style), the 104 active members of San Paolo (all members, excluding
those who died, were expelled, joined the clergy, did not attend
at all, or reached age 55 during 1480 and thereby became exempt from
normal obligations) came, on the average, to 18 meetings. Attendance was
highest during the first 4 months of the year (January-April), the period
encompassing the Lenten season, the Annunciation, and Easter Week.
During this period the typical member attended an average of 7.3 days. The
attendance continued to drop during the rest of the year, averaging 5.6
visits per member during the spring and summer (May-August) and 5.4
visits per member during the fall and early winter (September-December).
The average attendance for the entire year, 36.5 members, or 35% of the
active membership per meeting, was subject to seasonal variation. During
the first 4 months of the year, an average of 44.4 members attended each
meeting (42.6% of the active membership). For May through August, an
average of 34.0 members attended each meeting (32.7%), and for the last
third of the year, 31.3 members came on the average Saturday (30.1%).

In its organizational form San Paolo was republican and corporate. Its
republican features were similar to those of the Florentine republic. Office
holding was brief, lasting 4 months. Turnover was rapid: 41% of all active
members held office in 1480, and only 24% of the offices held in 1480 were
held by members who had already held a previous office that year. As a
corporate body, the beneficial actions of the "body" were shared by all
members in good standing. A small group of members performed rituals
whose benefits accrued to the entire company. For San Paolo, as for many
other companies in the city, the "body" having the responsibility of performing liturgical and related activities was the "body" of officers:

> Thus we have one body with diverse members, each having a different function, and
> thus we are all one body in Christ, each a different member. Since, I [Saint Paul]
> desire that my sons should refer all their diverse services to one and the same lord,
> the Governor shall publish, on the day of his entrance, [the names of his choices for]
> one Master of Ceremonies, one Provisioner, two Masters of Novices, two Sacristans,
> two Ministers, four Visitors of the Sick, and four distributors of Charity.[16]

---

16. *Capitoli,* 29, statutes of the company of San Paolo, 11r.

Si chome noi habbiamo in uno solo corpo molti membri et tutti non hanno uno medesimo acto et
exercitio, chosí siamo noi tucti uno corpo in Christo ciascheduno disperse membro l'uno dell'altro. Però,
desidero figliuoli miei che referendo diuersi seruigi a uno medesimo signore il Governatore publichi la
mattina di sua entrata uno cerimoniere, uno proueditore, dua maestri de nouizi, dua sacrestani, dua
ministri, quattro infermieri, et quattro limosineri.

This corporate conception of the governing group was common to confraternities. See, for

Table 3.10
Total Attendance by Office Holding[a]

Attendance	Nonofficer	Officer	Total
	Observed values		
1-10	41	5	46
11-20	10	5	15
21-30	4	15	19
31-40	4	5	9
41+	2	13	15
Total	61	43	104
	Row percentages		
1-10	89	11	100
11-20	67	33	100
21-30	21	79	100
31-40	44	56	100
41+	13	87	100
Total	59	41	100
	Column percentages		
1-10	67	12	44
11-20	16	12	14
21-30	7	35	18
31-40	7	12	9
41+	3	30	14
Total	100	101	99

[a] Chi-square $= 42.55$ with 4 degrees of freedom; $p < .001$.

Office holding was clearly one major determinant of attendance. Table 3.10 compares the distribution of meetings attended on the 52 Saturdays of 1480. Of those who attended fewer than 11 gatherings, 89% held no office in 1480, whereas officers, on the other hand, constituted 87% of those who attended 41 times or more. Of rank-and-file members, 83% attended 20 times or less, whereas 77% of all officers attended at least 21 times or more. For the active membership as a whole, as has already been noted, the average meeting drew 35% of the members. This figure is composed of two groups: officers and the rank-and-file. Officers accounted for 67% of those

example, the statutes of the company of Santa Felicità Maccabea e Sette Figliuoli Martiri, *Capitoli,* 137 (1507):

> Ordiniamo che nella nostra compagnia sieno dodeci ufficiali come appresso si dirà, seguitando la doctrina del Salvatore El Quale elesse dodici apostoli, e quali hauessino a ordinare e formare el corpo mistico della santa chiesa de fedeli christiani e quali douessino reggere et ghovernare.

attending the typical meeting. The typical officer attended most meetings, whereas the typical rank-and-file member exhibited a pattern of attendance that was more sporadic. Rank-and-file members did, however, attend the most important gatherings of the year, particularly those scheduled during the weeks of Christmas and Easter. (See Figure 3.4.) And the celebration of Holy Thursday attracted more members than any other meeting of the year.

The high turnover of officers (41% of all active members held office in 1480) meant that the attendance patterns of most members varied between periods of high attendance (as officers) and lower attendance (as rank-and-file members). The attendance of the typical member during his term of office was twice as great as his attendance during the periods immediately before and after his term of office. Such a pattern of attendance was, of course, fully consistent with the republican practices of other Florentine corporate groups.

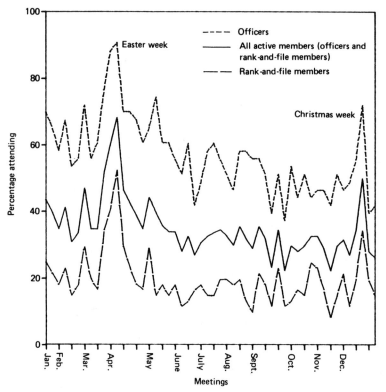

Figure 3.4. Percentages of officers, all active members, and rank-and-file members attending 1480 meetings.

The relationship between sacramental participation and office holding mirrors that of office holding and attendance. Only 15% of those active members who failed to confess during the year were officers. Officers made up 63% of those confessing twice or more. Only 12% of officers never made confession, whereas almost half of the active membership (48%) ignored this obligation entirely. The same set of relationships existed between communion and office holding. Of those members who failed to take communion during the year, 90% were rank-and-file. Only 7% of officers abstained from communion, whereas 62% of officers took communion twice or more. Of the rest of the company, 42% failed to take communion at all, and only 16% of the rank and file took communion more than once.

The statutes of the company required members to confess once each month and to take communion 4 times a year. The active membership of San Paolo confessed, on the average, 1.2 times and took communion 1.5 times annually. During the typical week, 2.4 confessions and 3 acts of communion were recorded. As with attendance, the officers of the company accounted for most sacramental acts. Nonofficers participated in .8 confessions and .9 acts of communion per member per year, whereas each officer, on the average, made confession 1.8 times and took communion 2.4 times. Figures 3.5a and 3.5b present the monthly percentages of officers, nonofficers, and all active members confessing and taking communion. The sacramental participation of officers was more than double that of nonofficers, but even officers failed to live up to the standards of proper membership behavior. Apart from the general requirements of confession and communion that applied to the whole membership, officers had special requirements. On the day of their installation and on the last day of their term of office, officers were required to confess to and to receive communion from the company chaplain, or to bring proof that such confession and communion had taken place elsewhere. Confession and communion thus served as sacred points demarcating the status transition from nonofficer to officer and from officer to regular member again. These acts of confession and communion often took place in a special public ritual observed by the entire confraternity. In part, sacramental participation was designed to serve as a means of promoting the honesty of office holding. In the transition from officer to regular member on the last day of the 4-month term of office, the sequence of confession and communion of old officers was coupled with a formal absolution of old officers by new officers for any transgressions of company statutes that had occurred during the term of office ending that day. The ritual confession and communion of company

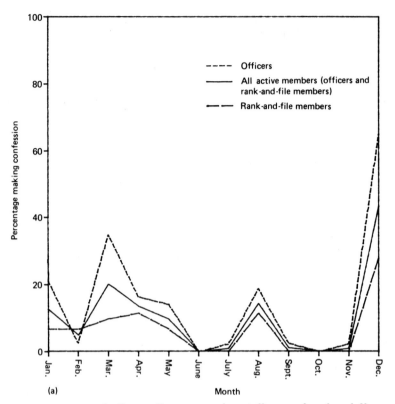

Figure 3.5. Percentages of officers, all active members (officers and rank-and-file members), and rank-and-file members making (*a*) confession monthly; and (*b*) taking communion monthly.

officers was taken seriously. Even Lorenzo de' Medici was not exempt from such obligations.[17]

Table 3.10, discussed previously, contains one anomaly. The row percentages of the table (the middle portion of the table) reveal that the percentage of rank-and-file members in each attendance category decreased as the number of meetings attended increased. Thus, of those members attending less than 11 times, nonofficers made up 89%; of those attending less than 21 times, nonofficers made up 67%; of those attending more than 41 times, nonofficers made up only 13%. The anomalous feature of the table is found

17. A record of the meeting of January 3, 1473, contains this item: "Addì detto fu inposto a Lorenzo de' Medici, vecchio ghovernatore, che infra 8 dì rechassi el sugiello della confessione dal suo confessoro o una fede i[n] suo mano." On January 9, 1473, Lorenzo brought the required proof of confession: "Addì 9 di giennaio recho Lorenzo di Piero de' Medici a una fede di mano del suo confessore come sopra confessato detto dì come gli fu inposto per ubidienza."

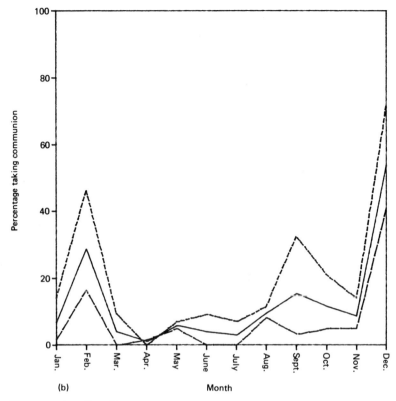

Figure 3.5. (continued)

in the third interval—those attending 31-40 times. In this category one observes a sudden rise in the proportion of those attending who were not officers. This reversal of the general tendency of nonofficers to constitute a decreasing proportion of members attending, as one groups members into categories of greater attendance, can be attributed to the activity of one group of nonofficers that does not follow this pattern—the novices.

Table 3.11 compares the relative frequency of attendance by brothers' length of membership in San Paolo. All members who held one or more offices during the year were excluded from this table in order to remove the effects of office holding upon attendance. On the average, only 16% of all rank-and-file members attended 21 times or more, whereas 67% of them attended fewer than 11 times. The one substantial deviation from this pattern is found in that group of rank-and-file who were members for less than 2 full years. None of the novices attended fewer than 11 times, and 75% of these new members attended at least 21 times or more.

Table 3.11
Days Attended by Length of Membership[a]

Number of years member	Attendance			
	1-10	11-20	21+	Total
	Observed values			
0	0	1	3	4
2	13	5	5	23
6	16	0	1	17
11	6	3	1	10
21	6	1	0	7
Total	41	10	10	61
	Row percentages			
0	0	25	75	100
2	57	22	22	101
6	94	0	6	100
11	60	30	10	100
21	86	14	0	100
Total	67	16	16	99
	Column percentages			
0	0	10	30	7
2	32	50	50	38
6	39	0	10	28
11	15	30	10	16
21	15	10	0	11
Total	101	100	100	100

[a] Chi-square $= 21.19$ with 8 degrees of freedom; $p < .01$.

Patterned after the novitiate in religious orders,[18] this trial period of membership lasted approximately 1 year and allowed the members to judge the novice and the novice to prove himself to the regular membership. Of all members ever expelled from San Paolo on "moral" grounds, 27% were expelled during their novitiate. The statute books do not reveal much about the special requirements of this period of the member's career in the confraternity, apart from excluding novices from most company offices, but the pattern of novices' attendance clearly indicates that novices were expected to conform to an ideal standard of behavior during this trial year.

18. On the novitiate in monastic orders, see Jacques Hourlier, *Histoire du droit et des institutions de l'église en occident: L'age classique (1140-1378): Les religieux* (Paris: Editions Cujas, 1971), 10:171, 177.

The statutes of the flagellant company of San Girolamo (1491), which required the novice masters to "take diligent care for a year, or for however long it seems to them, to record the novice's perseverence, and his on-time attendance," offer some confirmation of San Paolo's de facto practices.[19]

What was the pattern of recruitment of new members? No direct information exists on sponsorship in San Paolo. An examination of the ties of kinship linking the members does, however, provide some clues about recruitment. Of the 119 surnamed members of San Paolo in 1480 (those whose kinship ties are easiest to link), 46, or 39%, had a least one patrilineal kinsman who was also a member of San Paolo in 1480. Of the remaining members, 4, or 3%, had at least one relative precede them; 17, or 14%, were followed at a later date by one or more kinsmen, and 1 member had relatives both precede and follow him into the company. Those members who had been preceded in the company by a patrilineal relation had, on the average, 1.6 kinsmen enter before them. The members of San Paolo in 1480 who were followed by family members were, on the average, followed by 1.6 members during the period 1481-1493. The members who had preceded those currently enrolled in San Paolo included 14 fathers (17% of the relatives preceding those who were enrolled in 1480), 38 brothers (46%), 23 cousins (28%), and 8 paternal uncles (9%). Brothers preceded one another, on the average, by 4.3 years; fathers preceded sons, on the average, by 27.9 years. Members who sponsored their brothers for membership did so, then, early in their careers in San Paolo. Fathers, on the other hand, as should be expected, sponsored their sons during their final years in the company. Figure 3.6 provides a genealogy of the descendants of Ser Guido Paoli, an extreme example of family clustering in San Paolo. The members of this family who joined San Paolo included three separate family nuclei (including one solitary, Simone di Francesco).

Ties of kinship are not the only links between the members of San Paolo that can account for sponsorship and paths of recruitment. The entrance registers recorded, on occasion, the names of members of San Paolo with whom the novice was associated. A number of members of San Paolo appear to have sponsored their clients or boarders. Lorenzo de' Medici preceded two members of his retinue into San Paolo by 3 years, joining in 1471. In 1474 Niccolò di Michelozzo Michelozzi, Lorenzo's notary, and Poliziano, both residents at the Medici palace, entered the company. The following year, the father (Lorenzo di Bastiano di Ser Lorenzo) of one of Lorenzo's entourage, Sandro, joined the company. Antonio di Iacopo Car-

---

19. *Capitoli,* 81, San Girolamo 1491, chap. 9.

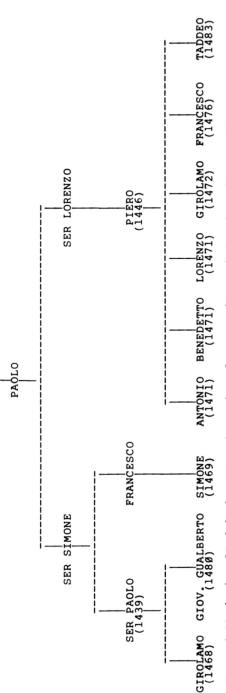

Figure 3.6. Membership of Paoli family in San Paolo. Members of company of San Paolo have dates of entrance following their names.

letti, joining the company in 1477, followed Carlo Attavanti, in whose house he dwelt, into the company by some 24 years but preceded Carlo's son Bernardo, who joined in 1483. Iacopo di Girolamo, a shoemaker, resided in the house of the grandfather of Andrea di Marco di Simone della Robbia. Simone preceded Iacopo in the company registers by 11 years. Agnolo di Moscardo, a student, and Giovanni di Otto Niccolini joined the company together in 1470. Agnolo lived in the household of Giovanni's father, several of whose relatives were already members of San Paolo. The information provided by the taxation registers of 1480 also reveals numerous cases of partners, landlords and tenants, and neighbors who were members of the company. Whether such links were paths of recruitment or were formed on the basis of common membership in the company is difficult to ascertain.[20]

Members appeared to have entered the company as the relatives, patrons, and clients of other members. The attendance patterns of members, however, reveal little clustering along the lines of previous social ties. A cluster analysis was performed on all members' attendance patterns to see if cliques of members attended together, or if groups of members came to San Paolo together with any regularity. This analysis revealed no cliques or clusters of members with similar attendance patterns. Once introduced into the company, the novices spent their first 2 years attending meetings with a frequency greater than that of any other period of their membership, apart from periods of office holding. The corporate nature of attendance and the frequent attendance of novices served to circulate the youngest and the most established members, to bring them together, and to integrate rapidly new members into the networks of their elders.

20. An examination of Florentine tax records submitted in the year 1480 reveals numerous links between members previously and currently enrolled in the company, some of them quite complex. Bartolomeo di Lagnino del Pace (joined 1477) and Bonaccorso di Ugolino di Ser Bartolo Corsi (joined 1457) shared a *ritaglatore* shop. Francesco di Agostino di Domenico Ciegia and Francesco di Domenico (both having joined in 1478) were partners in a fur-manufacturing firm. Giorgio di Mariano di Giorgio di Niccolo di Dante Ughi (1477) worked for Giovanni (1475) and his brother Francesco (1479) di Ser Martino Martini, both members of the silk guild. Tomaso di Neri Ardinghelli (1476) worked for a partner of Carlo di Lionardo Attavanti (1453). Similarly, Francesco di Agnolo di Antonio Tucci (1452) worked for the son of a partner of Francesco di Conte di Francesco (1454), a haberdasher. Michele di Christofano, guainaio (1455), rented his shop from a fellow guildsman and member of San Paolo, Ambrogio di Ser Baldassare (1465). Giovanni di Domenico Burci (1465) rented his shop from the brother of fellow confraternity member Palla di Carlo Strozzi (1474). Maestro Domenico di Ser Pagolo di Lorenzo Bencivenni (1480) lived next door to Francesco di Michele del Cittadino (1443) and his two sons Bartolomeo (1492) and Giovanni Battista (1482). Ser Antonio di Messer Benedetto Ubaldini (1465) rented his house from the widow and son (Niccolo, 1457) of Antonio de' Ricci (1439). Antonio di Pierozzo di Sandro Bocci (1472) rented his home from Tomaso Soderini (1440).

Membership and the Life Cycle

On this day, August 15, 1453, in the name of God, I was accepted into the Company of the Pilgrim [Jesus] which meets in Santa Maria Novella and this was arranged by Luigi di Zanobi Lapaccini who brought me [to the novice ceremony] and he was extremely diligent because today I find myself 58 years, four months, and twenty-six days old, and I thank God the Omnipotent for preparing my way to make penance for my sins. And so I beseech Him to make me persevere in good and fruitful penance, so that at the end of my life He will accept me into life eternal in His mercy, and to make me praise, thank, and glorify Him always as is only right and just. And so, on this day I, Domenico [Pollini] entered the company and there I was embraced by all the men that I found, who, almost to a man, were dressed in sackcloth. I said to each one, "The peace of God be with you," and then I was dressed in sackcloth like them and was placed in front of the altar together with Giovanni di Chante Chompagni and . . . di Ser Iacopo di Bastiano and there we were given the rules of the company, that is, that whoever enters ought to make confession and take communion three times each year, or to confess sincerely every month and take communion three times, and is obligated not to play at any games of dice or any table games and ought to fast one day each week and say penitential psalms and say one Paternoster and one Ave Maria at meals and to obey the captains in relevant matters and to recite 15 Ave Marias and 15 Paternosters every day.[21]

Were flagellant confraternities places of refuge for the elderly, like Domenico Pollini, who joined the flagellant Compagnia del Gesù Pellegrino at age 58 in order to prepare for death? What was the place of ritual kinship within the dynamics of Florentine household structure? In order to answer these questions, demographic profiles of San Paolo members will be related to two indexes of participation: continued membership activity and, for those continuing, the extent of their participation. The first variable, continued activity, divides the membership of 1480 into two groups: those who attended at least once during the year and those who never attended. The

---

21. BNF, ms. Magliabecchiana, VIII, 1282, *Ricordanze di Domenico Pollini,* 43r:

Memoria che questo dì v d'agosto 1453 chol nome di dio fuoi accettato nella chompagnia del Pellegrino che si raghuna in Santa Maria Novella e funo operatore e condussomi Luigi di Zanobi Lapaccini ebbelo molto charo maxime perche trovandomi questo dì detta d'anni 58 e mesi 4 e dì 26 ringratio l'Onipotente iddio che mi prepara la via a fare penitentia de miei pecchati. E cosi lo priego mi facci perseverare in buona e fructuosa penitentia si che alla fine mia egli per sua misericordia m'acetti in vita eterna e che io lo possa sempre lodare ringratiare e magnificare chome e degna e gusta cosa. Siche il dì sopradetto di Io Domenicho sopradetto in domenicha el dì del glorioso confessore Santo Domenicho entrai in detta compagnia e quiui abraccai tucti gl'uomini ui trovai che quasi tucti erano vestiti di saccho dicendo a ciascuno la pace di dio sia con voi e di poi fuoi vestito di saccho come loro e fui messo inanzi al altare insieme con Giovanni di Chante chompagni e di Ser Iacopo di Bastiano e quiui ci fu detto gl'ordini della compagnia cioè che chi v'entra si dee confessare e chomunichare ogni anno 3 volte o sinceramente confessare ogni mese e 3 volte chomunicare dee non guchare a niuno guocho di daddi ne a tauola dee digunare uno di della settimana e dire e salmi penitentiali e dire uno paternostro col ave maria quando ci pognamo a tavola et ubidire e chapitani nelle cose lecite e dire ogni di 15 ave marie e 15 pater nostri.

second variable, extent of participation, consists of the attendance of those members who were active during the year. The active members comprised only half the membership listed in the account books of the company in 1480. In addition to the 104 active members, there were 41 members (21%) who failed to attend at all, 4 (2%) who were expelled, 23 (11%) who joined, 6 (3%) who rejoined, 3 (1.5%) who died, and 25 (12%) who were *beneficiati,* that is who were entitled to enjoy the "benefits" of membership because of their previous service to the company. The *beneficiati* were those members who were 55 years old, were no longer in debt to the company, and who were therefore entitled to enjoy the benefits of membership (prayer, economic assistance, and eventual burial) without contributing anything more than their dues.

Was Domenico Pollini typical? As the records of Sant' Antonio and San Paolo indicate, members of flagellant *compagnie,* on the average, joined well over 20 years before their deaths. How old were they when they joined? Was the age at which a member joined a random event, or did members tend to join during a specific, narrow age interval? Figure 3.7 compares the distribution of ages at which Florentines who were members of San Paolo in 1480 joined with the general distribution of ages of all male Florentines aged 15-55, the lower and upper limits of the ages of individuals joining San Paolo (that is, based on the ages at which those members who were listed in the company accounts in 1480 and who could be found in the *Catasto.*) If members joined randomly with respect to age, that is, if they did not tend to join at a particular point in the life cycle, the distribution of percentage of males at each age (100% = all Florentine males aged 15-55) and the percentage of members joining at each age ought to be approximately equivalent. The distributions do not resemble each other in any manner (skew, spread, peakedness). Males between ages 21 and 27 joined San Paolo far out of proportion to their representation in the general population. After age 27, the distribution of males joining the confraternity declined at a much greater rate than the age distribution for the male population of Florence as a whole. The average age at entrance for San Paolo members was 23, less than half the age of Domenico Pollini when he joined a similar organization. Was San Paolo typical of other fifteenth-century flagellant confraternities? Figure 3.8 presents plots of the distributions of ages at entrance for several fifteenth-century or early sixteenth-century organizations. These plots describe three features of a statistical distribution: the median (the horizontal line bisecting the box), the middle 50% of the distribution (the entire box), and a robust estimate of the remainder of the distribution (the top and bottom whiskers extend to the estimated 97.5 and 2.5 percentiles, respectively). San Paolo and Arcangelo Raffaello were simi-

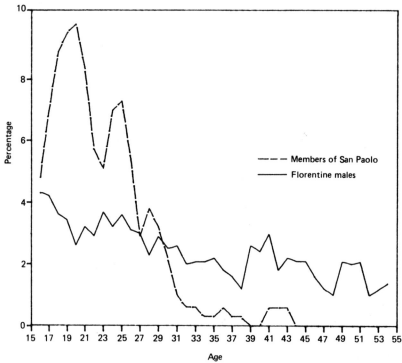

Figure 3.7. Percentages of members of San Paolo joining at age *x* and percentages of Florentine males of age *x*.

lar *disciplinati* companies. All three features of their distributions (central tendency, midrange spread, and full spread) reveal a similar pattern in the ages at which members entered. Sant' Agnese was a *laudesi* fraternity, meeting in Santa Maria del Carmine. The duties of the *laudesi* included the maintenance of the cult of the saints and the regular care of the dead, duties that had greater significance for older Florentines than for the typical entrant into a flagellant confraternity. The median age of entrance in Sant' Agnese was higher than the age of entrance into flagellant companies, and the middle 50% of members' ages were also much higher than the middle 50% of San Paolo.[22]

How old were members when they stopped coming to San Paolo? Table 3.12 presents the results of a test of the statistical significance of age differences between active and inactive members. The statistics reveal that inactive members were, on the average, 5.4 years older than active members, a difference having less than a 5% chance of being explained by "luck

22. *CRS*, 141 (A 146, vol. 3), Arcangelo Raffaello (il Raffa), *Ricordi, 1510-1561; Archivi delle Compagnie Soppresse* (archive 1, vol. 4), *Partiti, 1483-1509.*

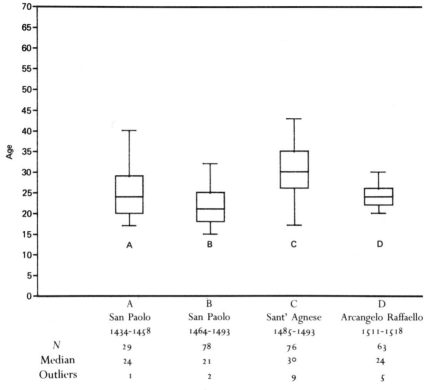

	A	B	C	D
	San Paolo	San Paolo	Sant' Agnese	Arcangelo Raffaello
	1434-1458	1464-1493	1485-1493	1511-1518
N	29	78	76	63
Median	24	21	30	24
Outliers	1	2	9	5

Figure 3.8. Ages at entrance.

of the draw" sampling variation. Active members were, on average, 31.2 years old; inactive members were 36.6 years old. The interval between these two ages represents the interval of most significant change in the life cycle of confraternity members and, for this reason, merits further attention.

The marital status of confraternity members is presented in Table 3.13. If

Table 3.12
Differences in Ages: Active and Inactive Members of San Paolo, 1480

Group	N	Mean	Standard deviation
Active members	53	31.2	10.1
Inactive members	21	36.6	11.4
t	*df*		Significance
1.89	34		$p < .05$

Table 3.13
Marriage Status by Age of Member in 1480[a]

				Age				
Marriage status	13-18	19-24	25-30	31-36	37-42	43-48	49-54	Total
			Observed values					
Unmarried	3	21	17	6	2	2	0	51
First marriage	0	2	3	15	6	7	4	37
Total	3	23	20	21	8	9	4	88
			Row percentages					
Unmarried	6	41	33	12	4	4	0	100
First marriage	0	5	8	41	16	19	11	100
Total	3	26	23	24	9	10	5	100
			Column percentages					
Unmarried	100	91	85	29	25	22	0	58
First marriage	0	9	15	71	75	78	100	42
Total	100	100	100	100	100	100	100	100

[a] Chi-square = 39.91 with 6 degrees of freedom; $p < .001$.

one isolates the age interval spanning the mean age of active membership and the mean age of inactive members, one discovers that this interval, approximately 31-36 years of age, witnessed a sharp rise in the proportion of members who were married. Only 15% of members 25-30 years of age were married, whereas 71% of those in the 31-36 age bracket were married. The proportion of married members continued to increase in the later intervals, but the most dramatic rise in the proportion of married males occurred in this interval of 31-36 years of age. A similar pattern is observed in the distribution of children by age of confraternity member (Table 3.14). No member below age 19 had children. Of members between ages 19 and 30, 90% were childless, but only 38% of members in the next interval, 31-36 years of age, were childless.

Table 3.15 describes the relationship between age and position in the household for members of San Paolo. The interval 31-36 years of age marks one of the two major shifts in household position (the other occurring after age 42). Between the ages of 30 and 37, the proportion of members who were heads of households more than doubled, from 19% to 43%, a figure that remained stable until age 43, when the proportion of household heads again doubled.

Table 3.14
Number of Children by Age of Father, San Paolo, 1480[a]

Number of children	Age							
	13-18	19-24	25-30	31-36	37-42	43-48	49-54	Total
				Observed values				
0	3	21	19	8	2	2	0	55
1	0	2	1	2	3	2	1	11
2-4	0	0	1	7	4	2	2	16
5+	0	0	0	4	0	4	1	9
Total	3	23	21	21	9	10	4	91
				Row percentages				
0	5	38	35	15	4	4	0	101
1	0	18	9	18	27	18	9	99
2-4	0	0	6	44	25	13	13	101
5+	0	0	0	44	0	44	11	99
Total	3	25	23	23	10	11	4	100
				Column percentages				
0	100	91	90	38	22	20	0	60
1	0	9	5	10	33	20	25	12
2-4	0	0	5	33	44	20	50	18
5+	0	0	0	19	0	40	25	10
Total	100	100	100	100	99	100	100	100

[a] Chi-square = 55.65 with 18 degrees of freedom; $p < .001$.

A direct relationship between status within the household and status within the confraternity is suggested by Table 3.16. The column percentages of the table indicate that active members were twice as likely to be sons of household heads as to be heads of households. This is reversed for inactive members, twice as many of whom were household heads as were sons of heads.

The average age at entrance into San Paolo was 23, 4 years less than the average age at which members stopped living with their fathers, for the mean age of members living in households without a reported father was 27.6 years. The typical member therefore joined San Paolo several years before his father's death, or before the member established a neolocal household separated from the authority of his father. The mean age of active members, 31, is below the mean age of first marriage of members,

Table 3.15
Position in Household by Age of Confraternity Member in 1480[a]

Position in household	13-18	19-24	25-30	31-36	37-42	43-48	49-54	Total
				Age				
			Observed values					
Head	0	3	4	9	4	9	4	33
Brotherhood[b]	0	3	4	5	1	0	0	13
Son of head	3	17	13	7	4	1	0	45
Total	3	23	21	21	9	10	4	91
			Row percentages					
Head	0	9	12	27	12	27	12	99
Brotherhood	0	23	31	38	8	0	0	100
Son of head	7	38	29	16	9	2	0	101
Total	3	25	23	23	10	11	4	100
			Column percentages					
Head	0	13	19	43	44	90	100	36
Brotherhood	0	13	19	24	11	0	0	14
Son of head	100	74	62	33	44	10	0	49
Total	100	100	100	100	99	100	100	99

[a] Chi-square = 34.54 with 12 degrees of freedom; $p < .001$.

[b] A household composed of brothers.

32.2,[23] the mean age of members at the birth of the first child, 33.4, and the mean age at the assumption of the head of a household, 36.5.[24] These last three ages (age at marriage, at birth of first child, and at assumption of head of family) all occurred in the interval between the mean ages of active and inactive membership. This suggests that one determinant of membership activity, that is, the choice of continued participation in the activity of the

23. The estimated age at first marriage for the members of San Paolo, 32.2 years, is only slightly higher than the age at first marriage estimated by Herlihy and Klapisch for all male Florentines in 1480, 31.4 years of age. David Herlihy and Christiane Klapisch-Zuber, Les Toscans et leurs familles: un étude du catasto Florentin de 1427 (Paris: Éditions de l'École des Hautes Études en Sciences Sociales, 1978), p. 207.

24. To estimate mean age at first marriage, at birth of first child, at separation from father, and at assumption of head of household, I have used the method of calculation first proposed by John Hajnal, "Age at Marriage and Proportions Marrying," Population Studies 7 (1953): 111-136. Although Hajnal's procedure was first applied to calculate age at first marriage, I have adopted his technique to estimate mean ages for other significant demographic events.

Table 3.16

Membership Status by Position in Household[a]

Position in household	Status in company						
	Active	Inactive	Expelled	Joined	Rejoined	*Benificiati*	Total
Observed values							
Head	17	12	1	1	3	16	50
Brotherhood	4	3	1	4	1	0	13
Son of head	34	6	1	5	0	0	46
Total	55	21	3	10	4	16	109
Row percentages							
Head	34	24	2	2	6	32	100
Brotherhood	31	23	8	31	8	0	101
Son of head	74	13	2	11	0	0	100
Total	50	19	3	9	4	15	100
Column percentages							
Head	31	57	33	10	75	100	46
Brotherhood	7	14	33	40	25	0	12
Son of head	62	29	33	50	0	0	42
Total	100	100	99	100	100	100	100

[a] Chi-square = 43.05 with 10 degrees of freedom; $p < .001$.

company, was linked to the life cycle: The typical period of active membership, for those who would eventually leave the company, was most probably that period immediately preceding the separation of fathers and sons and ending at the point at which they assumed the positions of husbands, fathers, and heads of their own households.

The crude distinction made between active and inactive members highlighted a phase of the life cycle during which members allowed their obligations to lapse. But such a distinction does not allow the effects of other variables—age, novitiate, office holding—to be controlled. The final section of this chapter presents a multivariate analysis that controls such variables, in order to assess the separate contributions of age, office holding, the life cycle, and the novitiate to a member's attendance.

Through multiple regression the factors influencing attendance at San Paolo in 1480 can be isolated from effects of other variables. Tables 3.17 and 3.18 present the results of two multiple regression analyses. Table 3.17 identifies variables that account for the attendance patterns of members

Table 3.17
Models of Attendance: Rank-and-File Members of San Paolo in 1480

Independent variables	Zero-order R	Dependent variable: Days attended in 1480															
		1		2		3		4		5		6		7		8	
		B	p	B	p	B	p	B	p	B	p	B	p	B	p	B	p
Novice	.453	18.91	.025			18.34	.024	17.25	.025	18.59	.018	18.00	.028	17.02	.046	17.52	.023
Age	-.165	-.05	.829			-.30	.248	-.80	.030	-1.10	.017	-.82	.034	-.81	.047	-.72	.05
Head of family	.292					13.29	.019	14.63	.009	14.06	.011	15.12	.010	14.94	.015	16.38	.005
Son of head	-.086					7.79	.132	7.69	.116	7.92	.104	7.37	.150	7.93	.145	9.71	.060
Married	.049							11.15	.059	11.92	.045	11.07	.072	11.08	.089	8.39	.179
Length of membership	-.041									.45	.246						
Family size	-.083											.35	.575				
Wealth	-.053													-.001	.705		
Social status	.152															2.44	.243
Intercept		10.08				8.79		18.96		23.35		17.02		20.13		13.85	
Multiple R		.454				.611		.683		.708		.690		.688		.708	
R-squared		.206				.374		.467		.501		.476		.473		.501	
Significance		.038				.018		.009		.012		.024		.043		.012	

$N = 28$

Table 3.18
Models of Attendance: Officers of San Paolo in 1480

		Dependent variable: Days attended in 1480													
	1	2		3		4		5		6		7		8	
Independent variables	Zero-order R	B	P	B	P	B	P	B	P	B	P	B	P	B	P
Offices held	.492	16.85	.012	17.03	.013	15.32	.050	14.50	.060	16.51	.016	16.75	.024	17.62	.010
Age	.020			−.05	.821	.10	.760	.10	.790						
Head of family	.021					−6.63	.670	−11.05	.510						
Son of head	−.138					−8.70	.580	−12.73	.550						
Married	−.224							−6.16	.600						
Length of membership	.140									.09	.752				
Wealth	−.100											<.001	.930		
Social status	−.040													−1.72	.510
Intercept		10.10		11.74		22.43		23.85		9.36		10.52		11.30	
Multiple R		.492		.493		.507		.533		.495		.492		.510	
R-squared		.242		.244		.257		.284		.246		.242		.258	
Significance		.004		.031		.174		.228		.030		.054		.024	
N = 25															

153

who held no offices during 1480, and Table 3.18 performs an identical analysis on those members who were officers during that year. For the company as a whole, office holding alone accounted for about 50% of the varrition in attendance (R = .697, R-squared = .485). But not all members were officers, and unless rank-and-file members all attended meetings with roughly the same frequency, the number of offices held (uniformly 0) certainly does not explain the variation in *their* attendance. It is assumed that sociodemographic variables affect officers, who were obligated to attend meetings, and the rank and file, whose obligations were much less rigorous, in different ways.

Column 1 of Tables 3.17 and 3.18 presents the raw correlation coefficients that describe the strength of each independent variable with the dependent variable, attendance, before these raw effects have been corrected for the influence of other variables. The raw correlation coefficient, zero-order R, varies between −1 and 1. The closer its value is to zero, the weaker is the relationship between the independent and dependent variable. Coefficients approaching −1 describe a strong negative correlation (an inverse relationship between the independent and dependent variable), whereas coefficients approaching +1 describe strong positive relationships. Columns 2-8 present alternative models of member attendance, isolating each variable included in the model from the effects of every other variable included in the model. Multiple R, the multiple correlation coefficient, found at the bottom of each column, describes the combined explanatory power of all the variables included in the model. It is interpreted in the same manner as zero-order R. R-squared, the square of Multiple R, describes the proportion of the variance in attendance that is explained by the joint effects of the variables in the model. The statistical significance of Multiple R describes the extent to which the multiple correlation coefficient might be the product of chance errors, that is, the "luck of the draw," since the data used in these regressions were derived from samples, not complete populations. The lower the value in the row labeled "significance," the smaller is the chance that random sampling errors account for the correlation of attendance and the relevant independent variables.

The main body of the table displays the regression coefficient and its associated probability (*p*) for each variable in the mode. The regression coefficient is equal to the number of additional days of attendance that are associated with a one-unit change in each particular independent variable, all other variables held constant. The variables are "offices held," "novitiate," "age," "head of family," "son of household head," "married," "length of membership," "family size," "social status," and "wealth." Another variable, a measure of distance between a member's home and the confraternity, is not included here, for its effect on attendance was zero. "Offices held" (found only in Table 3.18) varies between 0, no offices held in 1480, and 2, the maximum number of offices that a member could hold in any given year (since only officers are included in Table 3.18, the minimum score for this variable was 1). "Novitiate" (found only in Table 3.17, since no officers in the sample of all active members were novices that year) is a dummy variable, that is, it can take only the values 0, meaning that the member was not a novice, or 1, meaning that the member was completing his novitiate. (Novices who joined during 1480 were excluded from these tables because those joining in mid-year would not be able to share the same possible maximum attendance—52 days—as those members who were members on the first day of the year. For the same reason, members who died during 1480 or who were expelled were excluded from these tables.) "Age" describes the age of the member in 1480 and is measured in years. "Head of family" and "son of head" are dummy variables whose values are 0 if the condition is false and 1 if the condition is true. (A third category, a member of a household of brothers, a *fratellanza,* was excluded from the regression since it is the third category in a three-category dummy variable and is included automatically in the regression.) The variable "married" is also a dummy variable having two categories, 0, unmarried, and 1, married. "Length of membership" describes the number of years that had elapsed, as of January 1, 1480, since the member joined San Paolo. "Family size," excluded from Table 3.18 since its explanatory power was approximately 0, describes the number of related individuals living in the household of the confraternity member. "Social status" is a rank-ordered variable (0 = patrician, 1 = member of major guild, 2 = member of minor guild, 3 = *sottoposto*). "Wealth" describes a member's total household taxable assets in florins, after subtracting deductions, as recorded in the 1480 *Catasto; p* provides a measure of the probability that the regression coefficient is as large as it is because of chance effects. That is, it describes the probability (ranging from 0 to 1.000) that the coefficient is not truly statistically significant. Small sample sizes tend to produce somewhat higher correlations and regression coefficients than do larger samples. For this reason the statistical significance (p) of the regression coefficients and the Multiple R become quite important indicators of the degree of confidence that can be placed in these results. Given the very small sample sizes possible in this analysis, relationships that have a probability that is greater than .05 of being explained by chance will be ignored, except where unusual circumstances suggest a more tolerant interpretation.

For rank-and-file members, who attended, on average, 10 meetings each year, the best model of attendance is provided by Column 4. Novice status alone (Column 1, $R = .453$, R-squared $= .205$) accounts for only 20% of the variation in the attendance of these members. Correcting for age (Column 2) produces a coefficient for age that has an 83% chance of being the result of chance error and cannot, therefore, be trusted, and the gain in explanatory power is less than 1%. Controlling for age and for household status (Column 3) produces a 16% gain (the difference between the R-squared of this column and that of Column 2) in explained variance. Controlling for all of these factors plus marriage (model 4, the preferred model) adds an additional 7% to the explanatory power of our model and has the additional advantage of reducing the probability of chance error for two variables, age (from .248 to .03) and son of household head (from .132 to .116). Since son of household head is an integral category of the larger variable, household status, and since its other category included in this regression, head of family, has such a low probability of being produced by random error (.019), this variable may be safely included in the model. Model 4 as a whole has the lowest probability of being produced by chance effects (.009), adding further confidence in its reliability. Other models fail to meet the criteria established above. Column 5, which adds length of membership to the model, adds less than 2% additional explained variance, at the cost of adding a coefficient (length of membership) of weak reliability, given its p value of .246. Column 6 adds family size to Model 4, resulting in an increase in explanatory power of .7% and, at the same, introducing a coefficient whose probability of error is greater than 50%. Column 7 adds wealth to model 4, producing a model whose explanatory power is only .5% greater than Model 4. The final model, Column 8, adding social status, also contributes a miniscule amount of additional explanatory power, while introducing coefficients of dubious reliability.

What does Model 4 suggest about the attendance patterns of rank-and-file members of San Paolo? First, over the course of the year, novices attended 17.25 more meetings per year, all other variables held constant, than regular members of the company. If one compares the regression coefficients for novices for each of the models (that is, if one compares the effect of adding different control variables), one observes that the coefficients do not change much. Thus, the magnitude of the effect of being a novice (18.91 days), when one has merely controlled for age, is only 1.6 days greater than the effect of being a novice, after household status and marriage status have been controlled for as well. Did novices attend *because* their family life permitted attendance? The evidence suggests not. It appears that novices, irrespective of their domestic arrangements, followed the rules of San Paolo and attended with great regularity. For members who had finished their novitiate, however, domestic arrangements played a major role in patterns of attendance. All other factors held constant, heads of families attended seven more meetings (14.63 days) than sons of heads (7.69), and members of fraternal households attended very infrequently, attending 14.63 fewer meetings than household heads, and 7.69 fewer meetings than sons of household heads. Finally, married men attended 11.25 more meetings than did unmarried men.

For officers (Table 3.18), no model is more powerful than that of Column 2, the simple correlation between the number of offices held and attendance. Of the variance in attendance, 24% is explained simply by the number of offices held. As Column 1 indicates, each office held accounted for 16.85 meetings attended, which is hardly surprising given that the normal terms of office were 17 (first term), 17 (second term), and 18 (third term) Saturdays in duration. All other models add very little in explanatory power, while, at the same time, they introduce coefficients whose probability of error is quite high. Two of these models, Model 4 and 5, have overall significance levels (the probabilities that Multiple R is really the product of chance error) that are unacceptably high. The effect of office holding on attendance for officers appears, however, to be similar to the effect of the novitiate for rank-and-file members. No matter what controls are added, even those household and marriage controls that were shown to be statistically significant for rank-and-file members, the effect of office holding on attendance changes only very little, from a low of 16.51 days attended (excluding Columns 4 and 5, whose results are thoroughly invalidated by their high overall significance levels) to a high of 17.62. It is reasonable to assume, in the absence of other explanatory variables, that officers, like novices, attended not because their outside commitments permitted it but because they heeded the rules of the company. Their attendance patterns, even when social status and wealth were controlled, appear to have been relatively invariant.

Tables 3.17 and 3.18 estimated the number of days attended in 1480 that were attributed to the *separate* influence of each variable under analysis, after removing the effects of all other variables. Table 3.19 estimates the *total* yearly attendance for the members of San Paolo falling into each category of the table. This table is based on a regression combining rank-and-file members and officers. The total yearly attendance of members, not the partial attendance attributed to the influence of one specific variable, is presented here. Thus, the entry "Novice" in Table 3.17 estimates the number of days of attendance attributed only to the effects of being a novice. But one was not merely a novice or a continuing member. One was also a member of a household, an age group, and one was either married or unmarried. Each of these variables also contributed additional

Table 3.19
Estimates of Attendance, San Paolo, 1480

Selected estimates

Office holding

Regular member	9.25
1 Office	27.48
2 Offices	45.75

Novitiate, rank-and-file members

Novice	28.49
Continuing member	8.49

Household status, rank-and-file members

Head of household	11.52
Brotherhood	2.09
Son of head	8.93

Marriage status, rank-and-file members

Unmarried	8.73
Newly married	1.29
Parents	11.90

Household and marriage status,
rank-and-file members

	Son	Brotherhood	Head
Unmarried	8.32	1.48	10.91
Newly married	.97	0	3.56
Parents	11.59	4.75	14.18

Dependent variable: Days attended in 1480

Independent variables: office holding, novitiate,
household status categories, marital status categories,
age, length of membership

Multiple R	.785
R-squared	.616
Significance	<.001

$N = 53$

days of attendance over and above the effects of being or not being a novice. It is the sum of these combined effects that is presented in Table 3.19. And thus, by way of example, Table 3.19, by averaging the effects of all other variables, compares the total days attended in 1480 by novices, 28.49, with the total days attended by continuing members, 8.49. By adding together estimates of separate effects, as is done in Table 3.19, the total annual attendance of San Paolo's different member groups can be estimated.

After removing the effects of age, length of membership, and the novitiate on rank-and-file members, a model of the effects of the life cycle upon confraternal participation emerges from the data—a model that confirms conclusions made previously about the attendance patterns of active and inactive members.

Rank-and-file members of San Paolo attended, on the average, 9 meetings per year. Officers holding one office attended approximately 18 more meetings than those who held no office, and those holding two offices attended approximately 36 meetings more than those failing to be selected as officers. This estimate conforms quite well to the separate regression using officers alone, which estimated that members attended approximately 17 (16.85) additional meetings for each office held. Novices attended 20 more meetings than other rank-and-file brethren. Members who lived in households that included one or more parents or children had much higher attendance than did members living in fraternal households, the communal household of (usually unmarried) brothers. Ritual brotherhood was more prevalent among males lacking household blood-brotherhood than among members of *fratellanze*. All other variables held constant, sons of household heads attended more than four times as frequently as members of *fratellanze*, and heads of households attended five times as often as members of fraternal households.

Members who were married and childless were less likely to attend than were married members with children. Newly married members attended seven times less frequently than unmarried members, and ten times as infrequently as married members who were parents. All childless marriages in this sample were marriages of men whose ages conformed quite closely to the age of first marriage for males. One can safely assume, therefore, that these childless marriages were not infertile alliances but recent marriages. If this assumption is correct, then marriage was only a temporary obstacle to confraternity attendance. Increasing family obligations occasioned by the birth of children increased confraternity attendance as well. The mean ages at which members entered and were expelled offer further confirmation of the effects of recent marriage upon participation in this confraternity. The mean age of entrance, 23 years, plus the mean length of membership at time of first expulsion, 9.3 years, equaled 32.3 years. The mean age at marriage equaled 32.2 years. Members appear to have remained active participants until they married or formed *fratellanze.* Competing loyalties to these new household units diminished participation in many cases, leading, ultimately, to expulsion from the confraternity. As the final set of estimates of Table 3.19 (the combined effects of marital status and household cycle) indicates, recent marriage had the effect of reducing the attendance of sons of household heads and members of *fratellanze* to levels below the mandatory expulsion threshold of less than one meeting each third of the year.

The analysis presented earlier of active and inactive members suggested that the transition from active member to one risking expulsion occurred during the member's transition from bachelor to husband. This analysis of attendance helps to confirm that hypothesis. Marriage reduced attendance to a level below that required to maintain membership in San Paolo (three meetings each year), as did membership in a household of brothers. Such a community as a brotherhood may have been superfluous for members of *fratellanze,* already sharing ties of brotherhood. This, at least, is suggested by the very low attendance of members of these households. And the confraternity, capable of producing strong male bonds,[25] may have been perceived by the wives of members as a potential source of competition for the time and attention of newly acquired spouses. For those whose memberships survived marriage, additional household complexity and familial responsibility were accompanied by increased levels of participation in confraternal affairs.

Conclusion

The flagellant confraternity retained many of its members for one, two, and sometimes three or more decades. But the participation of members was not constant; it had its own seasonal rhythms. Over the course of the year attendance was greatest between Christmas and Easter. Confraternal attendance, then, reflected the emphases of the Christian calendar.

Over the course of their memberships members attended most frequently as novices or officers. The novice entered San Paolo through his family networks at the very time that his social relations were beginning to

---

25. On religious fraternities as sources of male bonding and identity, see Mary Ann Clawson, "Early Modern Fraternalism and the Patriarchal Family," *Feminist Studies* 6 (1980): 368-391.

The study of sorority in Florentine society is beyond the scope of this book. The reader is referred to the forthcoming doctoral dissertation of Sherrill Cohen, Princeton University, on sixteenth-century organizations for Florentine laywomen.

undergo fundamental changes. The typical novice was in the process of establishing his own personal networks of allies and connections. The negotiation of a marriage alliance, a growing independence from one's father, the prospective division of property among heirs, the establishment of business or political connections—these were difficult and even violent moments in the transition from dependent youth to married household head.[26] And it was precisely at the age (25) when many entered flagellant confraternities that Florentines qualified for public office. The presence of numerous politically active Florentines in San Paolo suggests that confraternal membership was quite compatible with Florentine politics despite the existence of laws forbidding politically active Florentines from joining confraternities.[27] More typical, perhaps, than the elderly Domenico Pollini, who entered late in life, was Bartolomeo Masi, who began his career in the adult brotherhoods at age 21, following his father and brothers into San Benedetto, and joining San Paolo at age 24, 2 years before he began to participate in Florentine civic life as a councillor for the Guild of Locksmiths.[28]

Social and ritual passages coincided in San Paolo. For Florentines about to broaden family and neighborhood centered networks and beginning to participate in the life of the city, the confraternity offered an introduction to the nature of citywide community, its republican institutions, and its civic values. And for older members, caught in the tense environment of competing obligations and extended networks, the confraternity offered the possibility of renewing and recreating a sense of obligation to broader communities.

26. David Herlihy, "Some Psychological and Social Roots of Violence in the Tuscan Cities," in *Violence and Disorder in Italian Cities, 1200-1500,* ed. Lauro Martines (Berkeley: University of California Press, 1972), pp. 143-149.

27. Despite the existence of communal prohibitions, San Paolo's membership was composed of many Florentines who themselves and whose families were politically active. Among the statesmen in the *balia* of 1480, were, for example, a number of currently active members of San Paolo, among them: Tomaso Soderini, Lorenzo de' Medici, Bernardo Buongirolami, Giovanni Borghini, Francesco Cambini, and Francesco del Cittadino. Numerous other *balia* members were the fathers, brothers, or sons of current members of San Paolo. On laws prohibiting politically eligible Florentines from joining confraternities, see pp. 167ff.

28. G. O. Corrazzini, ed., *Ricordanze di Bartolomeo Masi calderaio fiorentino dal 1478 al 1526* (Florence: Sansoni, 1906), *passim.*

Chapter FOUR

Pilgrims in the Desert
TRADITIONAL CONFRATERNITIES
IN CRISIS

Florentine confraternal organization and ritual practice underwent a radical transformation during the sixteenth century. Many traditional citywide confraternities became elite assemblies monitored by the Medici dukes. In the place of older associations new groups were founded having very different patterns of membership. The rites of brotherhood, too, were transformed. In Republican Florence, confraternal ritual provided a temporary suspension of class and neighborhood loyalties. Sixteenth-century confraternal celebrations were characterized by ritual expressions of *allegiance* to class, to neighborhood, and to the value of courtly, aristocratic culture.[1] The confraternities of the later sixteenth century underwent such transformations (to be examined in Chapter Five) in the aftermath of a general collapse of traditional confraternal life during the opening decades of that century. These difficulties, in the words of one confraternal scribe, left many organizations in the state of "pilgrims without any fixed abode." This chapter outlines the nature of the disruptions that led to the emergence of new confraternal organizations and values.

1. For a different view of when certain transformations among ritual groups occurred, see Richard Trexler, *Public Life in Renaissance Florence* (New York: Academic Press, 1980), pp. 399ff. Trexler believes that the appearance of artisan and neighborhood confraternities in the latter part of the fifteenth century was one element of a "ritual revolution" roughly contemporary with the rule of Lorenzo de' Medici. My own reading of the evidence we have from confraternal statute books (describing the kinds of organizations established in the city) and meeting records (describing the ritual content of fraternal gatherings), as well as contemporary chronicles and histories, suggests that a ritual transformation did indeed take place, but that it developed in the following century in the context of the emergence of the Medici principate and the Catholic reformation after the disruptions of confraternal life in the early years of the sixteenth century. Although craft and parish confraternities did appear in the fifteenth century, their significance should not be exaggerated.

Confraternities and Politics
in the Fourteenth and Fifteenth Centuries

> *The tyrant . . . prohibits congregations and assemblies, so that men will not form
> friendships among themselves, out of fear that they will conspire against him.* [2]

Savonarola's description of the tyrant's fear of conspiracy applied to
republics as well as tyrannies. The friar's own followers, upon coming to
power in Florence in 1494, suppressed the city's lay brotherhoods. These
ritual republics—the confraternities of Florence—could promote sentiments of public peace and concord. Like all corporate bodies in Renaissance

---

The following chart displays our data on the establishment of craft and parish confraternities in
Florence:

Dates by Which Confraternities Appear to Have Existed[a]

Period	Craft confraternity	Parish confraternity
1250-1399	6	1
1400-1449	1	1
1450-1499	3	0
1500-1530	5	0
1531-1549	3	4
1550-1599	11	14[b]

[a] No total for any period is certain to be complete. Only confraternities known to have been *parish*
organizations are listed here as parish confraternities. Trexler has linked several other fifteenth-century confraternities to neighborhood festive groups: San Michele della Pace, in the neighborhood of Sant' Ambrogio; the
Compagnia dell' Assunta in the area of Monteloro; the company of the Resurrection, in the area dominated by
the Kingdom of the Millstone. S. Michele became a parish society in the sixteenth century.
[b] At least 3 additional parish companies probably date from the late sixteenth century.

These figures, combined with Trexler's evidence of increasing neighborhood festive life, suggest
that a transformation in the social organization of confraternal ritual did occur, but that it took place
during the last 50 years of the sixteenth century. The statistics presented in this note give an indication
of the magnitude of this change in the sixteenth century. Confraternal change of this extent, as
Chapter Five argues, was the result of simultaneous institutional, social, political, and religious
transformations: the existence of widespread confraternal crisis and collapse following 50 years of
suppression, Florentine ecclesiastical reform following the Council of Trent and the Florentine Synod
of 1573, the transformation of the Florentine political class into a court nobility, and the creation of
courtly culture in Medici Tuscany. Precedents for the formation of craft and parish confraternities
certainly appeared before the sixteenth century. It was, however, not until the later sixteenth
century that the parish and craft confraternities became dominant forms of fraternal organization.

2. Girolamo Savonarola, *Trattato circha il Reggimento e Governo della città di Firenze,* ed. Luigi Firpo
(Rome: Bellardetti, 1965), vol. 2, pt. 2, pp. 458-459.

Italy, the confraternity could also, on occasion, serve as the focus for partisanship and discord, in the name of concord and the public good. Consequently, governmental intervention and suppression, although infrequent, did take place during the republican period. The outbreak of actual episodes of confraternal political activism early in the fifteenth century led to the enactment of a body of communal legislation that attempted to regulate or suppress confraternities. These groups were suppressed when there existed the slightest possibility that they mixed politics with religion. In 1377, during Florence's war with the papacy, flagellant peace processions were organized by the *disciplinati* companies of the city. The Signoria viewed these processions as part of a Guelph attempt to undermine domestic support of the war and temporarily suppressed confraternities.[3] In 1380 flagellant groups were again forbidden from meeting and from staging certain types of processions. The hooded garb of the flagellants permitted Florentines to march anonymously. Therefore, the Signoria permitted only those whose faces were clearly visible to march that year.[4] Two sacramental confraternities, one meeting in the cathedral and the other in Santa Maria Novella—companies accused of abetting the development of urban factions—were suppressed in 1391. The commune now required any similar society that wished to hold meetings first to gain the approval of the Signoria.[5]

The most thoroughgoing attempt at communal review of fraternities appeared in 1419:

> The lord priors . . . desire to eliminate the cause and occasion of scandals and to remove all suspicion from the minds of the authorities so that everyone can live peaceably. They have learned that as a result of the meeting of certain confraternities, the spirits of the citizenry have been perturbed, divisions have arisen, and many other inconveniences have occurred. Desiring to provide the proper remedy, they . . . have decreed . . . that every confraternity, whether penitential or dedicated to singing lauds . . . which is accustomed to assemble in the ecclesiastical foundations of the city of Florence . . . is henceforth to be dissolved and banned, and its meetings categorically prohibited. Whoever has . . . the custody of any of the books or documents containing the names of the confraternity's members, or their constitutions, observances, and regulations must bring them to the chancellor of the Commune of Florence during the month of October. . . .
>
> Item, the lord priors . . . are authorized, between now and the end of November, to dispose of all property, both real and personal, belonging to these

3. Gene A. Brucker, *Florentine Politics and Society* (Princeton, N.J.: Princeton University Press, 1962), pp. 320-321.

4. ASF, *Provvisioni*, 77, 215r-216r, December 2, 1388.

5. *Ibid.*, 80, 69r-70r, August 7, 1391.

confraternities . . . for the benefit of the souls, and for the remission of sins, of those who had given the property to those confraternities. . . .

Item, all of the furnishings in the buildings of these confraternities are to be totally destroyed . . . and the places of assembly . . . are to be used for other purposes or for habitation, or they are to be closed . . . so that no congregation or meeting can be held in them. . . .

Item, no person, lay or clerical, of whatever dignity, status, quality, or eminence may allow any company to assemble in his house.

Item, no confraternity may be newly created or established in the city of Florence or within a three-mile radius. . . . This provision does not apply . . . to any confraternity which is newly established with the license and consent of the lord priors.[6]

The law appears to have been more of a warning than an actual suppression. No company is known to have been dissolved for good, and all major companies founded in the thirteenth and fourteenth centuries survived beyond 1419. Throughout 1426 the priors received reports that secret meetings were taking place in many parts of the city with the purpose of manipulating tax assessment procedures on behalf of cliques. At the end of July the Signoria again raised the question of confraternities, fearing that discussions of communal affairs took place at confraternal meetings. The Signoria considered taking action against confraternities, "so that evil should not be done under the guise of doing good. . . . If they desire to pray or to whip themselves, let them do it in their own homes."[7] In September the Signoria acted, closing the societies again and requiring all companies to bring their account books to the Eight on Security.[8] The Eight apparently conducted an investigation of these societies, for on September 19, 1426, they declared the company of the Magi to be upstanding and proper and to pose no threat to the republic.[9] In 1427 the *Otto* began allowing confrater-

6. This 1419 provision was transcribed and translated by Gene A. Brucker in *The Society of Renaissance Florence* (New York: Harper & Row, 1971), p. 83.

An example of such approval to meet is contained in a decree affixed to the statute book of San Benedetto de' Camaldoli, September 1, 1419 (*Capitoli*, 635, 15r-16r). In 1435 the *Otto di Balia* granted permission for a hospital and fraternity to be created by the tailors under the protection of Saint Paul the Apostle. No record of any actual foundation exists, perhaps because the *sarti* were afforded membership in the shoemaker's company (del Migliore, 31r-v).

7. *Commissioni di Rinaldo degli Albizzi per il comune di Firenze* (Florence, 1873), 3:6:

Et ubi in ipsa lege reseruatur Dominis et Collegiis etc. auctoritas approbandi aliquas societates, amoveatur ista auctoritas et potestas, ut omnes iste societates penilus extirpentur, ne sub specie boni fiat mali, et ne alique congregationes amplius fiant, et ut qui uult orare uel se uerberare, id domi sue faciat.

8. Del Migliore, lv.

9. Gene A. Brucker, *The Civic World of Renaissance Florence* (Princeton, N.J.: Princeton University Press, 1977), pp. 313, 478-480.

nity officers to meet to administer bequests and to perform works of piety, but none of those officers allowed to meet could be among the *veduti*—those whose names were drawn for the three highest public offices—or the brothers, sons, or grandsons of *veduti* for communal offices since 1381.[10]

Fearing possible confraternal interference in electoral procedures, the Signoria in 1443 prohibited Florentines over age 24 who themselves, or whose fathers or brothers, had been drawn for the three major offices[11] from joining *laudesi* or *disciplinati* companies within 5 miles of the city. Those who violated this provision would suffer the penalty of a 1000 florin fine, and a 5-year disqualification from communal office.[12] This provision seems to have had some effect, for the secretary of the company of San Paolo complained that the number of members who attended meetings had dropped noticeably.[13] The rather complete membership records of this company suggest, however, that the *veduti* did not resign their membership. Attendance decreased in San Paolo, but the number of resignations did not increase. In 1452 at the urging of Archbishop Antonino, who was concerned that communal authorities disregarded the good that confraternities did for the soul, the 1443 law was suspended. *Veduti* could once again participate in confraternities but were subject to the original penalties of the 1443 legislation if communal or guild business was discussed at confraternity meetings.[14]

The confraternity of Gesù Pellegrino, just 2 years after Antonino's successful intervention, appointed special officers, *sollecitori,* for each *gonfalone* of the city to organize support for eligible confraternity members who might otherwise fail to qualify in the upcoming Florentine electoral scrutiny.[15] It is no surprise, therefore, that the following year, on June 19,

10. *Capitoli,* 635, San Benedetto de' Camaldoli, 17r-18r. On the *veduti,* see note 11.

11. The provisions of this act refer to the technicalities of Florentine government. The *tre maggiori,* or three major offices, were the three highest offices in which Florentines could serve: the Signoria, the Twelve Good Men, and the Sixteen Captains of the Standard-Bearing Companies. The names of all Florentines judged capable of serving in these three offices were placed in special pouches. A Florentine was said to be among the *veduti,* those "seen," if his name was drawn from a pouch. He was actually "seated," or *seduto,* if he was allowed to occupy the office. Disqualification could occur if the person whose name was drawn was in debt, or if he or a member of his family had served in the same or in a similar office recently.

12. *Provvisioni,* 134, 208v-209r, February 19, 1443.

13. *CRS,* 1579 (P 1, vol. 1), 13r-v, concerning the law of 1443. There is evidence that this law, at least, affected the companies. The secretary of San Paolo recorded (13v): "Pella non ben fatta legie de 1443 e privatione di tanti fratelli della prefata compagnia intervene che el detto luogo chominciò da pochi essere frèquentato e desercitato."

14. *Provvisioni,* 143, 32v-33v, April 5, 1452.

15. Nicolai Rubinstein, *The Government of Florence under the Medici,* 1434-1494 (Oxford: Clarendon Press, 1966), p. 119.

1455, "in order to avoid the scandals that many citizens in our city remember can occur," the Signoria disregarded the 1452 law and reinstated
the original 1443 provision, strengthening it by lowering the age from 24 to
20 at which the *veduti* were prohibited from confraternity membership and
extending the kin prohibition to include those whose sons were *veduti*.[16]
During the political crisis of the summer of 1458, in which secret meetings
were said to be taking place throughout the city,[17] the law of 1419 was
again invoked (on August 11), and confraternities were suppressed for 6
years.[18]

In September 1471 the provision against *veduti* participating in confraternities was invoked again. After recording the prohibition in San
Paolo's account books, the company secretary admitted that the members
of some companies committed mischief as much as they promoted good
works but lamented that because of those other groups, "I, Ser Lorenzo
Paoli, was one of those who was prohibited from enjoying the consolation"
that the confraternity of San Paolo provided.[19] The frequency with which

16. *Provvisioni*, 146, 147r-148r, June 19, 1455:

Per obviare agli scandali che potrebbono nascere nella nostra ciptà a ricordo di molti cittadini, si
provegha che qualunche di maggiore età d'anni venti conpiuti il quale o il cui padre, fratello carnale del
medesimo padre, o zio, o figliuolo in alcuno tempo fussi stato o sarà tracto ad alcuno de tre maggiori ufici
cioè fussi ueduto il quale per la uenire da calendi di luglio proximo in là si ragunera in alcuna compagnia
di laude o di disciplinati o qualunche altra sotto qualunche nome si chiamassono o in chiesa o case di
spedale o qualunche altro luogho per la deta materia nella città di Firenze o infra le cinque miglia esso
facto caggia in pena de fiorini mille d'oro per qualunche uolta e oltra a questo abbia divieto da qualunche
uficio de comune o pel comune anni cinque proximi che venissono poi che fusse facta la chiarigione che
di sotto si dirà. Et però ne sia sottoposto agli ufici degl'octo, della guardia e conservadori delle leggi del
comune di Firenze et al podestà et capitano della città di Firenze et di qualunche di loro.

17. Benedetto Dei, in his *Cronaca fiorentina* alludes to subversive meetings taking place during the
crisis of the summer months of 1458. BNF, Ms. II, 1, 394, 14r:

Correvono gli anni di Cristo 1458 quando el Potentissimo Popolo Fiorentino era stato anni 4 in pace e in
tranquilità stato di fuori e di drento e ll'arte lavorare assai e v'erano i cittadini drento inchominciatori
amanacciare assai e a fare mille vilanie l'uno con l'altro e restavano i maggiori del reggimento clamando
che pressa Luca Pitti e Chosimo de' Medici e altri di loro parte misono mano affare Parlamento e a punire
i pechati e i delitti che molti aveano chomessi e a tutare e a battere la superbia e ll'aroghanza di molti
cittadini drento. I schandolosi che cerchavano volere essere Maggiori che gli altri e Maggiori che alloro
non tochava d'essere e faciendo settuccie e ragunate e chogiggie e chongiure e intra versavano el
Paese . . . e il chomune era in triste disordine.

18. ASF, *Balie*, 29, 10v-11r, August 11, 1458.

19. CRS, 1595 (P 1, vol. 42), 33v:

Di poi addi i di settenbre 1471 fu pel chonsiglio maggiore che qualunche fusse stato ueduto al 34 'n ua a
uno de 3 maggiore egli o ssuo padre fratello di padre o zio e di padre o per la uenire sarà dattutto il mese
d'ottobre 1471 lla non si possa raunare ad alchuna compagnia di dì o di notte dassera o da mattina nella
città o nel chontado fralle 5 migla intorno sotto pena di Fiorini 500 larghi e di divieto 10 anni d'ogni

the prohibition against the participation of *veduti* in confraternities was invoked suggests that although Ser Lorenzo absented himself from the confraternity, others were less willing to comply with the law. Indeed, some confraternities circumvented the law. The 1477 statutes of the company of San Domenico were explicit in their concern to maintain secrecy, prohibiting members from revealing any "man or anything whatsoever of the company."[20] If the Signoria forbade *veduti* from membership, San Domenico's statutes specified that officers should be appointed to remove the names of *veduti* from the company pouches and that those pouches that must contain the names of all members should be hidden.[21]

Although the regulations against the participation of *veduti* in confraternities were reintroduced on several occasions during the late fifteenth century, there is no evidence that their enforcement, after each initial promulgation, was anything other than mild and sporadic. The entrance of numerous *veduti* into companies such as San Paolo, at or above the very age at which the provisions supposedly took effect, suggests that the commune no longer considered the participation of *veduti* in confraternities as serious a matter as it had earlier in the century. By the late fifteenth century, the confraternities of Florence were no longer singled out by the commune as special targets. Rab Hatfield suggested that the confraternity of the Magi, patronized by the Medici, was far from a threat to Medici rule. Its acceptance of Medici patronage fostered, in Hatfield's view, the confraternity's sense of the value of Medici rule. In their public pageant, the feast of the Magi, members of this confraternity ritualized Medici patronage itself.[22] During the final decades of the century, the confraternities of the city were viewed less as threats to civic order than as potential sources of political support for the Medici regime.[23] Lorenzo, through his participation in and support of a number of important confraternities, shared his patronage and his largesse with significant numbers of Florentines. His own membership in Florentine confraternities included the Magi, San Paolo, San Domenico,

---

uficio. Per la quale chosa parue al benigno iddio che a quelli che assimile compagnie andauano per altri dispetti che bbuoni e queli si uedeuano per l'opere fusse loro chiuso la uia per dimostrare che llauolontà sua non è che per tali dispetti si uada assimili luoghi. E Io Piero di Ser Lorenzo Paoli fu uno di quelli acché fu prohibito tal chonsolazione.

20. *Capitoli della Compagnia di San Domenico*, 1477, in Meersseman, 2:720.

21. *Ibid.*, p. 739.

22. Rab Hatfield, "The Compagnia de' Magi," *Journal of the Warburg and Courtauld Institutes* 33 (1970): 143.

23. On Lorenzo's use of confraternities as vehicles for expanding Medici patronage, see Trexler, *Public Life*, p. 412ff.

Gesù Pellegrino, Santa Maria della Croce al Tempio, and Sant' Agnese.[24] The political utility of Medici patronage of confraternities is revealed in the memoirs of one Florentine artisan, the coppersmith Bartolomeo Masi. In 1490, at the age of 10, Masi joined a confraternity of adolescents, San Giovanni Evangelista. Masi described with pride and wonder the marvelous celebration of Carnival in 1491, directed by a fellow *fratello,* Lorenzo de' Medici's 11-year-old son Giuliano. Lorenzo himself attended the Carnival feast. The boys were, after all, performing Lorenzo's own mystery play, the *Rappresentazione* of Saints John and Paul.[25] When Lorenzo died the following year, Masi left this entry in his diary: "8 April 1492: Lorenzo di Piero di Cosimo de' Medici, Florentine citizen, who governed Florence, died. He was a man skilled in all manner of things, and a man of such great counsel that he was considered one of the wisest men in Italy."[26] One can imagine the pride with which an artisan such as Bartolomeo Masi boasted that Giuliano de' Medici was his spiritual brother or that he shared his feasts with Lorenzo.

Records of Medici involvement in the affairs of one company, Sant' Agnese, exist in some detail. Sant' Agnese, one of the oldest *laudesi* companies in Florence, ran a hospital for poor women, helped to maintain the altars in Santa Maria del Carmine, and organized public feasts in the quarter of Santo Spirito. According to Vasari, Florence regularly celebrated certain major festivals that were organized around single quarters of the city. Santa Maria Novella celebrated the feast of Saint Ignatius; the quarter of Santa Croce hosted the feast of San Bartolommeo; and the quarter of Santo Spirito celebrated three feasts, the feast of the Holy Spirit (in Santo Spirito), Ascension (in Santa Maria del Carmine), and the feast of the Assumption of the Virgin (also in the Carmine).[27] The men of Sant' Agnese had primary responsibility for staging the feast of the Ascension.[28] If Sant' Agnese is any

24. See p. 117, n. 4.

25. G. Corazzini, ed., *Ricordanze di Bartolomeo Masi calderaio fiorentino, dal 1478 al 1526* (Florence: Sansoni, 1906), pp. 15-16.

26. *Ibid.,* pp. 17-18. Masi was, however, bitterly critical of Piero and applauded his expulsion from the city.

27. Giorgio Vasari, *Le Vite de' più eccellenti pittori, scultori, ed architettori* (Florence: Sansoni, 1906) (Vita di Cecca), 3:197-198.

28. On the staging of this feast, see Vasari's description, cited in n. 27. A very detailed description of the celebration in 1439 was left by the Russian bishop, Abraham of Souzdal, transcribed in A. D'Ancona, *Origini del teatro Italiano* (Turin, 1891), 1:246-250. Souzdal described the stage machinery of the representation of the Ascension of Christ as having the following elements: a stone castle representing the city of Jerusalem; a hill representing the Mount of Olives, 10.5 feet high, facing the castle; and a celestial sphere some 56 feet above the stage. When the company of Sant' Agnese

indication, these feasts were not only staged in a particular quarter of the city but also were staged by that quarter. Sant' Agnese drew its members principally from the area around Santa Maria del Carmine, that is, from the three neighborhoods into which the *gonfalone* of the Green Dragon was subdivided.[29] By actively participating in the affairs of Sant' Agnese, the Medici shared their prestige with the neighborhood in which the company met. To the extent that the Medici were actively involved in the celebrations of feasts in the other quarters of Florence it can be assumed that Medici prestige was diffused throughout the city, through fraternal organizations such as Sant' Agnese.

The Medici were frequently selected as officers of this company. Lorenzo was syndic in 1483, councillor in 1487, captain in 1489, treasurer in 1491, and captain again in 1491-1492.[30] Although Piero de' Medici was too young to meet the age requirements for confraternal office holding, the company voted to waive these regulations in his case "because the Medici House has always been the benefactor of our company."[31] And so, despite his youthful age, Piero was selected to be captain in 1488, and in 1489-1490.[32] Similar privileges were extended to Giuliano and Giulio de' Medici.[33] The favors shown the Medici included exemption from all actual duties, fees, and responsibilities, and these exemptions were called, repeatedly, the "privilege of the House of the Medici." Bartolomeo Scala, chancellor of Florence and loyal supporter of the Medici, entered Sant' Agnese in 1488. On the day his membership was approved the minutes of the confraternity read:

The captains . . . on this day, July 22, 1487, obtained and voted their approval, with five black beans [yea votes], that Messer Bartholomeo di Giovanni di Francesco

---

prepared for the celebration of 1488, the members were divided among these three staging areas, the castle, the mountain, and the heavens. ASF, *Archivi delle Compagnie Soppresse* (archive 1, vol. 4), *Libro di Partiti della Compagnia di Sant' Agnese,* 1483-1509, 18r-v.

29. See p. 72, n. 101.

30. *Libro di Partiti della Compagnia di Sant' Agnese,* 2r, 15r, 29r, 41v, 45r.

31. *Ibid.,* 17r:

Item adì 13 di gennaio 1487. E prefati capitani insieme coloro uficiali in sufficiente numero congregati, ottennonno et vinsono per loro solenne partito et per tutte 6 faue nere non ostante una biancha che Piero di Lorenzo di Cosimo de' Medici possa et sia gli lecito exercitare ogni ufitio di nostra compagnia benchè lui non habbia l'età conveniente che s'inchiede per capitoli nostri. Et in questo caso i prefati capitani et officiali predecti dispensorono a ogni età che s'inchiedessi a quantumque ufitio fussi tracto secondo i capitoli di nostra compagnia. Et questo hanno facto per chè la casa de' Medici è sempre stata benefactura di nostra compagnia.

32. *Ibid.,* 19v, 31r.

33. *Ibid.,* 55r.

Scala, Chancellor of the Signoria, is understood to be and is allowed to be one of the brothers of our company. And out of privilege they exempted him from every duty which is imposed and every tax that one is obliged to pay in this company, especially the yearly [dues], in that manner and form [granted to] Lorenzo de' Medici and his house.[34]

Scala, too, served as a captain of the company.[35] But Medici office holding was largely honorific. Lorenzo and Piero rarely attended meetings except when vital company business was discussed. During the 4-month term of office as captain that began in January 1492, Lorenzo missed every meeting except that of January 17, the meeting at which the company voted to give the captains full authority to manage the fiscal affairs of the company.[36]

What did the company gain from the presence of the Medici and their friends? It gained honor and patronage. Was it an accident that the next item of business following the approval of the membership of Bartolomeo Scala, "chancellor of the Signoria," was the dispatching of three members of the company to the Signoria to request "public subvention" of an upcoming feast staged by the men of Sant' Agnese?[37] Medici patronage operated more directly as well. The celebration of Christmas was a regular occasion for Medici gifts to Sant' Agnese. The loaves of bread that the company distributed on Christmas of each year came from grain donated by Lorenzo and, after his death, by Piero.[38] In return for their patronage of Sant' Agnese, the Medici received regular expression of gratitude for their patronage. Clientage also had its obligations. Lorenzo, at his pleasure, made use of the company meeting chambers to stage his private celebrations.[39]

It was certainly as useful to co-opt as to suppress the confraternities of

34. *Ibid.*, 14v.:

E prefati capitani, absente Biagio fabro, questo dì 22 di luglio 1487 ottennonno et vinsono per loro solenne partito et per cinque fave nere che Messer Bartholomeo di Giovanni di Francesco Scala, cancelliere della Signoria, s'intenda essere et sia de' frategli di nostra compagnia. Et per privilegio lo feciono exempte da ogni incharico et graveza l'infusse auuto et obbligato pagare in detta compagnia et maxime gl' anni et in quel modo et forma che è Lorenzo de' Medici et la casa sua.

35. *Ibid.*, 37r. Scala served as captain for the 4 months beginning January 1491.

36. *Ibid.*, 45r.

37. *Ibid.*, 14v.:

Item: e prefati capitani detto dì [22 July 1487] ottennonno che Maestro Antonio da Barberto et Francesco di Iacopo pupillo et Bandinello di . . . debbino domattina che saremo a dì 23 di luglio andare a Lionardo d'Antonio Ferrucci che al presente si truoua de' Magnifici Signori et allui exporgli tanto quanto hanno hauuto in commissione priori hauere la subuentione pubblica della festa.

38. *Ibid.*, 29v, 35v, 58v.

39. Lorenzo's use of the company quarters for his own celebration of the feast of the Holy Spirit is described on folio 27v of these accounts.

Florence. Suppression and rigid communal exclusions of the *veduti* had given way, by the final decades of the fifteenth century, to subtler forms of manipulation.

From Republic to Principate: The Crisis of Late Renaissance Confraternities

The relative stability of late fifteenth-century Florence contrasts sharply with Florence in the early sixteenth century. The suppressions of the fourteenth and fifteenth centuries rarely lasted for more than a few years. Applied in moments of social upheaval, not infrequently as part of general measures to retard the formation of opposition cliques, these suppressions appear to have had little lasting effect on confraternities, although the high turnover of members of San Paolo following its suppression from 1458 to 1464 suggests the extent of potential disruption that longer or more frequent suppressions might have brought. Signs of serious company disruption, like those that are to be found in abundance in the sixteenth century—radical loss of members, lack of members willing to serve as officers, loss of dues, accumulation and eventual cancellation of members' debts, mergers of confraternities, loss of meeting places, neglect of ritual and liturgical duties, open admission of crisis—were rarely mentioned at all prior to the end of the fifteenth century. Then came the real crisis.

From the Savonarolan period to the years immediately preceding the conclusion of the Council of Trent, internal political instability, and periodic plague and warfare created turmoil in Florentine confraternities, as each round of social conflict, warfare, or catastrophe brought renewed suppression. Almost every political revolution or change in government between 1494 and the beginning of the reign of Cosimo I (1537) was accompanied by a decree closing the confraternities of Florence, based on precedents set in the previous century.

Following the expulsion of Piero de' Medici, on December 2, 1494, the confraternities of the city were suppressed. The closing of these groups had become standard procedure in time of civil discord. The confraternities were outlawed because of "the inconveniences that follow in the wake of the meeting of the companies, intelligences, and sects, and to preserve liberty and peace, and to remove all causes of machination and sedition."[40]

40. *Provvisioni*, vol. 185, 6v, December 2, 1494:

Et più, hauendo inteso gl' inconvenienti seguitano del ragunarsi le compagnie et intelligentie et secte et

There is, however, no evidence that confraternities were actually involved in any seditious behavior. The decree outlawing the confraternities was article 19 of the general reforms enacted by the Signoria installed after Piero's expulsion. This provision included far more important edicts (among them, the abolition of the Medicean councils of Seventy and One Hundred and the establishment of the Consiglio Maggiore). The decree against the confraternities was the last in the list. The existing evidence indicates that by the end of the fifteenth century suppression of confraternities had become a preventive measure, rather than a response to actual sedition.

The company of San Frediano was suppressed, along with the other fraternities of Florence, in 1495. The account books of the company record no activity between the date of suppression and 1502.[41] The constitutional reforms of this company reveal repeated attempts to deal with the problems of frequent suppression. On March 25, 1518, after a suppression during the same year, the company voted to increase from two to three the number of its syndics, officials appointed for several years to oversee the fiscal and legal affairs of the company.[42] These officials were empowered to act in the name of the confraternity and to look after its fiscal affairs during periods of suppression.

By 1520, although it had continued to meet, its affairs had badly declined. The honorarium customarily paid to officers of the company, a ration of pepper, was withheld for nonperformance of duties. A reform dated October 20 of that year begins:

> How great is the disorder in which this company finds itself and its properties, not being able to make good on its accounts, nor to collect from its debtors, and the proper observance of the statutes has been neglected, and all this occurred because our meetings have no order. The captains and other officials, when requested to come to the company to take care of business, do not come to exercise the duties

---

per conseruatione di decta libertà et pace et atorre tutte le cagioni di machinationi et seditioni si provede che tutti e ueduti ad alchuno de tre maggiori o alla parte o al consolato di qualunque arti non si possino ragunare in alchuna compagnia, intelligentia o secta di dì o di nocte sotto le pene che nelle provisioni nominate nel parlamento del MCCCCLVIIJ o in epso '58 si contengono le quali qui tutte si ripetono et per ripetite s'hanno et più di fiorini cento larghi per ciaschuno d'anni venti o da indi in giu la quale s'applica al monte et in sua diminutione et per e maggiori di detta età di rimanere ammoniti per tre anni da tutti gli ufici di commune o pel commune et che di tutto ne sieno sottoposti a gli otto et a conservatori delle legge et come in decta provisione del 1458 si contiene et dispone hauendo luogo la proventione.

41. *Archivi delle Compagnie Soppresse* (archive 5, vol. 5.), 111r-112r.
42. *Ibid.*, (vol. 1), 16r-v.

that they ought to perform. The company, on account of this, remains abandoned and there is no one who looks after its affairs.[43]

This reform also lengthened the term of office for the company treasurer, who was no longer to be selected at random but was rather to be selected on the basis of administrative competence. Finally, the provision required those who failed to attend meetings to forfeit their offices.

San Frediano was not the only company to describe its condition, by 1520, as one of disorder and decay. The Compagnia del Raviggiolo reassembled in 1497, after the Savonarolan suppression. Although it appointed two procurators to oversee company affairs and the abbot of the Badia of San Pancrazio to be its chaplain, the company fell into a state of disorder and was not resurrected until the seventeenth century, and then in a new guise.[44] The brotherhood of the Opera di Carità (Work of Charity) experienced sustained crisis beginning with the Savonarolan suppression. Reunited in 1498, the company account books record:

> On this day, February 24, thirty men, together with the previously elected distributors of alms met to honor God. [They met to] consider that because of many disorders that occurred in our city a time ago, they were not able to meet, having been forbidden and prohibited from meeting by the Eight [on Security]. We have become very negligent, especially about performing those works that praise God, neither visiting the sick nor paying two soldi a week as our constitution requires.[45]

The debts that members owed the company were so extensive that they could not readily be repaid. Failure to pay regular dues was, in the traditional confraternity, a serious offense, and members who were so lacking in responsibility were charged additional sums. Once their debts reached certain limits, members were prohibited from holding office, then prohibited from voting, denied the "benefits" of membership (economic assistance in time of illness, use of the company physician, burial by the company), and, finally, expelled from the confraternity. Confronting an ever accumulating sum of unpaid dues in its debtors' book, the company was forced, in order to keep its membership intact and to encourage those who had become negligent to return to the company, to proclaim a *grazia,* general forgiveness of debts owed the company, leaving it to each member to decide for himself whether to pay debts anonymously into a general charity cash box.

43. *Ibid.,* 18r–20r.

44. *Capitoli,* 253, Santissimo Sacramento di San Pancrazio, p. 3. The company was refounded as a parish fraternity.

45. *CRS,* 1430 (M 112, vol. 42), Company of San Michele Arcangelo, 9r.

This *grazia* appears to have had little effect, for 8 months later, on October 27, 1499, the company complained of its recurring failure to gather its statutory quorum of 25 members. Because of this "gross negligence" (*grande negrigenza*), the company rarely gathered the 25 members needed to conduct confraternity business. Altering its statutes, the company voted to ignore the quorum requirement and to elect new officials and perform other duties with however many persons were actually in attendance at the meetings in question.[46] In 1500 the situation was little remedied, for in September of that year the company reported:

> Many, on account of their personal affairs, are refusing to participate in works of charity, and the others remain lukewarm and lack the fervor to do the work of God, even when it comes to raising a quorum to meet together, with the result that only with great difficulty are novices able to be admitted, nor can anything else be done for the utility of this consortium.[47]

Further worsening the problem, 2 months later, in November, 25 members quit or were asked to resign on account of absenteeism.[48] The excuse given by Antonio di Giovanni Buonafé for leaving the company was typical: "He said," wrote the company secretary, "that he was wrapped up in his own private affairs" ("Disse essere ochupato in sua faccende"). By July 1505, another 27 members had withdrawn from the company.[49]

During this period of declining membership, the company changed its name, placing itself under the protection of Saint Michael.[50] In the same

---

46. *Ibid.*, 10r:

Richordo questo dì xxvij d'ottobre, I nostri maggiori chom buon numero di frategli a honor di dio pensorno che al fare e nuoui ufficiali era sempre molto dificile per la grande nigrigenza delle persone per essere mal sollecitati a frequentare el luogho in modo che rarissime volte si raghunava il vero numero de xxv e per remediare a questo inconveniente che ccoresti che non si faccino chomese fatto molte volte per el passato che som rimasti indrieto che tornato in grande danno de' poveri e di detta partita vinsono el sopradetti per xxiij fave nere e 3 bianche che ogni volta che fa affare nuoui ufficiali si faccino chon quel numero di persone vi si trovassino.

47. *Ibid.*, 12v:

Ricordo questo dì xiij di settembre a honore di dio e nostri padri, veduto molti per avere grande ochupatione rinunziano a detta opera di charità e gli altri restanti essere freddi e pocho ferventi all'opere di dio per etiam a raghunarsi insieme numero perfecto in modo che dificilmente si può mettere nessun novizio o fare alchuna altra cosa che torni in utile di detto chonsorzio. E per remediare a questo inchonveniente e sopra detti nostri padri vinsono per xxv fave nere e v bianche che ogni prima domenica di mese si possa fare tutti qui e partiti che occhorreranno.

48. *Ibid.*, 13r.
49. *Ibid.*, 18r-27v (misnumbered as 28v).
50. *Ibid.*, 14r.

month (January 1500) the company, which had met up until this time in San Procolo,[51] appointed syndics to find a new meeting place.[52] Although no reason for this action was given, it appears likely that declining dues revenues could not provide for the rent and upkeep of the current meeting place and that, as the company of San Frediano did later in that century, the company of Saint Michael searched for a smaller, less expensive site. A week later such a site was found: the church of San Michele delle Trombe.[53] Within 2 years negotiations were underway with the newly founded (1501) company of Druggists to share the facilities of the Druggists located in that church.[54] An agreement between these companies, giving free use of the sacristy of San Michele delle Trombe to the company of San Michele, was finally signed in May 1505. Its language reinforces the interpretation that the change in meeting place was occasioned by declining membership and income. The reason for the agreement is stated as being "per conservazione di detta nostra compagnia" ("for the preservation of our company").[55] Saint Michael, however, proved no better a protector than had the previous advocate of the company. On November 15, 1506, the confraternity chaplain, Cipriano di Piero, of San Marco, addressed a stern letter to the company, scornfully suggesting that the company had come to its well-deserved end because of its iniquity and lack of charity. The friar recommended a complete revision of the company's constitution, hoping that this would spare the brotherhood from imminent ruin and annihilation.[56] And 10 years after the initial suppression of 1495, the company was still suffering its effects, "because," as the company recorded, "our brothers are very busy with their own affairs and many are still negligent, and for such a reason our statutes often go unobserved, [and] our company advances in disorder."[57] Now the company voted to restrict the number of members to a maximum of 72. As the membership continued to decline, an exclusive, "elite" principle of membership was introduced, perhaps as a means of increasing group cohesion and loyalty. This tactic worked no better than had other inducements enacted to regain and retain members. In 1513, in the aftermath of the Medici restoration, the companies of the city were

51. Ibid., 13v.
52. Ibid., 14r.
53. Ibid., 14v.
54. Ibid., 22r. On the company of Druggists, see p. 201, n. 18.
55. Ibid., 25v.
56. Ibid., 31r.
57. Ibid., 41r: "Perchè e nostri fratelli sono molto occupati nelle loro faccende et si anchora per negrigentia di molti e per tal modo che spesso manchano nella observanza de nostri capituli unde ne viene disordine in questa nostra radunazione compagnia."

again suppressed and were not allowed to meet until November 5, 1514.[58] Four years later the company account books still recorded complaints that "charity is lacking in the men [of the company] as much on account of weakness as on account of age and illness, and on account of the fact that members have become heads of families, and on account of preoccupation with business affairs, so that our statutes are not observed."[59] References to age and infirmity and to members progressing through the life cycle to the point at which they married and raised children (which normally did not occur until well after age 30) testify to the continuing failure of San Michele to recruit younger members. By 1521 the company again was forced to change meeting places, now moving to a room in Santa Maria degli Alberghi.[60]

Few surviving confraternity meeting records predate the end of the sixteenth century. Those that do exist, as in the case of San Michele Arcangelo, record the plight of the confraternities of this period. The repeated suppressions and confiscations and fires and floods of sixteenth-century Florence, as well as the siege of 1527-1530, succeeded in destroying most account books. The possibility of recovering the records of those companies that fared the worst and disappeared entirely is, of course, quite low. The discussion of San Frediano and San Michele has attempted to highlight the signs of confraternal crisis: the extension of *grazia,* the attempted union or sharing of facilities with other companies, the increasing average age of members, the decline in membership and attendance, the appointment of syndics to control company property and administrative affairs, and the suspension of key statutes. In the decades that followed, these signs appeared everywhere. During the period 1521-1540 the confraternities of Florence were more frequently in a state of suspension than in one of legitimate, approved operation. They were suppressed far more often than they met. Between August 1522 and December 1523 the *compagnie* were closed on account of plague.[61] Another outbreak of pestilence shut

58. *Ibid.,* 48r.

59. *Ibid.,* 55r: "MDXVIII, xxiij di Maggio. Perchè veduto la charità essere manchata sì per essere gli huomini indebiliti che per vecchiaia e che per infermità e che per essere venuti in famiglia e che per exercizij, in modo che nostri chapitoli non si observano."

60. *Ibid.,* 61r.

61. *CRS,* 1869 (S 163, vol 4), Saint Sebastian, 33v: "Ricordo questo dì primo di genaio chome Lorenzo Sancti . . . nostro padre Governatore, e suo chosilieri furno trati inanzi a questo tenpo iiij mesi inanzi e per chè le copanie si serono per amore del morbo non poterono esercitare e loro uficio." CRS, 1583 (P 1, vol. 9), 17r: "Per prohibizione fatta dal pubblicho della nostra cipttà di Firenze rispetto a tempi che sono seghuiti della pestilenzia non ci siamo raghunati dal mese d'aghosto 1522 in sino a questo dì [24 December 1523]."

down the *compagnie* from March 6, 1523, until February 11, 1524.[62] Plague was again the cited reason for the closing of confraternity doors from March 25, 1527, to November 1, 1528.[63] On March 6, 1528, the companies were again forbidden from meeting.[64] During the siege of Florence the confraternities were suppressed.[65] Reopening briefly after the fall of the republic in 1530, the confraternities were, for the most part, soon prohibited from organizing or meeting until 1540.[66] The unusually detailed records of the (adult) company of Arcangelo Raffaello describe the following periods of suppression: September 4, 1512-March 12, 1513,[67] September 1513-April 1, 1515 (excepting Holy Week, 1514),[68] Easter, 1515-Lent, 1516,[69] August 20, 1516-November 8, 1516,[70] November 8, 1521-February 8, 1522,[71] September 6, 1522-December 19, 1523,[72] March 5, 1524-January 28, 1525,[73] April 6, 1527-December 5, 1528,[74] January 4, 1531-May 1534,[75] and

---

62. *Ibid.*, 171r:

Ricordo questa sera cioè, adì xi di Febraio 1524 se ditto l'ufizio de defuntiti passati di questa presente uita e quali erono di questa penitente chasa in questo tempo che detta compagnia è stata serrata per prohibizione fatta dal publicho della nostra ciptà di Firenze che ci fu proibito el raghunarci da dì vi di marzo 1523 per insino a questa sera detta di sopra cioè adì xj di febraio 1524 per essere istato infetto di pestilenza la nostra ciptà di Firenze.

The period of allowed meeting was so brief during these years that several companies spoke of a continuous 3-year suppression: *CRS*, 1646, Compagnia della Purificazione di Maria Vergine e San Zanobi (P 30, vol. 8, 80v: "Nota che quelle compagnie stettono serrate presto a 3 anni per conto della peste poi si riaperto la prima domenica di quaresima nel 1524 che funo a dì 5 di marzo."

CRS, 1869 (S 163, vol. 4), 41v: "Chonsiderando el nostro Padre Ghovernatore cho sua consilieri che sendo istata a chasa nostra d'anni 3 in qua più tempo sanza raghunarsi respetta ala pesta e chattiui temporali."

63. *CRS*, 1646 (P 30, vol. 8), 85v: "Nota che da dì 25 di Marzo 1527 in sino al sopradecto dì primo di Novembre 1528 non ci apparisce alcuna comunione perchè stettono serrate le compagnie per causa della peste."

64. *CRS*, 1583 (P 1, vol. 9), 193v.

65. *CRS*, 1646 (P 30, vol. 8), 15v: "Nota che a tempo di sopradecti Maestri di Novizi non si fecie alcuna entrata perchè stette quasi semp' allor tempo serrata la nostra compagnia per causa della guerra."

66. *CRS*, 1583 (P 1, vol. 9), 82v: "Nota come la nostra compagnia dal settembre 1529 fino al mesi di marzo 1540 non si ragunò mai respetto alla assedio e di prohibitione fino adetto mese di giugno 1540."

67. *CRS*, 141 (A 146, vol. 3), Arcangelo Raffaello, *Ricordi*, 10v.

68. *Ibid.*, 14v.

69. *Ibid.*, 15v.

70. *Ibid.*, 18v.

71. *Ibid.*, 51r.

72. *Ibid.*, 54v.

73. *Ibid.*, 56r-v.

74. *Ibid.*, 76r.

75. *Ibid.*, 80r.

September 5, 1535-January 18, 1540.[76] When the members finally met in January 1540 they found that another company, Sant' Alberto, had taken over their residence without permission.[77] The company ceased meeting again from July 2, 1541 to January 4, 1544.[78]

The company of San Paolo, flourishing at the end of the fifteenth century, was by 1525 in a state of disorder. The company had appointed eight *operai* (literally, workers; figuratively, supervisors) to direct its business.[79] Unable to continue meeting at the company oratory, the company transferred its meetings to the Medici palace, where the company was reformed. The sons of San Paolo, record the *operai,* "hanno bisogno di reformatione, et non pocho" ("they are in need of reform, and not a little"). The *operai* examined and considered "how great the decline has been, and that it has been going on for many years, and how little the statutes are observed, and that not only do members not observe the constitutions, but many even publicly desire to disobey them.[80] In the same year the company of Saint Sebastian, founded in the thirteenth century, appointed six men to oversee the reform of the company, which had reached a similar state of decline:

> Our Father Governor, with his councillors, considering that our house has not met for three years on account of the plague and the evil times, and that the said house has many expenses, for the ill and the making of vestments, and many other expenses, and how day by day they increase, and wishing to remedy this, Our Father Governor has called six worthy men of our house to meet together and decide what they ought to do so that our house will be healthy, peaceful, and at rest.[81]

On January 17, 1527, when the company was closed by health officials because of plague, the members elected syndics, giving them a 1-year license to oversee company affairs.[82] The company met again 8 months later

76. *Ibid.,* 80v.

77. *Ibid.,* 82v.

78. *Ibid.,* 84r-v.

79. *CRS,* 1583 (P 1, vol. 9), 186v-187v. The *operai* were: Carlo di Cortona, papal legate in Tuscany, Messer Giovanni di Messer Bernardo Buongirolami, Messer Bartolomeo di Messer Francesco Gualterotti, Antonio di Guglielmo Pazzi, Bartolomeo Benintendi, Luigi di Tomaso Sartini, Giovambatista di Francesco del Cittadino, and Lorenzo di Iacopo Violo.

80. *Ibid.:*

> "Havendo prima bene inteso et examinato in quanta declinatione da molti anni in qua è venuto la detta compagnia di Santo Paolo et con quanta poca observantia de capitoli di quella in si vive et che non solo molti non si observono ma etiam ardiscono publicamente a contrafar alla dispositione di quelli."

81. *CRS,* 1869 (S 163, vol. 4), 41v.

82. *Ibid.,* 51v.

but had not recovered its membership, for in January 1529 the company proclaimed a general *grazia* for debts.[83] The confraternity was suppressed shortly thereafter for a 2-year period and was one of the few confraternities that reopened in 1531. Membership allegiance had shifted during the period of suppressions, for when the company reopened many members were reported to have dual memberships in this and other companies, which created factions in the membership.[84] By 1533 the company membership had, however, reached the respectable number of 176 men, but this figure is misleading, for the company could succeed in attracting only 27 members to meetings.[85]

Other companies, too, had, on paper, regained members, but entrances in account books often hid the weak loyalty that these members owed the confraternity. Three times between March 1533 and August 1535, *grazie* for debts were declared.[86] Despite the large number of enrolled members, on November 29, 1535, the secretary recorded that "at more and more meetings of the company only seven or eight members are in attendance, and no more, so that . . . the company suffers wounds."[87] Since the company did not have enough members in attendance to conduct business, it began to conduct its affairs with however many members the meeting happened to attract.[88] This policy was reaffirmed in 1536, with the inactivity of members continuing as before.[89] *Grazie* were extended in 1537, 1538, and 1539,[90] and in 1540 the officers of the confraternity met to discuss three different schemes for granting *grazia* to attract members.[91] By 1542 the extension of *grazia* was made not only to attract old members but also to encourage those few remaining members to carry out normal responsibilities. On November 11, 1542, *grazia* was offered to those who would actually assist at the burial of member Antonio,[92] and in 1544 the same offer was made to anyone willing to serve as company sacristan. Despite the offer of a partial cancellation of debts, an offer made yearly for 17 years,[93] in January 1551

---

83. *Ibid.*, 66r.
84. *Ibid.*, 88r.
85. *Ibid.*, 89r-93v, 95r.
86. *Ibid.*, 99r.
87. *Ibid.*, 102r: "Fo ricordo di questo dì 29 di novembre 1535 che più e più tornatte che in detta compagnia si raghunava i dette tornatte o sei o otto frategli e no più di modo che uedutto questo che la compagnia pattiua feri."
88. *Ibid.*, 102v.
89. *Ibid.*, 110v.
90. *Ibid.*, 115v, 118r, 120r.
91. *Ibid.*, 123r.
92. *Ibid.*, 128v.
93. *Ibid.*, 142r, (1546), 145r (1547), 147r (1548), 148r (1549), 153r (1550), 155r (1551).

the company reported that "considering the disorder of the company, with respect to the [number of] men, whose debts were small enough to qualify them to hold office, the drawing of men for office cannot be held." The company voted to require all those members selected for office to pay existing debts on the spot or to be charged a fine if they refused to hold office.[94] Partial cancellation of debts was again proclaimed in 1552 and 1553,[95] but in 1553 there were so few members eligible to hold office that those currently in office were confirmed for a new term.[96]

Grazia continued to be extended through 1555,[97] and the records reveal the continuing problem of locating enough men of limited indebtedness to qualify for office.[98] To attract recruits, more radical reforms were passed in 1556:

> As the house has gone into decline, with respect to the rare attendance of the men, and since it is desired that the house should augment its membership, it was proposed and passed that the entrance tax shall be reduced by half for anyone who should want to enter, and so too, that whoever enters should enjoy the benefits of membership just as if he had not paid only half the entrance fee.[99]

Sixteenth-century confraternities developed special membership categories, balancing the payment of dues and service requirements, offering either high service requirements and low dues payment or exemption from performing administrative and service duties and payment of double dues. To attract members, San Sebastiano reduced both service and dues. In 1557 this act, referred to as the *grazia della entrata de' noviti,* was reaffirmed.[100] In December of the same year company election procedures were again modified because there was "no one free from debts," and no company business could be transacted.[101] In January 1557 the officers reaffirmed in detail the measures designed to reinvigorate the company:

> Our Father Governor, with his counsellors, having considered the small number and little fervor of those who today come to the companies, because of evil times

<hr />

94. *Ibid.,* 155v: "Chonsiderando il disordine della chonpagnia circha alli omini che non ci era tanti netti che si potessi fare la tratta."

95. *Ibid.,* 157r, 158r, 159r.

96. *Ibid.,* 155v.

97. *Ibid.,* 163v, 167v.

98. *Ibid.,* 162v, 163v.

99. *Ibid.,* 170r: "Come la casa andava in declinatione rispetto alla pocha frequentia delli omini e desiderano che andase in aumento propose e uinse che l'entrata della casa fusi per metà per quantunque che volesi entrare e così chi avese benefitio come chi non d'avesi pagasi per metà."

100. *Ibid.*

101. *Ibid.*

that allow men to run up their debts so that order cannot be imposed on this house, finding the men without payment and allowing debts to pile up, therefore, so that the men with love and zeal should attend and should reform this house, the Governor and Counsellors instituted a *grazia* for the entire period, so that anyone who should find himself in debt to the house of such a sum and should want to return to the former state, can pay our treasurer fourteen *soldi* and his entire debt shall be cancelled, and these men should remain for eight months without being able to enjoy the benefits of the house, that is, if anyone should fall sick or dead, and having paid within eight months of that time, he shall not have any benefits or office at all. . . .

And furthermore, another *grazia* of entrance was passed and instituted, namely, that should it seem to those men who have friends desirous of being members of our consortium that the expense is too great, these brothers should be able to bring their friends here, diminishing the entrance tax by half.[102]

Despite these enactments, there were still too few men in attendance in 1558 to elect officers, and the old officers were kept for another term.[103] The administrative officer at the heart of most companies was the *proveditore,* the provisioner, to whom all illnesses suffered by company members, all requests for charity, and all company deaths were reported. The *proveditore* directed the administration of charity, the celebration of masses, and all exceptional confraternity activity. He assigned specific tasks to members and was in charge of all social services performed by the confraternity. The deplorable state of the company of Saint Sebastian in 1559 is revealed by the minutes of a meeting that concerned this office: "Since many times in the past it has been attempted to chose a *proveditore* for sick members, and because of the number of times that this was not accomplished, this house has found itself negligent in performing this work."[104] A year later the election of the governor seemed problematic. Unable to be elected by lot, the governor was elected at the company altar

---

102. *Ibid.,* 163 (bis):

Considerando il nostro Padre Governatore con sua cosiglieri il pocho numero e poco fervore a che son venute ogi le compagnie rispetto a tenporali catiui che gli uomini si lasciano i corere i debito e non si può fare li ordini della casa trovando li omini senza pagamenti e lacantosi i corere il debito aciò che li uomini con amore e fervore vengino e riformino alla casa loro fecano e statuirno una grazia per tucto il tenpo loro che qualunque si trovasi in debito con la casa di che soma e si fusi e uolendo ritornare nel primero stato pagino al nostro camarlingo soldi quattordici e sia cancelato tucto il debito . . . e debino stare mesi otto senza benefitio di casa, cioè, si l'alcun cascasi ifermità o mortte e pagando da otto mesi ila sie non i benefitio e ufitio di tucto. . . . Ancora vinsono e statuirno una altra gratia della entratta aciò che li omini auesino delli amici disiderosi d'essere del nostro consortio e che e paresi la spesa troppo aciò che detti fratelli posino condurci delli amici disminuendo la entratta per metà.

103. *Ibid.,* 165 (bis).
104. *Ibid.,* 168r (bis).

by those members who happened to be present.[105] The *proveditore* was finally elected governor, leaving vacant the provisioner position. The minutes continue:

> I record this day, September 8, 1560, that Donato calderaio [boiler maker] who had been *proveditore*, having been elected governor of our company, and not being able to exercise the office of *proveditore* on account of our company having few men willing to accept responsibilities, no one could be found who would accept the responsibilities of being *proveditore*. [106]

One willing member, a notary working for the archbishop, was finally located. He yielded to company pressure, "but only," he said, "out of obedience, and in order to keep our company open, do I accept."[107] On December 1, 1561, at the time of new elections, no one accepted the office of governor. An absent member was elected, and the *proveditore* was dispatched to beg him to accept the office:

> And so, on the following Monday, which was December 2, I, the *proveditore*, went to the shop of the aforementioned Benedetto in Borgo San Lorenzo, and finding him, told him that he had been elected governor, and I begged him to accept for the love of God and for our advocate, if he desired that the company should not close, because there was no one to be found here who wanted to accept. I did not know whether the Lord wanted to provide for our needs or for the maintanence of this house of His good servant and our advocate, S. Sebastian, as He then provided, since the aforementioned Benedetto answered me, saying that he did not desire to accept the position and if this meant closing the company, well, then, let is close![108]

The company did not close its doors, instead it revived slowly, making offers of *grazie* as late as 1580.[109] The disruption in the affairs of San

---

105. *Ibid.*, 169r.

106. *Ibid.*:

Ricordo questo dì octo di settembre 1560, come essendo stato electo governatore della nostra compagnia Donato calderaio quale era proveditore di essa et non potendo essercitare il proveditore per essere la nostra compagnia povera di huomini che voglino brighe non si trovando chi acceptarsi detto peso del proveditore.

107. *Ibid.*

108. *Ibid.*, 170v:

Et cosí il lunedì proximo che fumo alli dua di dicembre Io proveditore andai a bottegha di decto Benedetto in Borgo San Lorenzo et cosí trovandolo gli dissi come era stato electo governatore et lo pregai acceptassi per lo amor de Dio et del nostro advocato si desideraua la compagnia non si serrassi per chè qui ui non si trovava chi uolessi acceptare non sapendo Io che il Signore uolessi provedere a bisogni nostri et mantenimento della casa del suo buon seruo et advocato nostro Santo Sebastiano come di poi provedde il detto Benedetto mi rispose che non uoleua acceptare et che se la si uoleua serrave serrassisi.

109. *Ibid.*, 186v.

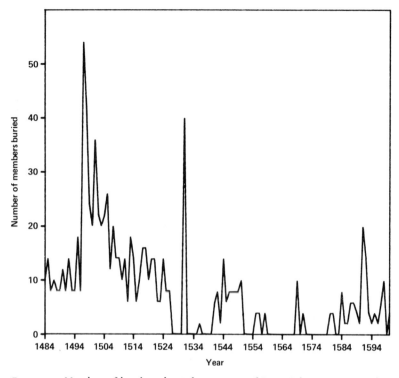

Figure 4.1. Number of brothers buried, company of Saint Sebastian, 1484-1600.

Sebastiano is revealed by its burial statistics (Figure 4.1). The number of members buried by the company declined throughout the sixteenth century, apart from a brief peak in 1529-1530 during the siege, and showed evidence of recovery only at the very end of the century. Assuming that the death of members offers a very rough indication of the relative pattern of earlier enrollment, and assuming further that members who died did so after approximately 14 years of membership (the length of membership at time of death for members of San Paolo and Sant' Antonio was 23 years, and it is assumed that members enrolling in the *laudesi* company of Saint Sebastian were, on average, at least 9 years older than those who entered flagellant companies, which is what a comparison between Sant' Agnese and San Paolo novices joining at the end of the fifteenth century reveals), the relative number of members joining Saint Sebastian can be crudely estimated (Figure 4.2). These estimates conform to the known record of sixteenth-century suppressions. Following the brief suppression in 1478, company entrances began to rise sharply but fell in the mid-1490s during a new round of suppressions and fell even further during the turbulent years

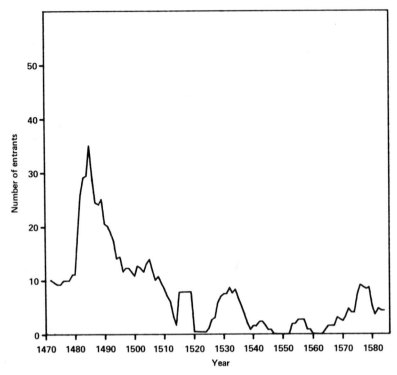

Figure 4.2. Estimates of number of entrants into Saint Sebastian, 1470-1587 (five-year moving averages).

surrounding the Medici restoration in 1512. Enrollment dropped again throughout the 1520s. The bulge in "enrollments" in the 1530s is, if one examines the raw data in Figure 4.1, attributable not to entrances but to an unusually high mortality during the siege, which the 5-year averaging procedure does not filter out. Enrollments appear to have been negligible during the 1540s and 1550s and did not begin to climb again until the 1570s.[110]

The suppressions of the sixteenth century forced companies like San Sebastiano to halt virtually all customary activity, including such basic tasks as the recitation of masses for the dead. Between 1527 and 1541, apart from the 21-month period January 15, 1532—October 25, 1533, the company recited no masses whatsoever.[111] The *laudesi* company of Sant' Agnese, as early as 1508, reported that the suppressions had resulted in a near total cessation of its customary liturgical activity, causing

110. *CRS*, 1872 (S 163, vol. 1, pt. 4), San Sebastiano, *Fratelli Morti*, 1r-45v.
111. *Ibid.*, 25v-26v.

the ruin and great disruption of our company, since we could not perform the necessary business at the appropriate times . . . the business being . . . the satisfaction of the obligations and bequests of those who have willed movable and fixed property to the company in order to celebrate divine Offices, or [to distribute] charity, or to recite *laude* for their souls.[112]

The meeting records of the company of the Purification of the Virgin Mary and San Zanobi, a boys' confraternity administered by adults, tell a similar story. In June 1527 the company reported the general closure of companies in Florence: "Public health officials ordered that the companies be shut down, so that from that day forward, our company could no longer meet. And then, because the plague intensified, many youths who were our brothers died of this pestilence."[113] The guardian himself having perished, the company received permission to meet, a year later, to elect a new guardian, who was most reluctant to assume the leadership of a suppressed organization:

Ser Giovanni di Ser Ghabriello Simone, nominated by Benedetto, won with thirty votes in his favor. . . . When the election became known to Ser Giovanni he offered many excuses and said that by no means would he accept such a responsibility. After much insistence by many persons and by those that had some leverage [he accepted] this responsibility, but as procurator, not as guardian, only so that the companies could reopen.[114]

The confraternity finally began meeting legitimately in 1528. Although it

---

112. *Archivi delle Compagnie Soppresse* (archive 1, vol. 4), 133, November 19, 1508:

Per non si ragunato loro et loro officiali et per non avere tornate . . . ne risulta ruina e disordine grande di nostra compagnia per non potere fare a debiti tempi e provedimenti ochorrenti di quella né consultare né pratichare né consigliare quello sia necessarie dì per dì a quella . . . el più della occhorrenti chose che si fanno et tractassi in detta compagnia sono in satisfare agl'obrighi et lasci di quelli che anno lasciato a nostra compagnia beni mobili et immobili per fare celebrare offici divini o elemosine o dire laude per l'anime loro et quelli aspectano e detti suffragij et aiuti.

113. *CRS*, 1646 (P 30, vol. 8), 279v:

Ricordo come adì 3 di giugno 1527 havendo cominciato a multiplicar la pesta nella nostra città fu mandato per tal causa da li officiali che erano all'hora sopra la sanità uno bando che le compagnie se serrassino, per il chè da decto dì cominciamo a non ci raunare più in nostra compagnia; sí poi per chè decta peste andò crescendo, oltre a molti giovani di nostri fratelli che di tale influentia perirono come in questo al suo luogo se ne fa particular mentione.

114. *Ibid.*, 279r:

Ser Giovanni di Ser Ghabriello Simoni come nominato da Benedetto nel sopradecto modo, il Quale fu uinto per partito con xxx fave nere. . . . Il quale Ser Giovanni predicto poi chi li fa pervenuta alli orecchi tale electione, per niente non uoleva acceptare tale peso allegando molte cause per le quali diceua non essere a proposito. Et dopo molta instantia factali varie persone et da quelli che quodammodo li potevano comandare [acceptarse] tal peso come procuratore et non come guardiano tanto che le compagnie si riaprissino.

closed during the siege, the company reopened again on August 7, 1530,
voting to aid its many members in financial distress.[115] The fragile state of
the confraternity depended on the administrative talents of a few members.
When the guardian of the company died in 1531, the company was left in
disarray: "I record that on the first of October, 1531, at the hour of twelve,
Ser Giovanni Simoni, our fifth guardian, left this present life, leaving our
company in terrible disorder, it having been closed for many months, and
all its furniture and equipment were stolen."[116] Although all companies
were formally closed, the company met on May 25, 1532, to elect a new
guardian. Having lost its residence, the company, when it opened several
months later, began meeting in the Badia of Florence and made a general
offer of grace to all company debtors. The company appears to have been
suppressed again in 1535, for no meetings are recorded until July 13,
1539, when the company recorded that "the boys' companies having been
closed for a long time, were given license to meet again, but only those
boys sixteen and younger."[117] Still lacking a permanent meeting place,
they met in the residence of the Compagnia della Carità. A week later
they met again in the Badia, for, it appears, during the suppression the
friars of San Marco occupied their meeting place, and permanently dis-
lodged them. Despite formal approval to meet, the company had clearly
lost momentum. By 1546 its account books describe a new state of disorder; ceremonies fell into disuse, and even the company guardian lost
interest in the affairs of the confraternity.[118]

At the beginning of the sixteenth century, the company of San Rocco,
meeting in the church of San Felice in Piazza, had spawned a second
confraternity across town, on the Via San Gallo. The turbulence of the 1510s
and 1520s was no kinder to San Rocco than to other Florentine fraternities.
San Rocco reopened briefly in January 1531, reabsorbed its offshoot on Via
San Gallo, and, in addition, merged with the company of San Iacopo.[119] On

---

115. *Ibid.,* 280v, 281v.

116. *Ibid.,* 280v:

Ricordo come adì 12 di octobre 1531 a hor 12 Ser Gioanni Simoni nostro quinta guardiano passò dalla
presente uita, lasci[a]ta la compagnia in grandissimo disordine per essere quelle stata serrata più mesi et
per essere schonfitto tucto il legname di quella, et le robe di epsa qui et quà per chè si pono più pericolo
di perderla per monache et soldati presenti.

117. *Ibid.,* 286r: "Essendo state le compagnie de fanciugli più tenpo serrate tandem ebbono
licenzia di ragunarsi ma solamente e fanciugli a anni sedici in giù."

118. *Ibid.,* 291r-v.

119. The tribulations of this company are recorded in *CRS,* 1704 (R 2, vol. 6), *Partiti e Ricordi,*
12vff.

February 25 all companies were ordered to close, and San Rocco appointed 12 men to oversee the company. The company was allowed to meet briefly in 1532 and took the opportunity to ask San Felice in Piazza to return the "vestments, money, belongings, and furnishings of the company" that the church had appropriated during the suppression,[120] a request that was unsuccessfully renewed 6 months later. In October 1532, 7 men were appointed to search for a new meeting place, the company having long since lost its quarters in San Felice. The company was, apparently, allowed to meet sporadically during the 1530s. *Grazie* were declared throughout 1534 and 1535, and to diminish open quarreling and infighting, the company voted to forbid anyone from talking at all, except officers, when present in the company chambers, a provision that had to be renewed 6 months later. Penalties were introduced for those who refused the offices of sacristan or visitor of the sick. Penalties were reaffirmed to punish those who besmirched the good name of the confraternity in public. None of these provisions appears to have had much of an effect on restoring loyalty or morale. The company treasurer and sacristan had to be threatened with expulsion to induce them to return "borrowed" company property. In 1535 the company drafted new statutes, but the affairs of the company continued to decline. *Grazie* were offered to the membership in 1535, 1536, 1543, 1547, 1555, and again in 1558. By 1556 the company did not have enough members to conduct its affairs and was forced to reduce its entrance fees.

The years of warfare and suppression were particularly damaging to Florentine confraternities in two respects. First, as several cases have already indicated, this period witnessed a decline in active confraternity membership. When the Compagnia dello Scalzo reopened in 1530, after the siege, it reported that 98 members, most of the active membership, had died since the suppression began.[121] The popular boys' confraternity, the Compagnia del Arcangelo Raffaello, which met in the chapel of the hospital known as La Scala, was thrown out of its accustomed meeting place in the aftermath of the siege. Moving out to make room for the monks of San Martino, the company moved into the chambers of the Compagnia della Carità in Santa Maria Novella, as had the company of the Purification of the Virgin Mary and San Zanobi, a move made possible because of the deaths of most of the members of the Compagnia della Carità since 1527. Three other companies meeting in Santa Maria Novella were incorporated into the

120. *Ibid.*, 4v.

121. Rita Marchi, "La compagnia dello Scalzo nel Cinquecento," in *Da Dante a Cosimo I: Ricerche di storia religiosa e culturale toscana nei secoli XIV-XVI*, ed. Domenico Maselli (Pistoia: Libreria Editrice Tellini, 1976), p. 179.

company of Archangel Raphael, because all four companies had greatly reduced membership.[122] The company of San Silvestro recalled its first meeting after the major cycle of suppressions: "Our city, having been oppressed by war and plague, remained rather depopulated, and the confraternity languished in a state of exhaustion, but in 1537 was revived by those few brothers who survived."[123] On July 28, 1540, the Compagnia di Santa Maria della Quercia recorded:

> Having come to the year 1540, out of need to put itself in order, the company being short of money and frequented by few brothers, and having come the time to prepare for the [annual] feast [of our patron], it was decided that the organizers of the feast, [*festaiuoli*] should spend money parsimoniously.[124]

To compound the fraternity's problems, it had lost its meeting place and was forced to meet where and when it could find a place to assemble.[125] The company merged with that of the Madonna del Carmine, called *il crocefisso,* in 1541 because both had few members.[126] In 1510 the company of Santa Maria in Verzaia had over 42 active members. A statute book described the reasons for the merger of that company with San Giovanni Decollato after the siege, by which time membership had decreased:

> The aforementioned election supervisors of both parties [the two companies] having considered the disorder in which the above mentioned companies find themselves, having been struck by the cruel plague and also because the ruination inflicted by the wars has diminished the entrances [of new members], and ruined, for the most part, their goods and reduced their [combined] number to forty men.[127]

---

122. Del Migliore, 59r-v. The boys' company of Arcangelo Raffaello should not be confused with the adult company of the same name.

123. *Capitoli,* 369, Compagnia di Sacramento di San Silvestro e San Felice, 1r-v:

Oppressa quindi la città nostra da guerra, e da peste, e rimasta quasi spopolata, anco la compagnia restò come spenta, ma nel 1537 fu ravvivata da quei pochi fratelli che sopravvissero, i quali continuarono le loro tornate in chiesa fino all'anno 1560, nel quale la compagnia lasciata la chiesa predetta già ceduta da monaci camaldolensi alle monache di San Pier Martire.

124. *CRS,* 1324, (M 51, vol. 1, pt. D): "E pervenuti all'anno 1540 per bisogni di rassettare il testo et essendo la compagnia scarsa di denari e pochi fratelli venuto il tempo di fare la festa fecero che si spendessi da festaioli con parsimonia."

125. *Ibid.*

126. *Capitoli,* 731, Santa Maria de Poveri. Instances of company unions following the Medici restoration and suppression could be multiplied. In 1535, the Company della Pietà and the company of the Virgin Mary, "la pace", combined their membership, neither company having enough members. See *Capitoli,* 55. The companies of Santa Maria del Morbo, "della capella," and Santa Maria della Quercia continued to suffer declining membership as late as 1553 and united in that year. Passerini, p. 423.

127. *Capitoli,* 167, p. 2. "Considerando i sopradetti elezionari d'una parte e l'altra ne i disordini

As late as 1573 the secretary of the adult company of Arcangelo Raffaello could still complain that "the expenses of the company were in disorder because many brothers are enrolled in the company, but few actually come here, and thus most fail to pay their dues."[128]

The second major problem confronting confraternities was the loss of income property and meeting places. The threat of war and its eventual outbreak in addition to providing the rationale for confraternity suppressions did much to weaken their economic stability. In the course of the war, confraternities were forced to vacate their properties and to see much of it destroyed. In 1529 the Signoria, preparing for the siege, sought to despoil the Florentine countryside rather than to allow it to provide the advancing enemy with food and shelter. Structures within several miles of the city were ordered demolished.[129] A number of buildings were destroyed by the besieging forces themselves. Additional confraternity properties and meeting places were lost, in the aftermath of the Medici restoration, to religious orders whose own property had been destroyed. These clerical groups used their political influence in Florence and Rome to legalize the occupations and confiscation of confraternity property. In 1529, during the siege, the meeting place of the company of San Giovanni Decollato, which had met for decades in the church of San Giovanni fra l'Arcora, outside the Faenza gate, was demolished.[130] Until the siege, the company of the Ten Thousand Martyrs had met in the church of San Salvatore. "In the year 1529," wrote a company official,

> on account of the war that came into the city of Florence, they [the members of the company] were thrown out of their meeting place, and their site was taken from them and demolished, and therefore it was necessary to meet in various and diverse places, especially in the Carmine, as Pilgrims without a stable abode, until the year 1555, when they chose a place . . . under the vault of S. Pancrazio in Florence, and these things that had occurred cooled off not a little the ardor of the members in frequenting the place, and on account of the great change and variation of the times, and change of persons, the old statutes came to be exercised little, or not at all.[131]

---

che si trovano le prefate compagnie sí per essere stata la crudel peste, sí ancora per la rovina della guerra che aueua loro diminuire l'entrata e rovinata loro più beni e diminiuto il numero di 40 uomini."

128. *CRS*, 141 (A 146, vol. 4), Arcangelo Raffaello, *Ricordi,* 58r, May 19, 1573: "Atteso che la compagnia era in disordine di spese per che erano schritti molti fratelli e pochi al venirci, mancho al paghare le tasse."

129. Benedetto Varchi, *Storia fiorentina,* 2 vols. (Florence: Salani, 1963) book 10, chap. 29.

130. Del Migliore, 55r. The oratory of the company of Santa Maria della Croce al Tempio, located outside of the Porta la Croce was likewise destroyed during the war. Passerini, p. 484.

131. *Capitoli,* 386, Compagnia dei Diecimila Martiri, p. 2:

The company of San Niccolò, nicknamed *del Ceppo,* meeting near San Miniato, was forced to vacate its residence in 1527 because of the threat of war. By 1530 its meeting place had become the property of San Miniato.[132] The company of Santa Maria in Verzaia had its residence destroyed during the siege.[133] The company of San Niccolò da Tolentino was forced to relinquish the keys to its house on April 6, 1529, and only after special pleading did the company regain its quarters in 1530.[134]

Siege warfare, especially as it affected the Oltrarno section of the city, was one major factor in the loss of confraternity property. It was, however, not the only factor. Encircled from without and economically isolated, the Florentines had to exploit their existing and ever-dwindling resources to pay the cost of their self-defense. In 1529 the commune ordered the sale of property belonging to ecclesiastical institutions.[135] Included as targets of this measure were the major confraternities of the city. Clerical confraternities suffered the heaviest losses as a result of the application of this legislation, but lay confraternities suffered as well. The Compagnia degli Orafi lost a cottage; the company of San Zanobi, a house; and San Piero Martire, a house, a farm, three parcels of land, and five shops.[136] Much of the property, sold by cameral officials, is only vaguely described in the communal accounts of these sales, and for this reason confraternal losses are not always visible. Communal officials recorded, for example, sale 436, July 30, 1530: "½ nella chasa posta in popolo di Santo Friano" ("one half of a house located in the parish of San Fr[ed]iano").[137] This house, offered to communal officials by the nuns of the convent of San Frediano, who were anxious to avoid handing over more valuable assets, was, in reality, the property of the lay confraternity of San Frediano and was the company's

---

E perchè insino dell'anno 1529 per causa della guerra che venne alla città di Firenze furan cavati dal detto luogo, e tolto loro il sito, e demolito, li fu necessario radunarsi in varie e diversi luoghi come Peregrini che non hanno casa ferma e specialmente nella chiesa del Carmine fino all'anno 1555 di dove partendosi si elessere un luogo . . . sotto le volte di S. Pancrazio di Firenze, e per esser' trascorsi e raffreddati non poco tutti nel frequentare detto luogo; e per la lunga variatione e diversità de' tempi e variatione di persone, si esercitavano poco o niente nell'osservanza de' capitoli vechi.

132. BNF, *Conventi Soppressi,* D. 3. 270, *Capitoli della Compagnia di San·Niccolò detta del Ceppo,* 1561 reforms.

133. *Capitoli,* 167, pp. 2-3.

134. *Capit.,* 446, p. 10. Similarly, the Compagnia del Pellegrino di San Donato fra' i Vecchietti was thrown out of its meeting place in 1529 (*Capitoli,* 209, 1575).

135. *Provvisioni,* 208, 58v-59v, December 20, 1529; Varchi, *Storia Fiorentina,* book 10, chapter 8.

136. ASF, *Monte,* 1296, *Beni di chiese venduti, 1529-1530,* 7or (Compagnia degli Orafi), 4v (San Zanobi), 1r, 1v, 7r, 15v, 19v, 23r, 41v, 43v (San Piero Martire).

137. *Ibid.,* 94r.

meeting place.[138] After vigorous protest and the intercession of the papal emissary in Florence, the residence was finally restored to the confraternity in 1531.[139]

The religious history of the sixteenth century is dominated by moments of high drama and intense symbolism. Sixteenth-century history has become a form of exegesis.[140] In the same manner that the church fathers interpreted the Old Testament in the light of the New Dispensation, so too have church historians interpreted the pre-Tridentine period in terms of the Council of Trent and its aftermath. Although it is no longer fashionable to compile lists of abuses begging for correction, it is still customary to search for early sixteenth-century reformers who announce or "prefigure" the coming of reform.

The history of Florence in the decades prior to Trent is not a history of reform movements or reformers. Rather, it is a history of reconstruction and reconstitution, of Florentines engaged in rebuilding a community shattered by warfare and natural disaster. As far as the task of reconstructing confraternities was concerned, even by the 1560s the work was not complete. Some companies disappeared; others, such as the company of San Martino, whose meeting place outside the Porta al Prato was destroyed in 1529 were not revived until the end of the sixteenth century.[141] The gradual attempt to restabilize the *compagnie* suffered a major setback in 1557, when Florence was devastated by one of the worst floods in its history. The company of Santa Maria in Verzaia lost all of its possessions and records in the flood.[142] The company of Santo Stefano was forced to change its

138. The religious activities of the company took place in chapels in the church of San Frediano. Business meetings were conducted in the house near San Frediano sold by the nuns.

139. *Archivi delle Compagnie Soppresse,* (Archive 5, vol. 120), p. 1. For other examples of confiscations of confraternity property, meeting places in particular, and the legal battles to regain this property, see ASF, *Conventi Soppressi,* 103, vol. 81, items 41, 42, and 44, which describe the half-century-long attempts of several companies to force the convent of San Giovannino to return confraternal furnishings and places of worship.

140. On the historiography of the Counter-Reformation in Italy, see Eric Cochrane, "New Light on Post-Tridentine Italy: A Note on Recent Counter-Reformation Scholarship," *Catholic Historical Review* 56 (1970): 291-319.

141. *Capitoli,* 167, pp. 2-3. This company was refounded in 1596.

142. *Capitoli,* 62. This company, founded in 1538, had to change meeting places four times in less than 20 years. After moving from San Tommaso and San Biagio to the church of Santo Stefano, it was again forced to vacate its premises: "Et quiui si raghunorno fino all' anno 1557 che venne la piena. Et avendo loro guasto l'acqua tutte le loro masseritie nè potendo loro habitare più in detta uolta." Other companies devastated by the flood of 1557 included San Bernardino (*Capitoli,* 3), San Niccolò del Ceppo (BNF, *Conventi Soppressi,* D.3.270), and the company of the Assumption meeting in San Niccolò Oltrarno. The meeting place of this company was abandoned in 1527 because of the plague, evacuated in 1529 because of the war, and, finally, heavily damaged in 1557 because of the flood. Italo

residence.[143] Sant' Antonio Abate and San Lodovico were forced to merge in the aftermath of the flood, for the survival of both groups,[144] and both lost all their account books, as did Santa Maria de' Raccomandati[145] and the company of the Assumption.[146]

Confraternities were, by nature, slow to change. The bonds of friendship, kinship, and economic exchange that provided the major routes of entrance into these societies and extended tenures of membership, had given them a stable character. The half century of crisis and suppression effectively disrupted this continuity. Without this disruption, the confraternities of Florence would have been less likely to respond to the changed culture of the city. But the years of suppression were long enough and severe enough to occasion the loss of confraternity oratories, a decline in membership, and a collapse of loyalty. The confraternities were "rebuilt," in a literal sense, from the ground up after a half century of neglect, without the cultural limitations imposed by the continuous membership of persons in regular contact with confraternal tradition, anxious to preserve "their" traditions. Lacking contact and commitment to older confraternal traditions, those who revived the confraternities of Florence would create new models of confraternal organization based on their own perceptions of piety and community.

Moretti, *San Niccolò Oltrarno* (n. d.), pp. 29, 32. The company of Santa Maria della Croce al Tempio lost all of its records in the same flood, (Passerini, p. 484), as did the company of the Pure in Santa Maria Novella *CRS,* 1690 (P 35, vol. 3). The secretary of San Niccolò da Bari in Santa Maria del Carmine described the flood in great detail, calling it a divine punishment. The company staged processions to mollify God's wrath and stop the flooding. *CRS,* 1542 (N 22, vol. 5), *Partiti,* 50v-51r.

143. *Capitoli,* 167, pp. 2-3.
144. *CRS,* 108 (A 98, vol. 4), 7r.
145. *Capitoli,* 798, p. 3.
146. *Capitoli,* 811, 2r.

Chapter FIVE

The Courtiers of God
RITUAL BROTHERHOOD IN
GRAND-DUCAL FLORENCE

By mid-sixteenth century, the social foundations of the traditional confraternity had undergone great changes. Florentine republicanism had owed
its survival to the existence of multiple, competing centers of power and of
social cleavages that divided members of the patriciate from one another as
much as from other social groups. The revolt of the Florentine wool
workers in 1378 (the Ciompi revolution) began a long process by which the
patriciate became a united class. Increasingly, from that time onward, the
ruling elite came to view patrician factionalism as a threat that endangered
patrician control of the Florentine state. In addition, by the end of the
fifteenth century, the multiple centers of power and patronage—which
provided an oligarchical counterweight to princely rule—had been linked
together in a centralized patronage network focused around the Medici.
After the Medici restoration of 1530 only one major source of power
remained—the Medici, whose papal ties outstripped the power and connections of the rest of the Florentine elite, a number of whom had suffered
during the decades of civil strife that culminated in the ruinous siege of the
city. The Medici dukes, at every opportunity, attempted to exclude the
patriciate from positions of independent power in the city and went so far
as to appropriate for themselves all symbols of Florentine collective allegiance. Alessandro de' Medici, upon coming to power, even minted new
coins, replacing the image of San Giovanni Battista, the patron saint of the
city, with Saints Cosimo and Damiano, the private patrons of his own
family. His successor, Cosimo I, decisively changed the character of Florentine rule and privilege. He replaced the informal patronage system, by
which Florentine patricians secured privileges for one another and their

clients at the official centers of civic power, with a formal bureaucracy staffed by foreigners removed from neighborhood and family networks and by select members of the Florentine patriciate who served at his pleasure. All significant favors, mediation, and patronage flowed from one source: the duke himself. In 1532 the principal political bodies of republican Florence—the Signoria, the Twelve Good Men, and the Sixteen Standard-Bearers—were replaced by new ducal institutions: a 48-member Senate, a Council of Two Hundred, and four Supreme Magistrates. Members of the Council of Two Hundred were drawn from the city's patrician families and held office for life. Vacancies in the council were filled by the duke. This body was originally conceived by the Florentine elite as the vehicle for preserving a modicum of "mixed government," a means of maintaining oligarchic influence within the new Medici dukedom. From the ranks of this council the duke selected the 48 members of the Senate, who also held office for life. Every 3 months 4 senators were selected for the Magistrato Supremo, the official inner council composed of those 4 senators and a fifth appointee of the duke. The council and the Senate were, in theory, the embodiment of the representative rights of Florentine citizens. In reality, after 1537, these bodies lost effective power to a host of newly created magistracies and offices, the most important of which was the office of First Secretary, the chief functionary of the Medici dukes. What the patriciate lost in power it gained in honor, for the status conferred upon councillors and senators was so great that by the seventeenth century, descendants of these officials were the recipients of noble titles and came to be considered members of a nobility of the blood.

The transformation of the old politically independent patriciate into a dependent bureaucratic nobility and a class of courtiers was, thus, the culmination of a century of change in the relations between and within Florentine classes and status groups. Between the late fourteenth and the early sixteenth centuries, Florentine patricians exchanged neighborhood ties and vertical alliances with other social groups for strong horizontal ties to members of their own class. The perception that the patricians had about themselves as a class changed as well. By 1494 the patriciate had become a closed caste. In that year, following expulsion of the Medici, a Great Council was established consisting of all males, age 29 or older, who themselves or whose ancestors had been selected for the three major governing bodies of the republic. Members of this caste were known collectively as the *beneficiati,* those "privileged" to have taken part in governing the State. Although the descendants of the chief republican office-holders were not legally recognized as constituting the highest rank of an official Florentine nobility of the blood until 1750 (when legislation singled out those whose ancestors had been among the *tre maggiori* prior to 1530), the *beneficiati* were given social recognition as Florence's hereditary nobility by the middle of the sixteenth century, as the membership practices of Florentine confraternities and the aristocratic passion for genealogy so clearly indicate. Evidence of patrician ancestry, for Florentines and non-Florentines alike, was required for admission into the knightly Order of Santo Stefano established by Cosimo I in 1562. Whereas honor in fifteenth-century Florence had been linked to the ability to exercise patronage, honor in sixteenth-century Florence was now equated almost exclusively with elite ancestry and with titles and honors bestowed by the duke. For the patriciate, a strong sense of class cohesion took the place of interclass collaboration. Patrician desire to lay claim to inherited honors and to demonstrate social exclusivity replaced the desire to mobilize popular support for political action. The new patrician sense of honor depended upon lineage rather than on the ability to wield independent political power. It was an honor devoid of real political power, an honor that could not threaten the prestige and authority of the duke.[1]

The confraternities of Florence assimilated these changes in domestic social and political relations. They also responded to fundamental changes in the organization and practice of religion brought about by the mobilization of the church against the growing threat of heresy and schism. Responding to the Protestant challenge, the Catholic church sought to extirpate heresy, promote reform at the local level, and restore its lost prestige and discipline throughout Catholic Europe.

The confraternities reformed and newly founded during the sixteenth century, especially its second half, embody the changed sociocultural envi-

---

1. On sixteenth-century Florence, see Rudolf von Albertini, *Das florentinische Staatsbewusstsein im Übergang von der Republik zum Prinzipat* (Bern: Verlag, 1955); Danilo Marrara, *Studi giuridici sulla Toscana medicea* (Pisa, 1965); Samuel Berner, "Florentine Society in the Late Sixteenth and Early Seventeenth Centuries," *Studies in the Renaissance* 18 (1971): 203-246; G. Spini, "Questioni e problemi di metodo per la storia del principato mediceo e degli stati toscani del Cinquecento," *Rivista Storica Italiana* 63 (1941): 76-93; *Cosimo I de' Medici e l'indipendenza del principato mediceo* (Florence, 1945); Antonio Anzilotti, *La crisi costituzionale della Repubblica fiorentina* (Florence, 1912); *La costituzione interna dello stato fiorentino sotto il Duca Cosimo I de' Medici* (Florence, 1910); and Furio Diaz, *Il granducato di Toscana: I Medici* (Turin, 1976). A very complete bibliography is included in Arnaldo d'Addario *La formazione dello stato moderno in toscana* (Lecce, 1976). On the legal status of the Florentine nobility in the eighteenth century, see R. Burr Litchfield, "Office-holding in Florence after the Republic," in *Renaissance Studies in Honor of Hans Baron,* ed. A. Molho and J. Tedeschi (Dekalb: Northern Illinois University Press, 1971), pp. 537-538. On similar social change in sixteenth-century Venice, see Edward Muir, "Images of Power: Art and Pageantry in Renaissance Venice," *American Historical Review* 84 (1979): 16-52.

ronment of grand-ducal, Counter-Reformation Florence. In contrast to traditional confraternities of republican Florence, sixteenth-century confraternities reveal major departures in ideology, ritual, and social organization, introducing principles of hierarchy into confraternal membership, localizing new confraternities in parishes, bringing citywide confraternities under the control of the duke, stressing a new ethic of obedience, and replacing older rituals that emphasized community, equality, and the suspension of social differentiation and hierarchy with ritual celebrations of status, honor, and rank.

Organizational Reformation and Refoundation

The unstable fortunes of confraternities in the sixteenth century—frequent suppression, loss of meeting place and members, and economic disruption—persuaded many that more permanent institutional arrangements were needed to safeguard confraternities against the effects of future suppression. Special offices of long duration were created to oversee the affairs of the companies; wealthier members were given special privileges and status to help maintain the economic vitality of these organizations; and citywide, heterogeneous organizations, generally, began to be transformed into hierarchical, elite assemblies. The company of San Bonaventura, founded in 1581, set special membership requirements. Its membership was limited to 72, one-third of whom had to come from the "families" of the city, "that is . . . those families that have had *Gonfalonieri,* or *Signori* or Knights of Jerusalem."[2] The elitist devotional company of the Blood, founded in 1592, was composed entirely of nobles.[3] By 1590 the company of San Domenico had vested its authority in a group of operai who ruled for life, each of whom had to "be of a noble family."[4] Without the approval of the *operai,* no sums above five *scudi* could be spent. The company of the Conception in 1575 limited its membership to 72 persons, only one-third of

2. *Capitoli,* 638, 3r. The earliest evidence of explicit status divisions in Florentine confraternities was that of the Purification of the Virgin Mary. In 1482 this company voted to limit its membership to 144 men, 96 of whom had to be *veduti,* and the other 48, *artefici.* Each group was represented by its own officers who were selected from separate purses. *CRS,* 1687 (P 31, vol. 1), Purificazione di Maria Vergine, *Capitoli,* 1482. Status-based membership divisions also developed in Venetian confraternities between the fourteenth and early sixteenth centuries. See Brian Pullan, *Rich and Poor in Renaissance Venice* (Cambridge, Mass.: Harvard University Press, 1971), pp. 63ff.

3. Del Migliore, 7r.

4. *Capitoli,* 30, 10r.

whom could be artisans.[5] The 1588 reforms of Santa Maria della Quercia forbade the company to enroll public employees, cooks, dice players, cloth weavers, cloth beaters,"or anyone else who practices a shameful or prohibited craft."[6]

The company of San Frediano in 1565 vested all real authority in four *operai*, who held 3-year terms. Only those members over 40 years old could qualify for this position, and three of the four had to come from families that were *beneficiati* for the three major civic offices.[7] The company of Santa Felicità e Sette Figliuoli Martiri in 1532 appointed twelve conservators, who met regularly in secret to run the affairs of the company and held office for 3 years.[8] The company of San Iacopo Sopr'Arno, whose statutes, written in 1589, state that the company's governor must be a man of a noble name,[9] vested much of its power in syndics who ran the affairs of the company for 1-year terms. Santa Maria della Quercia vested its authority in seven *operai*, each of whom was from a prominent Florentine family, two of them Medici.[10] The chief rector of the noble company of the Blood (or, more appropriately, company of Noble Blood, considering its entrance requirements) was the grand duke of Tuscany."[11] Fifteenth-century statutes had drawn parallels between the republican confraternity and the republican commune of Florence. Sixteenth-century confraternities drew different analogies: "The Holy Spirit speaks to David the Prophet, saying 'Behold, I have made you Prince and Governor of my people.' Therefore we wish that

---

5. Filippo Moisè, *Santa Croce di Firenze* (Florence, 1945), p. 423. Among companies establishing numerical limitations on members were Sancti Martiri Innocenti, which limited its membership to 70 men in 1587 (*Capitoli*, 719, 38v), and Santa Concordia, which established limitations of 100 members when the company reopened in 1506. *Capitoli*, 194.

6. *Capitoli*, 620, *Capitoli della Compagnia di Santa Maria della Quercia*, 1588, pp. 5-6.

7. ASF, *Archivi delle Compagnie Soppresse* (archive 5, vol. 2), San Frediano, *Capitoli*, 1565, 4v-5r.

8. *Capitoli*, 137.

9. *Capitoli*, 171, p. 52.

10. *Capitoli*, 620, *Capitoli della Compagnia di Santa Maria della Quercia*, 1588, pp. 28-29:

Essendosi la nostra Compagnia e Horatorio per insino al giorno d'oggi governata sotto la custodia di Operai come si trova essere stati e primi nel principio li infrascritti

Il Magnifico Hippolito del Signore Ducha Giuliano de' Medici
Francesco di Ruberto Martelli
Pagholo di Piero di Messer Orlando de' Medici
Piero di Lionardo Salviati
Giovanfrancesco di Ugho di Francesco della Stufa
Giovanmaria di Lorenzo Benintendi
Piero di Bernardo Nasi.

11. Del Migliore, 6v.

our Father Governor should be obeyed by our brothers in all things and honored as our superior."[12]

The informal social relations existing in traditional confraternities between members of different social classes were replaced in the sixteenth century by the formal recognition of social differences and the formal adoption of hierarchy as a principle of social organization and recruitment. Informal relations between patron and client gave way, as the character of social networks changed, to formal relations between individuals no longer tied by the bonds of patronage. Patrician honor now rested on the claim of social exclusivity, not on entourage, and the character of fraternal relations was also transformed.

The same weakened condition of confraternities that allowed elitism and hierarchy to reshape their character provided the excuse and the opportunity for the Medici to gain control of the major citywide confraternities. The company of San Zanobi, one of the city's oldest companies, met at the center of civic pride, the cathedral. After the first period of forced closure, the officers of the company voted to protect the confraternity against the damages of future disruptions. The officers declared that during periods of suppression company authority would be vested in an ad hoc committee.[13] During the suppression that followed, from 1526 to 1546, this strategy of appointing committees did not function as expected; in 1546, when the company resumed meeting, its officers found its affairs in total disorder.[14] The chaotic state of San Zanobi provided the pretext for what was essentially a takeover of its finances and affairs by the grand duke:

> Having appreciated the aforementioned pious works [accomplished by the confraternity], His Excellency wishes to participate in the spiritual benefits of the Company and to be counted among our members. . . . However, the aforementioned Duke, illuminated by God, and by His sweetest mother, Madonna Saint Mary, Ever Virginal, and by our Pastor and Advocate, San Zenobio, orders the aforementioned captains and councillors to add eight men as Reformers, who ought, given the things that have happened in the past which have damaged the Company not a little because of the bad custody and negligence of its ministers, to reform and correct all errors and conserve and maintain the accounts and property of this holy house and protect the affairs of the Company from decline and usurpation. And these men created and elected by His Excellency ought to remain in this office for

12. *Capitoli* 649, *Capitoli della Compagnia del Sacramento di Santa Trinità*, 1594, p. 19: "Lo Spirito Santo parla a David Profeta dicendo: 'Ecco, che io ti ho constituito principe et governatore del popolo mio,' e però vogliamo che il nostro Padre Governatore sia da tutti li fratelli ubbidito e honorato come maggiore e rendutoli quello honore che si richieda."
13. *Capitoli*, 154, 35v.
14. *Capitoli*, 155, 8r.

life. . . . and their authority ought to be as great as the whole body of the confraternity . . . and at least four of the Reformers must be present with the captains and
councillors at all deliberations and decision making sessions regarding the affairs of
the Company. And in the event that some doubt or hesitation should arise between
the captains, councillors and ministers in the correction of delinquents . . . the
chaplain, chancellor, or provisioner ought to expose such cases to the Reformers.[15]

The Medici, through actions such as this, came into control and supervision of one of the main potential sources of citywide organization, the
major confraternities of the city. The six captains of the Misericordia
became appointees of the grand duke, holding office for life.[16] Cosimo I
joined San Paolo and helped to appoint its *operai;* this process was continued by his successors, who felt free to pack confraternities with their
functionaries.[17]

The history of the citywide companies of Florence in the sixteenth
century reflects the growth of rigid social distinctions in the city of the
Medici dukes. In an increasingly aristocratic milieu, tradesmen and artisans
found themselves excluded from the most prestigious citywide associations.
The new exclusivity of older confraternities left tradesmen with few modes
of association beyond those of their parish and craft. The adoption of
elitist practices by citywide confraternities was accompanied by the formation of confraternities composed solely of artisans and tradesmen organized
around craft and parish ties.

A few parish and craft fraternities had existed in the fourteenth and
fifteenth centuries. They were not, however, the dominant forms of fraternal organization that they would become in the sixteenth century, when
they became, for all Florentines save the patriciate, the principal forms of
fraternal association. Five craft confraternities were founded in sixteenth-
century Florence before the establishment of the principate: the company
of druggists and physicians (1501),[18] the company of barbers (1509),[19] the

15. *Ibid.,* 28v-29v.
16. Ser Giovanni Maria di Baccio Cecchi, *Sommario de' Magistrati di Firenze secondo che si truovano
questo anno 1562,* transcribed in part by Arnaldo d'Addario, *Aspetti della controriforma a Firenze* (Rome:
Ministero dell'interno, pubblicazioni degli archivi di stato, 1972), p. 404: "Al governo di questi sono
sei Capitani cittadini, eletti dal signor duca, uno cancelliere e uno proveditore; e questi stanno a
vita."
17. On San Paolo, see *CRS,* 1583, 205rff. See note 10 for the *operai* of Santa Maria della Quercia.
18. San Cosimo e San Damiano dei Medici e Speziali, *Capitoli,* 189, 1743. This company was
founded on April 6, 1501 in the church of San Michele delle Trombe. Following the disturbances of
the early sixteenth century, the company was forced to unite with the parish confraternity
Santissimo Sacramento in San Firenze and later moved to its own site.
19. *CRS,* 316 (C 8, vol. 1, pt. A), *Doti,* 1509, Santa Caterina da Siena. The earliest statutes of the
company date from 1518: *Capitoli,* 589.

company of pork butchers (1509),[20] the company of carpenters (1520),[21] and the company of bakers (1529).[22] After the fall of the republic (1530), such associations proliferated. Definite foundation dates establish the creation of companies of innkeepers and cooks (1542),[23] gatekeepers (1547),[24] scrap iron dealers (1560),[25] woolen cloth weavers (1576),[26] cloth beaters (1579),[27] weavers of fine fabrics (1595),[28] and masons (1604).[29] Evidence for other companies is more circumstantial and permits only the specification of a date by which a company is known to have existed. Nevertheless, these dates follow a pattern similar to that of dates of foundations, clustering in the last half of the sixteenth century. Thus, a company of cloth finishers existed by 1543,[30] another confraternity of cloth weavers by 1566,[31] booksellers by 1568,[32] haberdashers by 1575,[33] employees of the Mercanzia by 1575,[34] butchers by 1577,[35] mattress makers and secondhand-clothes dealers by 1595,[36] and millers by 1602.[37]

Craft associations, unlike the parish societies that will be described later in this chapter, were rather narrowly conceived organizations providing members of the working class, at their own expense, with a primitive form of social insurance. Through group prepayment of mandatory dues by all members of a craft, sufficient capital was generated to provide dowries for members' daughters, burial benefits, and weekly cash payments to members who fell ill. These associations were chartered and regulated by the grand-ducal court. Provisions requiring mandatory enrollment of all practitioners

20. Riccardiana, ms. Moreniano, 54, *Capitoli della Compagnia di San Bartolomeo de' Pizzicagnoli*, 1509.

21. San Giuseppe de' Legnaiuoli, *Capitoli*, 348; del Migliore, 21r-v.

22. Del Migliore (4v) found rental agreements for the company of Sant' Antonio e San Lorenzo de' Fornari dating from 1529. The sixteenth-century statutes of this company are preserved as Laurenziana, Ms. Antinori, 24. Other company documents dating from the 1570s are contained in *CRS*, collection A 99.

23. San Martino degl' Osti, Albergatori, e Cucinieri, *Capitoli*, 197.

24. San Pietro de' Gabellieri e Stradieri, *Capitoli*, 458.

25. Santa Trinità de' Ferravecchi, ASF, *Conventi Soppressi*, 89, 136, *Capitoli*, 1560.

26. San Giovanni Evangelista e San Michele Arcangelo, cited by del Migliore, 44v.

27. San Cosimo e San Damiano, *Capitoli*, 492.

28. San Francesco di Pagola, *Capitoli*, 22.

29. San Matteo de' Muratori, *Capitoli*, 797.

30. San Pietro, Riccardiana, ms. Riccardiano, 2577.

31. Santa Maria del Chiodo de' Tessitori de' Panni Lani, *Capitoli*, 608.

32. Natività di Maria Vergine, *Capitoli*, 709.

33. San Donato de' Vecchietti de' Merciai, *Capitoli*, 209.

34. San Iacopo e San Filippo, *Capitoli*, 178.

35. Sant' Antonio de' Macellari, *Capitoli*, 623.

36. San Leone Papa, *Capitoli*, 5. This company provided services for members of these crafts but was founded earlier in the century as a company free of craft ties.

37. Sant' Antonio de' Mugnai, *Capitoli*, 745.

of a trade were enforced by the Medici dukes.[38] Through these fraternities
the state monitored and attempted to control the behavior of the Florentine working class. Mandatory enrollment guaranteed that most workers
would be provided for in the case of personal catastrophe and in such a way
that they might be less tempted to seek the patronage of the Florentine
patriciate.

In 1588 Florence suffered a major famine. The response of Florentine
authorities, civil and ecclesiastical, to this calamity reveals how the city's
craft fraternities could be used as instruments of state manipulation of the
working class. Widespread fear of a potential grain shortage caused a 33%
rise in grain prices in May of that year. Grand Duke Ferdinand I opened his
stores of grain to the poor, ordering that the commodity be sold to them at
the old price.[39] In gratitude, the craft fraternities of the city collaborated
with the grand duke, enabling him to eliminate a potential mode of
working-class organization. The chronicler Agostino Lapini describes this
collaboration, with the grand duke and against the city's taverns:

> Almost every day the preachers, especially at the Duomo, railed against the taverns
> of our city, Florence. They said that the taverns are, if not absolutely, then generally
> the ruin of our young men and boys, and that it would be excellent to get rid of
> them. They spoke so often about this and hurled so much abuse that many persons
> decided not to frequent the taverns any longer, especially when it was known
> everywhere, to everybody that it was a matter of great importance to the grand
> duke that no one visit the taverns. And so the cloth weavers, cloth beaters, fabric
> weavers, wool washers, and dyers, each one of them in their own companies, began
> to discuss the matter because it would be an act of gratitude to our patron for us to
> stop frequenting the taverns, and it would be good to vote that in the future one
> should not go to the taverns, since one sees and hears that our Grand Duke
> Ferdinand cares so much about this; and this is why the grain this year has been so

---

38. A letter from the company of Masons to the grand duke dated March 23, 1657, requesting
the assistance of the Medici in establishing compulsory membership requirements for their company,
cited numerous craft fraternities whose members were *sottoposti* to these societies as precedents for
such regulations:

> Il Governatore, Consiglieri, Ufiziali e tutti i Fratelli del Membro e Compagnia de' Muratori tutti
> Vmilissimi Serui, e Vassalli di V.A.S. umilmente gli espongono, come essendo in questa Città di Firenze
> assai Muratori, che esercitano il mestiero, e non si fanno descriuere di detta Compagnia, come segue in
> altre Compagnie, e Membri in questa Città di varij esercizij, quali unitamente s'adunano insieme, come
> Tessitori, Torcitori, Filatoiai, Pettinatori di Lino, Barbieri, Osti, Fornai, e molte altre Compagnie, e
> Membri, quali tutti auendo il suo luogo, e Compagnia, tutti di detti mestieri in esse s'adunano, e sono
> sottoposti, e tenuti quelli, che fanno tali esercizij di pagare alli loro membri le Tasse in quella quantità
> contenuta nelli loro Capitoli.

Capitoli, 797, San Matteo de' Muratori.

39. Giuliano de' Ricci, *Cronica (1532-1606)*, ed. Giuliana Sapori (Milan: Ricciardi, 1972),
pp. 516-517.

subsidized that it returned to 3 *lire* per *staio* and less. And so, everyone having become inflamed and zealous, each company put it up to a vote that, from now on no one should go there [the taverns] any longer, under penalty of losing one's dowry and the charity [to which one is entitled] when one is sick, and the other benefits about which the statutes speak. These provisions, having won approval, were confirmed by the grand duke and the archbishop of Florence.[40]

Members of the Florentine working class, with increasing regularity, were required by law to join craft fraternities. Now, they "voluntarily" agreed to regulate their own behavior according to the wishes of their patron, the grand duke, at a time of grave social insecurity, by agreeing henceforth to lose all the benefits of their compulsory fraternity membership if they should be caught frequenting taverns. Taverns had been, in republican Florence, associated with working-class culture and revolutionary activity. The term *Ciompi,* used to describe the working-class revolt of 1378, is said to have originated as a term descriptive of working-class tavern sociability.[41]

In his attempt to monitor the activities of the Florentine lower classes and remove them from locales traditionally associated with working-class organization and rebellion, Duke Ferdinand acted according to what appears to have been a calculated and consistent policy. The same year in which the craft fraternities fulminated against the taverns at Ferdinand's instigation, the Venetian ambassador to the Medici court evaluated Ferdinand's internal policy as one in which the lower orders of society were kept pacified by relative economic security. Potential upper-class opponents of Ferdinand were generally forbidden from meeting together in private gatherings (*radunanze*), a policy quite in keeping with the Medici practice of appointing the officials and packing the membership of elite confraternities.[42]

The relationship between charity and social control was expressed symbolically on May 22, 1588, when 200 members of the company of dyers, preceded by trumpeters, marched in procession with lighted candles, accompanying 4 bushels of grain loaded on carts. Members of this fraternity

40. Agostino Lapini, *Diario fiorentino dal 252 al 1596,* ed. Giuseppe Corazzini (Florence: Sansoni, 1900), p. 267.

41. Samuel Kline Cohn, *Laboring Classes in Renaissance Florence* (New York: Academic Press, 1980), chap. 3. Both Ricci and Lapini express a certain sense of wonder at workers' collaboration in the suppression of taverns. On the basis of the evidence of 1588 it appears that the tavern culture of the *popolo minuto* did not die out by the end of the fifteenth century, as Cohn has hypothesized.

42. *Relazione delle cose di Toscana di Tomaso Contarini, ambasciatore al Cardinale Granduca,* in *Relazioni degli ambasciatori veneti al senato, 1588,* 2 vols., ed. A. Ventura (Rome: Laterza, 1976), 2:301.

acted out ceremonially the dual roles of recipients of grand-ducal charity and distributors of that charity as they carried their ceremonial offering to the poorest nunneries and monasteries of the city. The procession culminated in the ritual distribution of grain, an offering made, in part, to ensure the success of the campaign against the taverns, a campaign formally inaugurated by the procession.[43] The offering of grain symbolized the gifts and subsidies made to the working class by the grand duke and the role of the craft fraternities in providing for their own members under the grand duke's watchful eye. The procession marked the beginning of a holy enterprise: the enforcement of social and moral orthodoxy on the working class, using the working class as the instrument of its own regulation.

However emblematic of social transformations the rise of craft fraternities and the growing elitist and hierarchical character of traditional confraternities might have been, it was the rise of parish confraternities in grand-ducal Florence that signaled the most profound restructuring of piety and community, for it was in the rise of the parish confraternities that the major threads of social change coalesced.

The neighborhood had long been a fundamental unit of social interaction; however, the confraternal geography of the city had not been aligned according to this fact. Flagellant piety had made the escape from neighborhoods a quasi-sacred experience; confraternities were organized on a citywide rather than on a narrow neighborhood basis. Such piety released the Florentine from the tight bonds of the local community and allowed him to participate in broader communities. The city of Florence rather than its individual neighborhoods was the locus of the sacred. The *laudesi* confraternities, too, recruited a good number of their members from throughout the community, although a greater proportion of their membership came from the quarter of the city in which each company met. The churches in which *laudesi* chose to worship were all major centers of civic devotion. The sixteenth century, however, witnessed the decline of those institutions—such as guilds and a widely influential political class—that provided the practical basis for constructing broadly based communities that crosscut neighborhoods. By the middle of the sixteenth century, the foundation of heterogeneous cross-parish, and cross-*gonfalone* communities had been severely weakened.

Whatever the fate of confraternities, the regular ritual obligations of the community had to be carried out. The dead required solemn burial and permanent memorial, and the living required ongoing communion with

43. Lapini, *Diario fiorentino*, p. 268.

God through the sacraments of the church. The *laudesi* companies of Florence had regularly performed these tasks for their members. But we have seen how such ancient companies as Sant' Agnese and San Sebastiano had been forced to allow those functions to lapse during the turbulence of the early sixteenth century. One would expect that in the absence of confraternal burials and masses, Florentines would have been forced to rely upon the ritual life of their neighborhood communities. It is no coincidence then that the first reports of regular, active parish religious activity appeared during the second and third decades of the sixteenth century, that is, during precisely those years that witnessed the suppression and collapse of traditional Florentine confraternal life.[44]

A new form of confraternal association blossomed in Florence following the Medici restoration in 1530: parish confraternities dedicated to the Holy Sacrament. Between the Medici restoration in 1530 and the early seventeenth century at least 24 such organizations were founded in Florence.

While older forms of confraternal organization continued to exist, one finds no mention of the foundation of *laudesi* confraternities in this period and scant reference to new flagellant companies. By the time that *laudesi* confraternities began to revive in the 1540s, 1550s, and 1560s, their ritual services were somewhat superfluous: The cultic life of Florentines had already begun to center in the parishes of the city. When the *laudesi* revived, they tended to become, like San Zanobi, elite clubs, or, like Sant' Agnese, formal neighborhood groups. Traditional penitential companies appear to have suffered as well. Although the term *disciplina* appeared everywhere, it lost its traditional meaning. By the late sixteenth century, *disciplina* had acquired the connotation of zeal, sanctity, and reverence. Many companies described themselves as wearing the *"veste da battuti"*—the slit robes of flagellant confraternities—without mentioning, in any discussion of ritual, the actual practice of flagellation. Only rarely does one find mention of flagellant practices in the late sixteenth century, but everywhere one reads of flagellant garb symbolic of discipline and piety.[45] In a culture dedicated

44. On May 3, 1518, a general procession was held in Florence to stir up enthusiasm for a crusade against the Turks. Every parish priest in Florence, bearing the relics found in each parish, marched in the procession. On May 7 and 8 of that year the residents of the parishes went on processions throughout their parishes, singing psalms and *laude*. (G. Corazzini, ed., *Ricordanze di Bartolomeo Masi calderaio fiorentino, dal 1478 al 1526* (Florence: Sansoni, 1906), p. 233: "Et ancora tutte le chiese parrocchiale di Firenze, a' di vij et a' di viij del presente mese di magio, andorno a procissione per tutti e Popoli loro. . . . E dette chiese di priorìa portavano la crocie, e non l'altre, e passavano per tutte le vie di loro Popoli, cantando inni e salmi e cose i'lalde di Dio." In 1530, during the siege, the parishes of Florence sponsored 2 months of parish processions (Richard Trexler, *Public Life in Renaissance Florence* [New York: Academic Press, 1980], p. 543).

45. The *Bianchi* company in Santo Spirito continued to wear flagellant garments but never referred to flagellant practices (*CRS*, 4 [A 8, vol. 4], *Partiti*, 18v). Their practices emphasized

to social distinction and pomp, traditional penitential piety, as we shall see, came to be perceived as something of an anachronism, something quaint, old-fashioned, and even rather distasteful. The old citywide companies that had emphasized penance became social clubs for the Florentine elite, monitored closely by the Medici dukes.

The rise of the parish confraternity must be charted against the decline of civic institutions. But the parish confraternity was more than a reaction to the decline of broader communities. It provided a solution to the problems of order faced by church, state, and confraternity. For the church, the parish—the unit of social control—offered a potent range of possibilities of restoring discipline and of guarding against the introduction of heresy into the community. The concentration of social interaction at the neighborhood level also made political supervision and control by the state that much easier. In Februrary 1549 Cosimo I divided Florence into 50 neighborhoods, giving to each two informers. The exaggerated remark of Vincenzo Fedeli, Venetian ambassador to Florence, that "the terror of spies has reached such a state that . . . there is not a person who is not suspicious of his closest relatives and friends" at least conveys something of the continuing tensions of neighborhood life exacerbated by Cosimo's fear of plots and assassination.[46] Fedeli wrote to the Venetians in 1561 about Cosimo's use of the parish clergy as his eyes and ears:

> The Prince even wishes to know from the parish priests the number of Hosts distributed during communion, because he is accustomed to say that alterations and changes in religion bring with them the manifest danger of changes of State, and therefore he remains warned.[47]

The parish provided confraternities with a stable institutional base that linked them to the parish church. Parish confraternities formally bound

---

veneration of their crucifix and the Eucharist. Similarly, the sacramental company of Santa Trinità, founded in 1541, called themselves a *compagnia di disciplina* but referred often to sacramental reverence and never to flagellation (*Capitoli*, 649, 1594). The Compagnia di San Bonaventura, refounded in 1581 to aid prisoners, also referred to the wearing of flagellant garb without referring to flagellation (*Capit.*, 638, 1605). Companies of male children, parish companies, and companies devoted to public assistance are all found wearing the garb of the *disciplinati*. Even if occasional flagellation did take place in some of these companies—and scant trace of it exists—the practice has clearly moved from center stage to the periphery of confraternal ritual, replaced by sacramental devotions. On these devotions, see pp. 228-241.

46. Quoted in Berner, "Florentine Society," pp. 239-240.

47. *Relazione di messer Vincenzo Fedeli segretario dell' illustrissima Signoria di Venezia tornato dal duca di Fiorenza nel 1561*, reprinted in *Relazioni degli ambasciatori veneti*, ed. Ventura 2:213. The use of the parish clergy to monitor the sacramental participation of parishioners was not new in Florence. Antonino had listed this as one of the duties of parish priests (1455) and required them to report to curial officials all residents of the parish who did not avail themselves of confession and communion.

themselves to these churches through notarized contracts. In exchange for the long-term use of a meeting place, these companies were obligated to make a yearly ceremonial offering to the parish clergy, in public recognition of the clergy's dominion over the confraternity. In addition, the parish societies were obliged to bury deceased residents of the parish, to assist at parish masses, and to arrange the celebration of the feast of the patron saint of the parish. The obligations that gave these societies their common name, companies of the Blessed Sacrament, were those of carrying the host on parish processions, surrounded by torches and protected by a canopy, and bringing the sacrament to ill parishioners.[48]

The sixteenth century witnessed both the emergence of newly created parish confraternities and the transformation of older companies into parish groups. The company of San Iacopo Sopr'Arno, which had been a flagellant company in the previous century, reappeared in 1589 as the flagellant company of the Sacrament of San Iacopo, a parish society.[49] The company of Santo Stefano was founded in 1538; after the flood of 1557 it reappeared, on July 27, 1568, as a parish company.[50] The confraternity of Santa Felicità and Her Seven Martyred Children was founded in 1507; its statutes, at this time, specifically allowed the company to elect its own clerical chaplain and confessor. By 1532 the company had taken over parish duties, and its dependence upon the parish was clearly recognized, for it was now required to have as its chaplain the priest of the parish of Santa Felicità. And by 1560 neighboring San Felice in Piazza established its parish group.[51]

The transformation of traditional confraternities into parish companies dedicated to the Blessed Sacrament is well illustrated by the evolution of the company of the Sacrament of Santa Maria Novella. The Compagnia della Carità, founded in 1379, had met in Santa Maria Novella until the chaotic decades of the early sixteenth century. In 1538 the company rees-

---

Richard C. Trexler, "The Episcopal Constitutions of Antoninus of Florence," *Quellen und Forschungen aus italienischen Archiven und Bibliotheken* 59 (1979): 258.

48. For examples of contracts between parish confraternities and parish churches, see *CRS*, 177 (A 149, vol. 2), *Libro de' contratti della Compagnia del Sacramento dell' Assunta e Pace in San Piero Gattolini*, 1565-1726, contracts dated January 4, 1565, January 10, 1585, and April 1, 1609; *CRS*, 183 (A 152, vol. 1), *Capitoli della Compagnia dell' Assunta e del Santissimo Sacramento, in San Niccolò Oltrarno*, 1581, pp. 26-27; *CRS*, 1880 (S 180, vol. 2, pt. A), *Contratti e Testamenti della Compagnia del Sagramento in San Felice in Piazza*, 1560-1762, copy of contract dated 1560; *CRS*, 1759 (S 6, vol. 2), Compagnia del Sacramento di San Salvatore in Borgo Ognissanti, *Ricordi*, 1569-1578, 11v-12r; *Capitoli*, 499, *Capitoli della Compagnia del Sacramento di Santa Lucia de' Magnoli*, pp. 41-43, contract dated January 26, 1640.

49. *Capitoli*, 171.

50. *Capitoli*, 62.

51. *Capitoli*, 137. On S. Felice, see *CRS*, 1880 (S 1, vol. 1).

tablished itself as the company of the Blessed Sacrament of Santa Maria Novella. Six years later, two other companies united with this sacramental confraternity. The company of the Pure, founded in the cemetery of Santa Maria Novella in 1472, had, according to its statutes, fallen into a state of grave decline by the time that it was allowed to reopen in 1531. In 1534 the brothers of the Pure united their company to that of another severely damaged confraternity, San Niccolò da Tolentino, which had been accustomed to meet in Santa Maria Nuova. In 1544 this recently combined group was absorbed into the Company of the Blessed Sacrament, which became the group of overseers (*opera*) for Santa Maria Novella itself.[52] The desirability of merging with this company is not hard to understand, for the company of the Blessed Sacrament of Santa Maria Novella had become, by 1540, one of the most attractive Florentine confraternities. In that year it became linked to the influential Roman archconfraternity of the Most Holy Sacrament of Santa Maria Sopra Minerva. The members of the company of Santa Maria Novella enjoyed the considerable spiritual privileges granted to the Roman group, as was customary for all affiliates of sixteenth-century archconfraternities.

This Roman company, founded in the church of Santa Maria Sopra Minerva, was the model sacramental confraternity of the Catholic Reformation. Its constitutions, approved by Paul III in 1539, had as their goal the propagation of honor and reverence for the sacrament of the Eucharist. This was to be achieved by sponsoring annual parish processions around the parish church on Corpus Domini, by ensuring that the sacrament was carried to the sick of the parish, by incorporating parish wives into the company to add to the store of prayers offered by the parish, by the celebration of a solemn mass every third Sunday of the month, and by the granting of spiritual privileges to encourage other confraternities to affiliate with the archconfraternity.[53]

Before the flood of 1557, the church of San Remigio had housed one of Florence's two companies dedicated to Santa Maria della Neve (the other was located in the parish of Sant' Ambrogio), but by 1568 this company had collapsed. In that year, the prior of San Remigio granted permission to the men of the parish to take over the older, now defunct company and to found the company of the Sacrament of San Remigio for the purposes of burying parish dead, accompanying the sacrament on parish processions, and assisting at communion services.[54] Sacramental companies had been

52. *Capitoli*, 455, Compagnia della Purità di Maria Vergine e Santissimo Sacramento, 1564.
53. November 30, 1539, *Dominus noster Iesus Christi.*
54. *Capitoli*, 181, Santa Maria della Neve in San Remigio, 1569.

founded in the parishes of Santa Maria in Verzaia (San Giovanni Decollato e Santissimo Sacramento) by 1535,[55] Santa Trinità by 1541,[56] San Piero Maggiore by 1550,[57] Ognissanti by 1565 (Sacramento del San Salvatore),[58] San Iacopo in Campo Corbolini by 1574 (San Giovanni Battista alla Cavalieri di Hierusalem),[59] San Niccolò Oltrarno by 1581 (Assunta e Santissimo Sacramento),[60] San Biagio by 1584,[61] San Paolo prior to 1595,[62] Santa Maria Maggiore prior to 1601,[63] San Piero Gattolini prior to 1607 (Madonna dell' Assunta),[64] Santa Lucia de' Magnoli in 1640,[65] and San Pancrazio some time between 1630 and 1640.[66] The parishes of Santa Cecilia and San Michele Berteldi also were the sites of parish confraternities created between the late sixteenth and early seventeenth centuries.[67] Between 1569 and 1582 at least two of the four *Bianchi* companies founded in 1399 around specific quarters of the city—Santa Lucia de' Bianchi (in Santa Lucia sul Prato), and the Bianchi (which moved from San Piero del Murrone to San Michele Visdomini in the fifteenth century)—reemerged as parish societies.[68] By midsixteenth century San Firenze had its parish group.[69]

The older Florentine confraternities provided a ritual space that was socially much broader than the parish; the new sacramental companies concentrated their sacred energies on the parish itself. In republican Florence, the confraternities had shown their splendor to the community on the vigil of the feast day of John the Baptist, a day on which the holy city of

---

55. *Capitoli*, 167, San Giovanni Decollato e Santissimo Sacramento, in Santa Maria in Verzaia, *Capitoli*, 1743.

56. *Capitoli*, 649, Santissimo Sacramento di Santa Trinità, 1594.

57. *CRS*, 182, (A 151), Assunta e Santissimo Sacramento in San Piero Maggiore, *Libro dei Contratti*, 1550. The earliest known statutes for this company, damaged by the flood of 1966, date from 1601 (*Capitoli*, 271).

58. *Capitoli*, 516, Santissimo Sacramento di San Salvatore in Borgo Ognissanti, *Capitoli*, 1565.

59. *Capitoli*, 63, *Capitoli della Compagnia di San Giovanni Battista alla Cavalieri di Hierusalem*, 1574.

60. *CRS*, 183 (A 152, vol. 1).

61. Ms. Moreniano, 56.

62. *CRS*, 120 (A 99, vol. 2), SS. Paolo e Antonio, *Ricordi e Contratti*.

63. The *CRS* series (S 5) contains documentation for this company as early as 1601, although no evidence for a foundation date has been found.

64. *Capitoli*, 828, *Capitoli della Compagnia della Madonna dell' Assunta in San Piero Gattolini*, 1607 reforms.

65. *Capitoli*, 499, *Capitoli della Compagnia del Sacramento di Santa Lucia de' Magnoli*, 1650 reforms.

66. *Capitoli*, 253, *Capitoli della Compagnia del Sacramento di San Pancrazio*, 1668 reforms.

67. The earliest extant statutes of the company of the Conception and the Holy Sacrament, in Santa Cecilia (*CRS*, 655 [C 143, vol. 1]) date from 1671, but they speak of an "antichissimo tempo" when the company was founded. The archival collection for San Michele Berteldi (S 4) contains documents as early as 1626 but mentions no definite date of foundation.

68. *CRS*, 1769 (S 8, vol. 1); *Capitoli*, 45, *Capitoli della Compagnia di San Michele Arcangelo*, 1569, p. 36.

69. On San Firenze see p. 201, n. 18.

Florence proudly entwined itself in a citywide procession. The new parish confraternities altered the ritual geography of the city. The statute books of the parish confraternities reveal a preoccupation with sacralizing the parish, and the parish procession is the central procession mentioned in confraternal records. Even the feast day of John the Baptist became a parish affair, as one company of the Holy Sacrament recorded: "On the 24th [of June 1576], the day of Saint John the Baptist, the organizers of the feast assembled our company, and a solemn procession was made through our parish, with great devotion. And there were three companies, San Giovanni, San Paolo, and ours.[70]

The principal feast day observed by the sixteenth-century parish confraternity, Corpus Christi, was also a feast day celebrated by citywide processions, but, in addition, each community celebrated its own sacred uniqueness. On Corpus Christi, the sacramental companies marched not only on the traditional processions throughout Florence but also on parish processions, demarcating the sacred boundaries of the parishes and quarters of the city.[71] The two processional occasions of special importance to sixteenth-century sacramental confraternities were Corpus Christi and the particular feast day of the patron saint of the parish. Thus, the company of San Giovanni Battista, in San Iacopo in Campo Corbolini, marched on two processions yearly: on the day of its patron and on Corpus Christi,[72] as did San Frediano, San Niccolò Oltrarno, and numerous other companies.[73] Certain parish societies—the Sacrament of San Iacopo,[74] San Silvestro e San Felice, San Biagio,[75] and San Niccolò Oltrarno[76]—went on more frequent parish processions, perhaps as often as did Santissimo Sacramento di Santa Lucia or the sacrament of Santa Maria Novella, which carried the host through the parish every third Sunday of the month.[77]

The citywide confraternity had provided a refuge from neighborhood

70. CRS, 1759 (S 6, vol. 2), Sacramento di San Salvatore in Borgo Ognissanti, Ricordi, 1569-1578, "A dì 24 detto [June, 1576] il dì di Santo Giovanni Battista doue e festaiuoli avevono tornate la nostra compagnia si fiece una solenne pricisione pel nostro popolo e furno 3 compagnie, San Giovanni, San Paolo, e la nostra e con gran divozione di poi si disse l'ufizio solenne alla Santa messa.".

71. The company of the Pure, the parish company of Santa Maria Novella, marched on three processions for Corpus Christi: a parish procession, a procession around the cathedral, and a procession around the quarter of Santa Maria Novella (Capitoli, 455).

72. Capitoli, 63.

73. Capitoli, 179, 28v-29v; CRS, 183 (A 152, vol. 1), pp. 26-27; Capitoli, 45, pp. 72-73; Capitoli, 828, 14r; Capitoli, 253, pp. 12-13; Capitoli, 63; Capitoli, 649, p. 69.

74. Capitoli, 171.

75. Ms. Moreniano, 56.

76. CRS, 183 (A 152, vol. 1), pp. 18-19.

77. G. Richa, Notizie istoriche delle chiese fiorentine (Florence, 1754-1762), 3:106-107; Capitoli, 455.

social ties and neighborhood scrutiny, in short, from the "parochialism" of
the parish. The parish confraternity, on the other hand, reinforced parish
boundaries and parish ties as well. Most parish confraternities were under
the direct supervision of the rector of the parish church.[78] The only
sacramental companies that were not obligated to have the rector of the
parish church as chaplain appear to have been those companies in parishes
where the resident clergy had rights of habitation but not the care of
souls.[79]

The cross-parish confraternity lessened the density of social relations,
but the parish confraternity included the whole neighborhood in its moral
domain. Although wives and sisters of members were not admitted into the
confraternity meeting chambers, the parish confraternities admitted them
into the spiritual community of the confraternity and allowed them to
participate in the celebration of parish feasts.[80] Women were considered
members in spirit, but they did not perform the services that male members
performed. Sisters were required to offer prayers at home but they did not
join the brothers in burying the dead.[81] The membership of women in
Florentine sacramental companies offered them spiritual rather than physical community. *Sorelle* were allowed to come to company meetings only
once annually:

> It is prohibited and forbidden, not only to our sisters, but to every other woman as
> well, under penalty of expulsion, to enter our oratory in any manner, except for the
> Sunday of the octave of Corpus Domini, and not at any other time, so that the

78. On the clerical control of parish confraternities, see the statutes of the following companies:
Assunta e Santissimo Sacramento in San Niccolò Oltrarno, *CRS*, 183 (A 152, vol. 1); San Biagio, ms.
Moreniano, 56; Santo Stefano, *Capitoli*, 62; Santa Felicità Maccabea e Sette Figliuoli Martiri, *Capitoli*,
137; San Michele Arcangelo, *Capitoli*, 45, pp. 4, 29; San Pancrazio, *Capitoli*, 253, pp. 4-5; San Frediano,
Archivi delle Compagnie Soppresse (archive 5, vol. 2), 7r; San Salvatore, *Capitoli*, 224.

79. The nuns residing in the monastery of San Piero Martire were only too willing to turn over
parish duties to the company of San Felice in Piazza (*CRS*, 1880 [S 180, vol. 2, pt. A]). Similarly, a
decree of October 6, 1551, gave Franciscan friars rights of residence in Ognissanti but gave the
parishioners of Santa Lucia sul Prato the right to "pigliare i sacramenti"—the right to "take control
of the sacraments" themselves, that is, to appoint their own parish clergy and arrange for parish
masses (*CRS*, 1769 [S 8, vol. 2a], company of Santa Lucia sul Prato, *Interesse Diverse*). The same friars
also granted similar rights to the company of the Sacrament of San Salvatore in Borgo Ognissanti
(*CRS*, 1759 [S 6, vol. 2], *Ricordi*, 1569-1578, 11v-12r).

80. On the status of women in parish confraternities, see the statutes of the following companies:
Santo Stefano, *Capitoli*, 62, chap. 17; San Giovanni Battista, *Capitoli*, 63, chap. 24; Santa Felicità
Maccabea e Sette Figliuoli Martiri, *Capitoli*, 137; San Iacopo Sopr' Arno, *Capitoli*, 171; San Frediano,
Capitoli, 179, 40v-41r.

81. *Capitoli*, 63, *Capitoli della Compagnia di San Giovanni Battista alla Cavalieri di Ierusalem*, capitolo 24:
E perchè è una delle sette opere della misericordia seppellire li morti delle quali opere al finale iuditio dal
tribunale de dio saranno ricerche ma perchè non possono così le nostre Sorelle essere habili a seppellire li
morti però possono loro tale opera eseguire spiritualmente bonum est pro mortuis orare ut a tormentis
liberentur eglie buono pregare con le orationi per li morti acciò che quelli sieno liberati de tormenti.

opportunity to expose or slander us will be removed and this is done for the salvation of the souls of each of our sisters.[82]

This participation of women, limited as it was, was more extensive than the opportunities allowed women in fourteenth- and fifteenth-century groups. The parish societies incorporated male children as well as women, organizing confraternities of Christian Doctrine[83] supervised by the parish confraternities of adults. Several fraternities of adolescents had been founded in the fifteenth century, and these, like the adult societies, had been citywide in membership.[84] At the end of that century Savonarola had organized his adolescent supporters into clubs, one in each of the four quarters of the city.[85] As parish confraternities of adults replaced more broadly based societies, so too parish organization replaced citywide organization for juveniles. The confraternities of Christian Doctrine, tied to the parish, were juvenile auxiliaries of the adult societies, enrolling boys aged 6-15. The company founded by the men of the parish of San Salvatore had two goals: First, to keep boys obedient to the sacred law and second, "that which inspired these devoted brothers [the adults], in their desire that their Company of the Holy Sacrament should not only maintain its present healthy size (thanks to God), but that it should grow even larger."[86] The company of Saint Michael, the parish society of Sant' Ambrogio, declared: "After age fifteen, the most able and expert boys should be allowed to enroll in our company."[87] The members of the adult companies instructed "these tender plants, our sons, in being good Christians, in chanting, reciting Psalms, and making sermons," preparing their sons to be the "fathers of the children of the future."[88]

---

82. Capitoli, 179, Capitoli della Compagnia del Corpus Domini di Sancto Fridiano, 1573, 40v-41r:

Prohibendo et uietando non solo alle nostre sorelle ma etiamdio a ogni altra donna che sotto pena d'essere rase non debbino in modo alcuno entrare nel nostro oratorio excettuato però la domenica del ottaua del corpus domini. Et non in altro tempo acciò si lievi ogni occasione di dire ha chi uolessi exporre et calumniare et per salute del anima di ciaschuna di loro.

83. The foundation of Florentine confraternities of Christian Doctrine was assisted and popularized by Ippolito Galantini (1565-1619). On Galantini, see D'Addario, Aspetti della controriforma a Firenze, pp. 45-47; and ms. Moreniano, 137, Memorie del b. Ippolito Galantini messe insieme dai Fratelli della Dottrina Christiana.

84. On these clubs and their similarity to the adult societies, see Richard Trexler, "Ritual in Florence: Adolescence and Salvation in the Renaissance," in The Pursuit of Holiness, ed. Charles Trinkaus (Leiden: E. J. Brill, 1974), pp. 200-254.

85. Principe Piero Ginori Conti, ed., Vita del Beato Ieronimo Savonarola (Florence: Olschki, 1937), p. 122.

86. Capitoli, 224, Capitoli della Compagnia del Santissimo Sacramento di San Salvatore, 1579, 1r-1v.

87. Capitoli, 45, pp. 68-69.

88. Ibid., pp. 69-70.

Dressed in white, to "preserve their innocence,"[89] the boys were admonished to be "faithful observers of the Holy Commandments of God and the Holy Church, and obedient to their fathers and mothers."[90] In the same manner that the feasts and festivities of adult fraternities in the course of the sixteenth century came to be transformed into or replaced by solemn devotions, so too in the juvenile companies mystery plays were substituted for festive activity at Carnival, "because it is good to keep the young occupied during times of dissolute behavior."[91] The parish procession of Corpus Domini was an event of special pride for the men of the parish companies. It was a time when the virtues of their young seedlings could blossom publicly. Fathers and sons marched together, the fathers in red, the traditional color of eucharistic companies, and the sons in white, "so that one should be able to see and recognize out of the same body of the same company, which are the fathers and which are the sons, [and see] that the Father guardians should be and are superior and govern the boys, their sons and subjects.[92]

These sacramental confraternities directed the religious and festive life of their parishes. The parish confraternity organized the burial of fellow parishioners, and one did not have to be a member of the confraternity to enjoy this privilege.[93] Those whose families were too poor to reimburse a confraternity the customary three florins for funeral expenses were buried for free, and the confraternity, which held the keys to the neighborhood

89. *Capitoli*, 224, 2r.

90. *Ibid.*, 13v-14r.

91. *Ibid.*, 9v.

92. *Capitoli*, 45, pp. 72-73:

Ragunati li sopradetti Capitani et uffitiali et altri fratelli in detta compagnia . . . dopo maturo deliberatione questo dì 16 di Giugno 1585 havere riceuuto nella loro compagnia l'exercitio della Santissima Dottrina Christiana il dì delle Domeniche e feste comandate al Vespro per publica utilità de' loro figliuoli et del popolo di Sant' Ambrogio non solo per ritenerli dal fare male, ma per condurli et darli occasione di far bene, et perchè l'altre compagnie dove si esercita detta dottrina sono andate, et uanno a pricissione secondo l'occorrenze et piacimento de loro superiori per più honor di Dio . . . e deliberato che si debba andare a pricissione generale le feste del Corpus Domini et la uigilia di San Giovanni Batista Advocato et protettore della nostra città con questo che s' debba portar sempre il nostro segno di compagnia et con le solite veste tutti gli huomini di nostra casa, et li fanciulli della dottrina da quindici anni in giù con ueste bianche perchè si uegga et conosca quali sien li padri, et quali sien li figliuoli del medesimo corpo della medesima compagnia, et che detti Padri custodi sian et son superiori et governano li detti fanciulli loro figliuoli et subditi et che in fronte dette ueste tanto bianche quanto rosse debbia havere il segno del miracolo e sulla spalla destra il segno di San Michele.

93. *Capitoli*, 171, p. 37: "S'ordina per el presente capitolo il modo si deve tenere quando ciascuno de' nostri fratelli o sorelle o altri del nostro popolo che lasciassi in vita che alla morte sua volessi esser della notra compagnia sotterato." See also the statutes of the company of the Sacrament of San Pancrazio, *Capitoli*, 253, p. 51.

cemetery, was paid by the parish priest.[94] Any member of the parish who fell ill was entitled to regular sacramental and social visits by the confraternity.[95] Sacred and secular feast day activity centered around the parish confraternity. Some fraternities such as the Sacrament of Santa Lucia sul Prato doubled as *potenze*, neighborhood festive groups (more properly, gangs) that staged street fights during feast days. In some cases, fifteenth-century *potenze* may have provided the secular organization that later took the form of a sacramental company.[96] In addition to the customary officers and the psalmists (who officiated at funerals and sang lauds at the company altars), Santa Lucia had "un capo di Paese, cioè l'Imperatore" (a "turf boss" or, should we say, an emperor).[97] The increased frequency of secular festive life, especially violent games and combats of all sorts,[98] may have compensated, to some extent, for the decline of liminal communal ritual.

For the feast of Santa Maria Impruneta, the parish societies went door to door throughout the parish, collecting gifts to bring to the Virgin.[99] The companies arranged the parish feasts, visiting each household on the feast day and giving each a loaf of bread.[100] Once each week the members of the confraternity fanned out in all directions, knocking on every door in the neighborhood, crying out, "Donations for candles for the Sacrament! Donations for the Company of the Sacrament!"[101] Taking charge of the upkeep of altars and the supply of candles and arranging for the singing of lauds in the evening, the parish societies appear to have taken over many of the cultic functions of the older *laudesi* companies, but on a far more local basis.

The parish confraternity, under the direction of the parish priest, exercised the functions of a neighborhood elite, maintaining order and discipline in the community. The role of the parish confraternity in maintaining order extended throughout the neighborhood. The statutes of the company of the Sacrament of the Holy Savior describe its responsibility to pacify its neighborhood:

94. CRS, 1759 (S 6, vol. 2), Compagnia del Sacramento di San Salvatore in Borgo Ognissanti, *Ricordi*, 1569-1578, records of November 25, 1571, and June 24, 1571.

95. *Capitoli*, 828, *Capitoli della Compagnia della Madonna dell' Assunta di San Piero Gattolini*, 1607, 14r.

96. Trexler, *Public Life*, p. 403ff.

97. CRS, 1769 (S 8, (vol. 1), *Capitoli della Compagnia del Sacramento di Santa Lucia sul Prato*, 1582, chap. 2.

98. Berner, "Florentine Society," pp. 225-227.

99. CRS, 1769 (S 8, vol. 1), chap. 8. See also *Capitoli*, 45, *Capitoli della Compagnia di San Michele Arcangelo*, p. 47, for the procession to Santa Maria Impruneta.

100. *Capitoli*, 828, 12r.

101. *Capitoli*, 649, capitolo 18; *Capitoli*, 828, 11r; *Capitoli*, 253, p. 35; CRS, 120 (A 109, vol. 2), Compagnia del Santissimo Sacramento di SS. Paolo e Antonio, 38v.

And we order that if any quarrel or difference should develop between the men of the parish, of whatever degree, we wish that the Governor, with his councillors, shall be held and obligated to elect two men of good fame and conscience, and they shall be held to make an accord between the contesting parties and to make them make peace and to unite them together, and these officials shall be called the Peacemakers of the parish.[102]

In the fifteenth century, the Florentine was apt to join citywide flagellant companies when he went from being a dependent son to being a responsible head of household and active citizen of Florence. The membership of *laudesi* societies, on the other hand, consisted primarily of members of the artisan community who were already established heads of households. The new parish confraternities of the sixteenth century appear to have had a focus on cultic activity that was similar to the *laudesi* of the previous century, although their membership was much more limited in terms of class and geographical origin. Figure 5.1 graphs the age distributions of persons enrolling in sixteenth-century parish confraternities.[103] Like the older *laudesi* groups, the age at entrance into parish confraternities was significantly higher than for the flagellant groups of the previous century. Among the *disciplinati* in the second half of the fifteenth century, about three-fourths of the members joined before reaching the age of 25. The *laudesi* companies drew members who entered at a significantly more advanced age. Three-quarters of the members of Sant' Agnese joined between the ages of 26 and 45, and the reader will recall that the typical member of the *laudesi* company of San Zanobi in 1480 was more than 15 years older than the average member of the *disciplinati* company of San Paolo in the same year. In the case of the parish societies of the sixteenth century, three-fourths of the members joined between the ages of 25 and 55. (Sant' Agnese officially limited its activities in the sixteenth century to its neighborhood.[104]) The average age at entrance is about the same for sixteenth-century parish groups and *laudesi* groups of the previous century, but the spread of ages is much wider (see Figure 3.8).

102. *Capitoli,* 516, pp. 80-82:

Ancora ordiniamo che se nacesti alcuna lite o differenza infra gli uomini del Popolo in qual grado si voglia, vogliamo che el Governatore con sua Consiglieri sia tenuto et obbligato eleggere due Uomini di buona fama et coscienza, e quali sieno tenuti mettere que' tali d'accordo e fare Loro fare pace et unire insieme tutti, e detti si chiamino pacigli del Popolo.

See also the statutes of the Compagnia dell' Assunta e Santissimo Sacramento, in San Niccolò Oltrarno, *CRS,* 183 (A 152, vol. 1); and the statutes of San Giovanni Battista, *Capitoli,* 63.

103. *CRS,* 1759 (S 6, vol. 2), San Salvatore, *Partiti,* 1569-1578; *Archivi delle Compagnie Soppresse* (archive 1, vol. 5), *Partiti,* 1547-1596; *Ibid.,* (archive 5, vol. 7), *Partiti,* 1577-1588.

104. ASF, *Acquisti e Doni,* 44, *Capitoli della Compagnia di Sant' Agnese,* 1584, 37v, 40r.

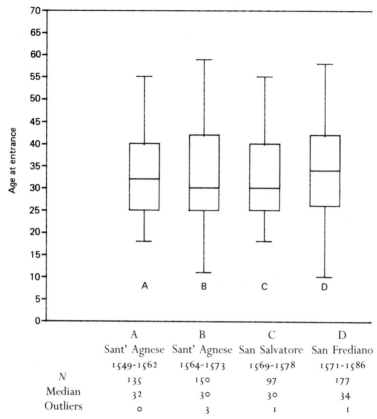

	A Sant' Agnese 1549-1562	B Sant' Agnese 1564-1573	C San Salvatore 1569-1578	D San Frediano 1571-1586
N	135	150	97	177
Median	32	30	30	34
Outliers	0	3	1	1

Figure 5.1.   Ages at entrance of members of sixteenth-century neighborhood companies.

The members of the parish confraternities were, almost without exception, men of modest means. Of the 136 members who entered the company of the Holy Sacrament of San Salvatore between 1569 and 1578, 15 were identified by father's first name alone; 11 were immigrants; 16 were identified by family name, almost all of which were names of artisans (a Gianfigliazzi, a Macinghi, and a Baldovini being the exceptions); 4 members were not clearly identified; and the remainder were identified by their occupation, at a time when almost all respectable Florentines were adopting surnames. In the case of San Salvatore, the occupations of nearly all the members were typical of the lower middle class, for the most part craftsmen and artisans providing goods and services for local consumption, plus a number of textile workers (Table 5.1). When the company opened in 1565 its governor was a weaver, Niccolò di Michele, and those who wrote the company statutes were Bartolomeo di Michele, goldsmith, Antonio di

Table 5.1

Occupations of Entrants into Parish Company of San Salvadore, 1569-1578

Occupations occurring once

Grave digger	Flag maker	Priest	Wool beater
Blacksmith	Goldsmith	Dyer	Fisherman
Vegetable dealer	Messenger	Notary	Silk guild employee
Porcelain maker	Wool worker		

Occupations occurring twice

Gardener	Barber	Cook	Glass maker
Shoemaker	Druggist	Painter	Bookbinder
Bricklayer		Second-hand-clothes dealer	

Occupations occurring three or more times

Carpenter (3)	Weaver (20)	Baker (11)	Sieve maker (3)
Mattress maker (3)	Miller (6)	Innkeeper (5)	Gold threadmaker (5)

Listed by	N
Occupation only	90
Town of origin	11
Father's first name	15
Family name	16
Unknown	4
Total	136

Piero di Meglio, Pellegrino di Niccolo, printer, Tommaso di Domenico di Tommaso, weaver, and Domenico di Agostino, weaver.[105] The limited incomes of the members sometimes complicated matters. Of 105 names drawn from the election purses during the three *tratte* of 1578, over 50% were disqualified because they were in debt to the company.[106]

The parish societies, then, attracted humble artisans of advanced age and, upon graduation from the companies of Christian Doctrine, their sons. As confraternity members, these men performed the functions of a neighborhood elite,[107] pacifying the community, administering its forms of charity,

105. *Capitoli*, 516, pp. 7-9.

106. *CRS*, 1759 (S 6, vol. 2), San Salvatore, *Ricordi*, 1569-1578.

107. Neighborhood ritual activity, by the end of the sixteenth century, was increasingly viewed as the preserve of the Florentine working class. Evidence exists suggesting that by the end of the sixteenth century, the upper middle classes, those called citizens, who nevertheless lacked noble status, were disdaining neighborhood and parish involvement. The parish confraternity of Saints Paul and Anthony reported in 1609 that the citizens (*cittadini*) of the parish, who used to carry the canopy over the host in local Corpus Christi processions "in order to render greater honor to God," were no longer willing to undertake that duty for the parish. *CRS*, 120 (A 99, vol. 2), *Ricordi*, 1570-1722, 58r, September 6, 1609.

socializing with the parish priest, assisting in the administration of the sacraments, and helping to perpetuate masses for their kinsmen and to maintain parish altars. In the Republic of Venice confraternities provided the Venetian middle classes—those excluded from political life—with a sense of power, public responsibility, and honor.[108] In an analogous way, the parish societies of Florence permitted members of the artisan community to claim their share of honor. Through the administration of their local communities and through their acts of ritual deference to one another, these neighborhood "governors" maintained order and participated in the culture of discipline and hierarchy of the later sixteenth century.

The sixteenth-century confraternity propagated a new ethos. The functions of the parish confraternity stressed the maintenance of social order and civil and religious orthodoxy and discipline. The older citywide companies had become elite clubs for those enjoying rank and privilege. It should come as no surprise to find piety, confraternal obligation, and even the nature of ritual equated with the principal virtue celebrated in the sixteenth century: obedience. The statutes of San Giovanni Battista described the goal of the company as encouraging members "to live in peace and tranquility, and to obey our superiors, and to observe unviolated the precept of Holy Obedience, in the name of which we should be most ready to obey."[109] Gone are the links between obedience and community found in the fifteenth century. Obedience, in its sixteenth-century usage, reemphasized one's subordinated status, and to a greater extent, the surrender of one's will to God and to earthly superiors. Hierarchical obedience became central to the nature of ritual experience in sixteenth-century confraternities. Suddenly whole chapters of statutes are devoted to discussion of the primacy of obedience among all the virtues.[110] For the members of the company of San Leo, writing in 1573, obedience lay at the heart of the most sacred event in Christian history:

> The wise man says, speaking through the mouth of the Holy Spirit, that obedience is the greatest and most worthy sacrifice that man can make, because he binds his will

108. Pullan, *Rich and Poor in Renaissance Venice,* 107ff.

109. *Capitoli,* 63, San Giovanni Battista, 1574.

110. See, for example, *Capitoli,* 793, Oratorio della Meditatione della Passione di Nostro Signore Iesu Christo, 1590, chap. 10, 11r-v. This statute defined disobedience as the first sin committed by man. God, it seems, wanted to test man in only one way. It was not humility, chastity, patience, or abstinence that God used as his test of human worth, only obedience. The chapter defined disobedience as the worst sin, the sin that is at the root of all other sins. Conversely, obedience is the greatest virtue, and no other virtue stands us in such good stead as obedience "when we negotiate with God about our deeds." The practical lesson drawn from obedience, according to this company's statutes, was the need to obey the company chaplain, the councillor, and the governor without demanding justification for any order and without any "question, contradiction, or excuse."

to the will of God. Because our ancient forefathers sacrificed animals, and because we have been regenerated through the precious blood of Jesus Christ Our Lord, let us sacrifice our own wills to our leaders and superiors.[111]

Ritual Reform in Counter-Reformation Florence

> *A Spaniard was in the noble city of Cosenza on the day of the celebration of Corpus Christi, and he was very indiscreetly saying that Italians were poor Christians because they never accompanied the Most Blessed Sacrament when He was taken through the city in a procession. On the other hand, he was boasting of the Spanish custom, saying that in Spain all the nobles participated in the procession. Irritated by all that boasting, a man said to him: "Brother, here He does not need a bodyguard, for He is carried among friends."*
> —Ludovico Domenichi (1515—1564)[112]

Actually, a few years after Domenichi published this anecdote, the exaltation of the Eucharist began to emerge as one of the principal forms of confraternal worship in Florence, and Christ would come to have His noble bodyguard. The new emphasis on sacramental piety was one element of a transformation that occurred in confraternal ritual between the Renaissance and the Catholic Reformation. Collective ritual experience, symbolic inversions, and ritual celebrations of brotherhood, equality, and friendship had been at the heart of traditional republican confraternal piety. In the years following the Medici restoration, the reawakening of confraternal life, and the Council of Trent, these traditional modes of confraternal ritual behavior were reevaluated; private devotions replaced collective celebrations; affirmations of rank, hierarchy, and obedience replaced inversions of status and the temporary creation of equality.

The sixteenth-century church emphasized those elements of cultic activity repudiated by Protestantism: the cult of saints, relics, indulgences, and communion. An active enthusiasm for these forms pervades the sources. A Franciscan preacher, Hannibal Santucci, urged the congregants at Santa Croce on the feast of the Annunciation to venerate the altar in Santa Croce

---

111. *Capitoli,* 5. On this theme, see also *Capitoli,* 209, *Capitoli della Compagnia del Pellegrino di San Donato fra i Vecchietti,* 1579; *Capitoli,* 827, *Capitoli della Compagnia dell' Assunta in via Tedesca,* 1575, p. 8; CRS, 1769 (S 8, vol. 1), capitolo 4; *Capitoli,* 516, p. 24; *Capitoli,* 455.

112. Charles Speroni, ed. *Wit and Wisdom of the Italian Renaissance* (Berkeley: University of California Press, 1974), p. 236.

dedicated to the Conception of the Virgin. Friar Santucci led the crowd on a procession to that altar, and listing the indulgences recently granted to confraternities that venerated the Conception, he founded, at that moment, the company of the Most Holy Conception of the Virgin Mary.[113] Cardinal Serletta, a patron of the oldest, and one of the two most important, sacramental companies in Rome, San Lorenzo in Damaso, was approached through Monsignor Giovanni di Matteo Dei, the brother of Benedetto Dei, a friar in Santa Croce, to allow the newly founded company of the Conception to share in the indulgences, privileges, and spiritual treasures of the company of San Lorenzo. Only 6 days later a procurator was appointed to seek additional indulgences from the pope, and in August the company published a copy of the privilege granting to all those who went on a procession to the altar dedicated to the Virgin a plenary indulgence. Within 4 months the original scope of the company—the veneration of the Holy Conception of the Virgin—had undergone a subtle shift. On November 29, 1579, the fraternity published a new decree granting a plenary indulgence to all who received *communion* in the chapel dedicated to the Conception or who accompanied the procession to the chapel organized by the confraternity on the second Sunday of each month. (The change in procession times from the first to the second Sunday of the month allowed members of the confraternity to participate in the devotions in honor of the Name of God.) The company's new spiritual privileges made it extremely popular. Its processions were so well attended that special officers had to be appointed to manage the processional throng. At a meeting in December:

> Francesco di Guglielmo Ciacchi, our *proveditore,* said that often, at the middle door of the church where the procession exits, because of the great crowd that passes through there, disturbances break out. He said that he could not, by himself, remedy the situation . . . and suggested that two brothers be elected, having the responsibility to stand by that door in order to exhort the crowd to march slowly, and to help those who, through bad luck or some accident should fall down, so that no one in the crowd should inadvertently suffocate.[114]

The company of the conception became so popular that other fraternities made the altar of this confraternity an object of pilgrimage.[115] The veneration of the crucifix of the company of the *Bianchi,* in Santo Spirito, when carried in eucharistic processsions, became equally popular. Although it was

---

113. *CRS,* 642 (C 21, vol. 5), 1v. These events took place in 1579.
114. *Ibid.,* 73r.
115. *Ibid.,* 43v.

on a work day, the ceremonial uncovering of the crucifix on March 5, 1598, was attended by an "infinite crowd."[116]

The Oratory of the Meditation on the Passion of Our Lord Jesus Christ, founded by members of the Florentine nobility at the end of the sixteenth century, promoted the veneration of saints in a novel manner: Each member chose his holy patron at random. The statute on the selection of patron saints declared:

> Many useful things are derived from the celebration of the Saints: their holy doctrines dispel the darkness of our ignorance, they teach us to adore God, honor the angels, detest vices and embrace the virtues; they exhort us to detest the world, to mortify the flesh, to attend to our prayers, frequent the sacraments. So much that is of value is brought forth in those who seek the protection of the Saints. And in order that we should have greater opportunity to render them the veneration that we owe them, we have deliberated . . . to write the name and feast day of each saint on a piece of paper, and place them all in a pouch. On the last day of each month everyone will draw from that pouch the name of a saint who will be his advocate for the month, and on that day all are obliged to confess and take communion.[117]

Of all the forms of devotion sponsored by confraternities in the late sixteenth century, the most popular and widespread was the cult of the eucharistic host. Even those companies, such as the company of the Holy Conception, founded to venerate a specific saint came, within a short time, to give eucharistic devotion equal importance in fraternal ritual practices. Eucharistic piety served as a "condensed symbol" of the many facets of Catholic renewal. Emphasizing the sacrament of communion reaffirmed the doctrine of transubstantiation in the face of the Protestant denial of the magic worked by the priest. This denial served as the focus of Protestant attacks on the power and authority of the church hierarchy and the clergy. Central to the Catholic doctrine of transubstantiation was the unequivocal affirmation of priestly authority. Administered in parishes, the Eucharist, linked to confession, reaffirmed in a most practical fashion the power of the clergy at the local level. The priest, able to withhold the sacrament from suspected heretics and those who had not properly confessed, was brought into contact with the entire parish community and could easily identify heretics. The celebration of the Eucharist, therefore, not only was the central rite of the church but also became central to the propagation of

116. *CRS*, 4 (A 8, vol. 4), Compagnia del Crocefisso de' Bianchi, *Partiti*, 19r.

117. *Capitoli*, 793, Oratorio della Meditatione della Passione di Nostro Signore Gesù Christo, Capitoli, 1590, 5r-6r.

orthodoxy and moved to the center of confraternal devotional practices.[118] The Florentine provincial synod of 1573 went far beyond the Council of Trent in stimulating sacramental worship and in regulating confraternities. The Tridentine decrees (Session 22, rubric 8) regulated confraternal life in only one way, requiring episcopal visitation and approval of all pious places. The 1573 synodal statutes adopted by the Florentine church went far beyond Trent. They encouraged the formation of sacramental confraternities in every parish,[119] and encouraged, in a similar fashion, the establishment of confraternities of Christian Doctrine for the boys of each parish.[120] All existing confraternities of every sort were forbidden from celebrating mass on Sundays and feast days unless they received prior permission from the priest at the parish in which the confraternity met.[121] In this way, even the older citywide companies came under increasing control by the parish clergy. The parish priests were given the task of inculcating sacramental reverence in their communities. If at all possible, parishioners were to take daily communion, and all parishioners were to be warned that they must take communion in their own parishes at Easter.[122] Each parish was to organize Corpus Christi processions.[123] Finally, all confraternal banquets were forbidden, except those in honor of Corpus Christi.[124] Following the synod of 1573, the archbishop began efforts in earnest to abolish confraternity feasts and to replace these and other fraternal practices with eucharistic worship.

118. On ritual reform during the Catholic Reformation, see John Bossy, "The Counter-Reformation and the People of Catholic Europe," *Past and Present* 47 (1970): 51-70; Jean Delumeau, *Il cattolicesimo dal XVI al XVIII secolo* (Milan: Mursia, 1976), pp. 225-229. The replacement of festive ritual celebrations with ritual solemnity, and the curtailment of folk ritual more generally has been referred to by Peter Burke as the victory of Lent over Carnival (*Popular Culture in Early Modern Europe* [New York: Harper & Row, 1978], chap. 8). For examples of how confraternal sacramental piety was used to combat Protestantism elsewhere in Europe, see Philip Benedict, "The Catholic Response to Protestantism: Church Activity and Popular Piety in Rouen, 1560-1600," in *Religion and the People, 800-1700*, ed. James Obelkevich (Chapel Hill: University of North Carolina Press, 1979), p. 168-190; and Mario Bendiscioli, "Finalità tradizionali e motivi nuovi in una confraternita a Mantova del terzo decennio del Cinquecento," in *Problemi di vita religiosa in Italia nel Cinquecento*, (Padua: Antenore, 1960), p. 93ff. For an example of Florentine Protestants challenging the Catholic doctrine of the Eucharist, see L. Bruni, *Cosimo I de' Medici e il processo d'eresia del Carnesecchi. Contributo alla storia della riforma in Italia con l'aiuto di nuovi documenti* (Turin, 1891), pp. 59-61.

119. J. Mansi, *Sacrorum Conciliorum Nova et Amplissima Collectio* (Paris: Welter, 1902), vol. 35, *Concilium Florentinum*, rubric 31, chap. 2.

120. *Ibid.*, rubric 21, chap. 1.

121. *Ibid.*, rubric 18, chap. 6.

122. *Ibid.*, rubric 31, chaps. 6, 8.

123. *Ibid.*, rubric 46, chap. 3.

124. *Ibid.*, rubric 51, chap. 3.

Confraternities appear to have been quite receptive to the clergy's efforts to foster eucharistic peity. In statute after statute one finds conspicuous reference to sacramental reverence. For fifteenth-century companies such as San Paolo, communion had been a rite of fraternity and a preparation for confraternal assembly. In the sixteenth century, fraternal rituals prepared the brothers for the now central rite of communion. The brothers of the Oratory of the Meditation on the Passion of Our Lord Jesus Christ selected as members only those applicants who had taken communion regularly for the previous 6 months, and they described confraternal obligations as duties undertaken "so that one can better prepare oneself for Sunday communion."[125] The company of Saint John the Baptist so revered communion that it voted 112-1 to abolish all nonliturgical confraternity meetings or affairs on those days when the company distributed communion.[126] In 1584 the archbishop paid a pastoral visit to one parish company of Sant' Ambrogio, the company of Santa Maria della Neve. In the aftermath of the visitation, Corpus Christi practices were transformed. Festive spontaneity was replaced by sacramental gravity:

> Because the works of God must be done purely and sincerely, out of love and honor for Him alone, in a manner that should reflect decency and decorum, far removed from any sign of gluttony or inebriation, especially those works that are performed in order to bludgeon and mortify the flesh, such as pilgrimages and processions and visits to holy places, they ought to be accomplished quickly with as much discomfort and trouble as they merit. And on feast days celebrated on behalf of divine worship and service to God, we ought, all the more, to abstain from that loose and scurrilous talk and lazy and idle behavior which is encouraged by wine, the minister of jokes and laughter, behavior scarcely appropriate to cloistered and holy places. Therefore in statute xxi we prohibit those banquets that the captains arrange for the morning of the feast and procession of the marvelous miracle of the blessed body of Christ our Savior, exhorting our brothers instead to offer charity or a meal for the poor of the parish, or to add to the dowry that is granted each year that is of major service to God and utility to one's neighbor, and that they ought to drink and relax in their own homes with their own families.[127]

125. *Capitoli*, 793, 6r-8v.

126. *Capitoli*, 86, *Capitoli della Compagnia di San Giovanni Battista*, 1579.

127. *Capitoli*, 606, pp. 52r-v. The trend toward replacing festive meals with sacramental adoration was still continuing in the seventeenth century. In 1635 the Compagnia della Santissima Annunziata replaced its annual feast day distribution of loaves of bread blessed by the company chaplain with the Perpetual Adoration (a ritual form discussed later in this chapter). *Ibid.*, 615:

> Havendo considerato il nostro Padre Governatore Lorenzo Cavalicci et altri Governatori quanto pregiuditio apportino all'anime nostre le difficultà et confusioni che nascono ogn' anno quando si celebra la festività della Santissima Nuntiata per la distribuzione che si fa del Pan benedetto, et uolendo per quanto

It would be incorrect to assume that all ritual reform in sixteenth-century Florence was directed by the clergy. Confraternities were quite capable of establishing their own ritual practices. Until the 1570s, the adult company of Archangel Raphael maintained the traditional ritual practices of fifteenth-century confraternities. But there was growing dissatisfaction among the membership. In 1575 the brothers initiated a debate about the most popular ritual found in trecento and quattrocento companies:

Holy Thursday usually has caused more disorder than order, considering that on many occasions it was disrupted by people unfamiliar with it, and by related problems, whence it followed that the celebration upset the men of our company and they remained, for the most part, little satisfied. It seemed, therefore, worthy of being done away with. And for this reason His Reverence [the governor], aspiring principally to satisfy the honor of God, his own conscience, and the minds of all our brothers generally, and not being able to think of a better way to resolve this than by meeting here together in the whole body of the company, giving license to each one of us to be able to give his own opinion about this issue, he thus allowed each one to say whatever occurred to him, one at a time. And it so happened that many opinions were voiced, and in particular that of our most Serene Grand Duke who, being present, said that the washing [of feet] and the supper were customs performed even in the chapel of the pope, and thus could not and should not be abolished. It seemed right to him that the feet of twelve poor men of this house, and only of those twelve, should be washed. They alone should be served the meal and with the sums that the festival organizers have been accustomed to spend, a simple meal should be prepared for only those twelve who are to be washed. The remainder of that sum should be given to them as charity. This opinion was applauded by many and our Reverend Father Governor put it to a vote to see if it pleased our brothers. It passed with more black beans [than white beans]. The vote was 24 white beans to 26 black beans. But then many said that they had not properly understood [the motion] and, moreover, one could not really make out whether several beans were black or white since they appeared to be grey. His Reverence saw that the members were beginning to stand up in a rather tumultuous fashion. Already people were leaving, and he saw that the hour was late and that everybody was tired from the other three evenings and two mornings spent at Santo Spirito in the sacramental processions. And so, they recited the Ave Maria, and he gave

---

si può provedere a simili disordini con introdurre in cambio del cibo corporale lo spirituale a benefizio dell' anime nostre et de fratelli e sorelle passati all' altra vita, Hanno però deliberato et ordinato quanto app. vz.

Che in avvenire ogn' anno il giorno che si celebrerà la festività della Santissima Nontiata nostra Signora Avvocata e Protettrice, non si distribuisca più il Pane benedetto con forme a che si è fatto per il passato, ma in quel cambio si esponga il Santissimo Sacramento con l'orazione della 40 hore et la spesa che per quella functione occorrerà farsi si deva cauare di dove si cauaua quella che si faceva in detto Pane dovandosi seguitare a eleggere quel medesimo numero de Festaioli con il modo et ordine che si è fatto sino al presente per la detta Festività.

everyone license to leave, leaving this in the care of those who will attend to it during another year.[128]

The traditional washing of feet had become a troubling issue for the men of Archangel Raphael. They had to balance the increasingly unfulfilling, even distasteful aspects of the *lavanda* and the sacred supper against the continuing reverence for tradition per se, particularly when tradition and orthodoxy became visible signs of social stability and political loyalty. Nevertheless, the vote was close—and the outcome, ambiguous. What was it about the washing rite and the holy supper that the brothers found so objectionable? Let us first recall the meaning attributed to the ritual in the previous century. Giovanni Nesi, preaching before the company of Saint Anthony of Padua in 1474, defined what was a common conception of the essence of the *lavanda* rite:

> And now, most worthy Fathers . . . we ought to discuss the most holy act of the washing of feet, the act that was performed with such great humility by the True God, the act that we celebrate on this day. . . . And humility, according to Tullio, is "virtù per la quale l'huomo con uerissima cognitione di sé medesimo uile si riputa." Humility is the virtue by which man, with truest understanding, comes to consider himself vile.[129]

128. *CRS,* 141 (A 146, vol. 4), Arcangelo Raffaello, *Ricordi,* 59r-v, meeting record of April 2, 1575:

> Era stato proposto da alchuni amorevoli di nostra compagnia qualmenti la cosa della colizione solita farsi il giovedì santo chaussaua più presto disordine che hordine, atteso che molte volte per essere agitato da genti pocho pratichi ho simili chose ne seghuiva che si teneva a disagio li huomini e ne restauano in maggior parte poco sadisfatti e che a molti seria parso si douessi levare onde sua R.rea aspirando principalmente di sadisfare al honor di dio e alla sua conscienzia et alle menti di tutti i fratelli universalmente e per venire a questo non aueua possuto pensar meglio che congreghando quiui un- itamente il corpo di compagnia dando facultà a ciaschuno di poter dire intorno a questa causa il suo parere e chosì diede facultà a ciaschuno dir quanto li occoreua a uno per volta intervennero adunque in questo fatto molti opinioni ma particularmente sendo presente il nostro Serenissimo Gran Duca disse che la cosa della lavanda e dela colizione si costumaua sino nella cappela del papa ne si potea ne si doua leuare ma che a lui seria parso pigliare 12 poveri della casa e che solo a quelli 12 si douessi lavare i piedi e fare la colizione e che la spesa erono soliti fare e festaiuoli facessino d'una semplice colizione per solo e quelli 12 et del restante far lhoro limosina il qual ragionamento da molti conmendato la R.va del nostro Padre Ghovernatore sudetto fece mettere a partito se di chosì piacceua a fratelli resoluerne e uincerne partito in corpo di compagnia da vincersi per le più fave nere il qual partito ebbe 24 fave bianche e 26 fave nere ande molti dissono non avere inteso e che ancho certe fave per pendere in bigio non si sapea discerne se erono nere ho bianche, la onde auendo S. R.rea righuardo al cominciarsi a veder con tumulto sollevare i popoli che già si partiscono e al hora che pure era tarda e al esser di tre altri sere di due mattine in Santo Spirito alla procissione del sagramento affaticati tutti chosì sono l'ave Maria e diede licenzia lassando questa cura a chi appurtirra il pensarui un altro anno chosì se resto.

129. *Oratione del Corpo di Cristo da Giouanni Nesi composta, et da lui nella Compagnia di Sancto Antonio da Padua recitata, die vij aprelis MCCCCLXXIIIJ,* in Cesare Vasoli, "Giovanni Nesi tra Donato Acciaiuoli e

When it came time to arrange Holy Week in 1576, a resolution changing the rite was adopted. The members' objections to the rite as performed the previous year appear in the following quotation. It is instructive to compare them with Nesi's interpretation of the ritual one century earlier:

> The washing of feet and the supper for the recently celebrated Holy Thursday . . . was such that this performance of the washing ought to be abolished, considering that on many occasions it has happened that only with much difficulty could there be found those who were willing to undertake that duty that they considered vile [*reputarsi chosa uile*]. This happened last year, when only seven persons were willing to participate, at which point the aforementioned Reverend Messer Matheo said some words that roused the people so that they voluntarily agreed to offer themselves as participants in this affair, some Gentlemen and some Artisans. All of this seemed to confirm the opinion expressed some meetings ago, and it seems better to adopt the resolution of last year that ordered a simple meal for those twelve who take part in the washing on a platform placed in the middle of the company. They should all stand with our Reverend Father Governor and kneel in turn at the platform, and all the other brothers should remain seated in their usual places in the choir.[130]

For Nesi, the essence of the rite was the public demonstration of one's baseness, that a member "uile si reputa," considers himself vile. For the

---

Girolamo Savonarola: Testi editi e inediti," in *Umanesimo e teologia tra '400 e '500 Memorie Domenicane,* n.s. 4 (1973): 132:

> Restaci, degnissimi Padri, solamente del sanctissimo acto del lauare e' piedi douere tractare, el quale con grandissima humiltà del uero iddio in questo giorno è celebrato. Ma perchè nel mio processo più ch'io non istimauo mi sono disteso, solo della humiltà, per la quale tal atto fu trouato, parlerò, credendo maximamente ciaschedun di uoi, per la frequentatione di quello meglio che le parole non potrebbero exprimere, suo significato interpretare. È adunque, humiltà, secondo Tullio, "*Virtus qua homo uerissima cognitione sui uilescit sibi ipsi.*" Humiltà è uirtù, per la quale l'huomo con uerissima cognitione di sé medesimo uile si riputa.

See also *ibid.*, p. 141. On the Holy Thursday rite in the earlier period, cf. pp. 99-104 of this book.
130. *CRS,* 141 (A 146, vol. 4), 61r:

> L'hordine tenuto giovedì sera proxima passato fu questo nella lavanda e nella colizione che posto prudentemente la R.rea del nostro Padre Governatore, messer Matheo Sanminiati e suo honoreuoli consiglieri messer Filippo de'Nerli e Messer Giuliano di Niccolò Sale come questo fatto dalla lauanda douesse terminarsi atteso che molte uolte era aduenuto trouar con difficultà chi uolesse tal charicho per reputarsi chosa uile ho da che si procedessi onde era chausato l'anno passato non essere uolsuti interuenire più che sette persone onde fatto per il sudetto Reverendo Messer Matheo sudetto alcuna parole conmosse e popoli che uolontarij si contentornono offerirsi per tal neghozio e intervennero parte gentilhuomini e parte artieri e questo più tornate in dreto opinione e parere ne uedendoci hordine di buona resolutione si atennonno più parere e meglio hordine conforme al partito del anno passato onde e quelli dodici che fecciono la lavanda fu a una panche posta in mezzo di compagnia hordinata una semplicissima cholizione stando tutti con la R.rea del Padre Ghovernatore genuflexi da torno a detta pancha e tutti gli altri fratelli stauono a soliti lhoro luoghi a sedere in choro.

men of Archangel Raphael, it was precisely this meaning—that man comes to "reputarsi chosa vile," consider himself made vile, by participating in a vile ceremony—that made members unwilling to participate in the rites of Holy Thursday.

What had happened to the rites of Holy Thursday? In elitist exclusive grand-ducal Florence poverty, humility, and low status—the traditional ritual attributes of *la lavanda*—had become signs of social impurity and pollution. A man undertaking a vile act might himself become vile. Given the collapse of guilds as units of political action and the growing irrelevance of neighborhoods as centers of patrician social and political power, encouragement for what had been collaboration, if not exactly affection, between social classes and status groups had diminished greatly. Gone were the impulses supporting communal fraternal ritual and corporate solidarity. The major rituals of Florentine confraternities—collective feasts and symbolic inversions producing equality through ritual degradation—were transformed into theater. A few members were delegated to feast, wash, and be washed, while the rest watched from a safe distance. Baroque pomp replaced medieval penance in this company's perception of piety.[131]

The transformation of the rites of Holy Thursday in 1576 was not without precedent in Florence. The archbishop had been accustomed to perform the *lavanda* by washing the feet of the canons of the cathedral. In 1569 Archbishop Altoviti introduced a new ceremony. In precisely the same manner that the members of Archangel Raphael ceased to play the roles of the poor and substituted the truly poor in place of officers or the general membership, Altoviti replaced the canons with 12 poor men, who were then treated to a meal at his expense and were covered, in public, with garlands. Patronage of the poor had replaced the symbolic adoption of poverty by the rich.[132]

When the brothers of Archangel Raphael voted to diminish the importance of the Maundy Thursday washing of feet, they did not reject ceremony per se. Indeed, a new form of devotion captured the enthusiasm of a number of the members. The first occasion on which the reformed Holy Thursday rites were performed was also the occasion on which another Holy Thursday ritual was introduced into the company:

> I record that on this morning, Holy Thursday [1576], having heard it said many times that very many of our brothers have continually lamented that we do not say Mass in our company on Holy Thursday and Good Friday, that therefore, on

131. For similar transformations in Venice, see Pullan, *Rich and Poor in Renaissance Venice*, p. 52.
132. Lapini, *Diario di Firenze*, p. 163, Holy Thursday, April 7, 1569.

account of my resolution, the sacrament was placed among us this year, and thanks to me this devotion went well, considering that it pleased every brother and was commended by everyone. Our brothers divided up all the hours, the hours of the day as well as the night, so that the sacrament was never alone, and it worked out quite well. Having recited the Mass on Good Friday, the procession was held, with a good number of men and torches. Some of our brothers, because of their devotion, desire this Mass also on Good Friday, and even, I note, on Holy Saturday as well.[133]

This celebration of mass on Holy Thursday was, in fact, the celebration of a new form of devotion to the Eucharist, the *Quarantore,* or the Forty Hours, as it came to be called, known today as the Perpetual Adoration of the Blessed Sacrament. The devotion began during the siege of Milan in 1527 as an attempt to placate God's wrath against the Milanese. The ritual spread throughout the Italian peninsula via the Cappuchins and acquired the following form: After a mass, the host was placed on a high platform where it was watched over by at least two men—men replaced every hour for 40 hours—in commemoration of the interval between Christ's death and Resurrection. At the conclusion of the fortieth hour another mass was celebrated. In the original rites of 1527, and at subsequent moments of public crisis, the 40 hours were divided among the major churches in the city. At the moment that an hour had elapsed, the adoration would conclude in one church and begin in another. The celebration of the Forty Hours as a form of popular devotion was given official approval by Clement VIII in 1592.[134]

By the final quarter of the sixteenth century, the *Quarantore* had become one of the most popular rituals in Florentine confraternities. The first *Quarantore* celebrated in the cathedral was on December 8, 1589, on the

---

133. *CRS,* 141 (A 146, vol. 4), 60v:

Ricordo come questa mattina del Giovedì santo auendo sentito più volte dire che molti e molti de' nostri fratelli si erano sempre lamentati che in nostra compagnia non fussi messa il Giovedì e'l Venerdì Santo onde per si expediente di mia risoluzione vi fussi questo anno e chi ui si ponessi il sacramento la quale devozione per la detta grazie mi venne ben fatta attese che piacque a ciaschuro universalmente e da ogniuno fu conmendata e scompartissi tutte l'hore i fratelli tanto del giorno quanto della notte a fine che il sacramento non stessi solo passo molto bene e il Venerdì santo detto la messa s'andò in processione e furno buon numero di huomini e di torce e certi nostri fratelli per lhoro devozione si uollono ancho la messa il venerdì santo anzi dico il sabato santo.

134. The company of Arcangelo Raffaello's meeting records contain details of the celebration, hour by hour. See *CRS,* 141 (A 146, vol. 4), meeting records for April 1594, 17v-19r. On the *Quarantore,* see G. Burigozzo, "Chronica Milanese, 1500-1544," *ASI* 3 (1842): 451ff.; Joseph A. Jungmann, *The Mass of the Roman Rite* (New York, 1950), 1: 150; Maurice Brillant, *Eucharistia* (Paris, 1957), pp. 363ff. P. Tacchi Venturi, *Storia della Compagnia di Gesù in Italia* (Rome, 1930), vol. 1, pt 1: 229-248.

For the approval of Clement VIII, see *Graves et diuturnae,* November 25, 1592.

Feast of the Conception, in the presence of the grand duke and most of the confraternities of Florence.[135] The Forty Hours had, however, been present for at least 3 decades. On May 29, 1558, following communion in the company of the Nativity, a confraternity of juveniles, the "father governor,"

> with the greatest devotion and ceremony, left on the altar the most holy sacrament in a ciborium, following the customary practice, with many lights which were arranged in different levels in a most beautiful design. The chamber was decorated in such a manner that it seemed to be a paradise and it greatly inspired all those who entered there. And so, in the name of God, the prayer of the XXXX hours was begun and it lasted until Monday evening at the sixth hour. Our father guardian and Iacopo Ferretti remained for the first hour in a separate place where they were neither seen nor disturbed by anyone and they were followed by the other brothers, going two by two, in the most solemn silence and devotion, until the end of the ceremony.[136]

The flood of 1557 destroyed much mid-century documentation, and it is therefore difficult to determine exactly when and where the *Quarantore* first appeared in Florence. The company of the Nativity lost all of its account books in the flood of 1557,[137] and the meeting records mentioning this celebration of the Forty Hours began again at the end of 1557. The Forty Hours rite is described as being "customary" (*consueto*), but for how long cannot be ascertained. Widespread reference to the ritual does, however, begin to appear shortly after 1567, just the time that the clergy had begun to emphasize eucharistic devotion. On May 15, 1567, Archbishop Altoviti entered Florence, amidst great celebration, to claim his bishopric, after years of struggle with Cosimo I. Two weeks later, on May 29, Florence celebrated the feast of Corpus Christi. Bishop Altoviti ordered that the facades of all the houses along the processional route be decorated festively to greet the sacrament.[138] Shortly thereafter signs of greater sacramental reverence appeared in Florence and in other parts of Tuscany. By 1568, 11 *disciplinati* companies in the Medici-controlled town of Borgo San Sepolcro had unified into a single company whose principal function was the organization and performance of monthly celebrations of the *Quarantore*.[139] On March 3, 1571, members of the company of Sant' Antonio Abate voted to

---

135. Lapini, *Diario di Firenze*, pp. 292-293.

136. CRS, 160 (A 147, vol. 6), Compagnia di Arcangelo Raffaello (adolescents), *Ricordi*, 5r.

Giovanni Lami dated the introduction of the *Quarantore* into Florence to the 1630s. G. Lami, *Diario fiorentino dal 1611 al 1717*, ms. Riccardiano, 3808. This dating is at least 70 years too late.

137. CRS, 160 (A 147, vol. 6), 19r-25r.

138. Lapini, *Diario di Firenze*, p. 157.

139. Pier Lorenzo Meloni, "Topographia, diffusione e aspetti delle confraternite dei *disciplinati*," in *Risultati*, p. 47.

celebrate monthly communion services.[140] Sacramental enthusiasm had evidently increased to the extent that 1 year later, on March 15, 1572, the company voted to begin celebrating the *Quarantore*.[141] During the decade of the 1570s references to the rite become numerous, and the ritual first finds mention or was formally established in the companies of San Salvatore (1570), San Benedetto (1570), Santa Croce in via Maffia (1571), San Frediano (1573), for which company the ritual became the central Holy Thursday rite, Santa Maria Maddalena (1574), Arcangelo Raffaello (il Raffa) (1576), San Bastiano e Sant' Alberto (1579), and Crocefisso de' Bianchi (1579).[142] Sometime around 1570 a system of exchange had been created for the distribution of hours of adoration among several of the confraternities of the city during major feasts. On December 24 of that year the parish company of San Salvatore in Borgo Ognissanti participated in the Forty Hours celebrations of the company of Saint Benedict in Santa Maria Novella[143] and the company of San Giorgio.[144] On April 7, 1571, the company was invited to participate in the devotion performed by the company of the Crucifix of the *Bianchi* in Santo Spirito.[145] The company of the *Bianchi*, in turn, went forth from Santo Spirito to celebrate the Forty Hours in Santa Croce,[146] and in Santa Maria Novella.[147]

One of the most complete descriptions of the celebration in a Florentine sodality was provided by the secretary of that company of the *Bianchi* in Santo Spirito, who left this record, September 6, 1601:

> This morning 44 of our brothers assembled with the required vestments, and torches in hand we marched to Santo Spirito. At the altar where our crucifix is located, the Fathers of Santo Spirito were celebrating the Mass of the Holy Spirit,

---

140. *CRS*, 108 (A 118, vol. 4), Sant' Antonio Abate, *Partiti e Ricordi*, 1557-1574, meeting record of March 3, 1570.

141. *Ibid.*, meeting record of March 15, 1571.

142. For San Salvatore, San Benedetto, San Giorgio sulla Costa, and Santa Croce, see *CRS*, 1759 (S 6, vol. 2), Sacramento di San Salvatore in Borgo Ognissanti, *Ricordi*, 1569-1578, 26r, 31v. For Santa Maria Maddalena, see *CRS*, 1395 (M 93, vol. 5), Compagnia di Santa Maria Maddalena, *Ricordi*, meeting records for April 3 and 11, 1574; For Arcangelo Raffaello, see *CRS* 141 (A 146, vol. 4), 60v, meeting record of April 19, 1576; For San Bastiano e Sant' Alberto, see *Archivi delle Compagnie Soppresse*, (archive 4, vol. 1), 10v; for the Compagnia del Crocefisso de' Bianchi, see CRS, 4 (A 8, vol. 4), *Partiti*, 5v.

143. *CRS*, 1759 (S 6, vol. 2), Sacramento di San Salvatore in Borgo Ognissanti, *Ricordi*, 1569-1578, 26r: "Richordo come ali 24 di dicembre 1570 chome la chonpagnia del Santissimo Sagramento di Santo Salvadore in borgo ogni santi è ita a ore chuatro del deto mese ala chonpagnia di Santo Benedetto in Santa Maria Novella, cioè al oratione dele chuaranta ore."

144. *Ibid.*

145. *Ibid.*

146. *CRS*, 4 (A 8, vol. 4), Crocefisso de' Bianchi, *Partiti*, 1576-1626, 5v.

147. Ibid., 42r.

and under our canopy we carried in procession the most precious body of our Lord Jesus Christ. Arriving there we carried the most Holy Sacrament onto the scaffold on the altar which had been erected and decorated not only with lights but with adornments as well. Reverend Father Monsignore Lorenzo recited a sermon. Everything was ready, and our brothers began the prayer. It was approximately hour 17. The bell rang and the brothers who had been so ordered came and with them two brothers assisting in the ceremony, their faces covered. They prayed at the foot of the scaffold, reciting the psalm Miserere, kissed the ground and then climbed up to their assigned places where they prayed secretly for the space of an hour until others came to take their places. And they came down from the altar through a secret door, reentering our company sanctuary where they kneeled again, said prayers, and recited the Te Deum Laudamus, then went to change their clothes.

At the end of the 40 hours:

> The hour having come enabling the Mass to be celebrated, the Mass was celebrated in our company at the altar supporting the scaffold. At the conclusion of the Mass the priest consumed the most Holy Sacrament and the Te Deum Laudamus was sung. Having recited prayers, given thanks to God, and sung the Ave Maria, each one of us was given license to go with the Peace of the Lord.[148]

Unlike the feasts and rituals that it replaced, the *Quarantore* was not a collective celebration in the traditional sense. It emphasized spectacle and ornate eucharistic display. The Forty Hours celebrated by the men of Santa Maria Maddalena for Easter of 1574, for example, was such an elaborate

---

148. *CRS*, 4 (A 8, vol. 5), Crocefisso de' Bianchi, *Partiti*, 39r-40r:

Ricordo questo dì detto chome in questa mattina d'ordine del Serenissimo Gran Duca et di Monsignore Vicario del Illustrissimo Cardinale Arcivescovo si sono poste publicamente nella nostra Compagnia l'Orazione delle Quarantore . . . in questa mattina raunatisi li fratelli in compagnia el numero di 44 con le solite ueste e torci ebi in mano siamo andati in Santo Spirito, et essendosi per li Padri de detta Chiesa all'altare del nostro Crocifisso celebrato la messa dello Spirito Santo, si è sotto il nostro baldachino portato processionalmente in compagnia il preciosissimo corpo di nostro Signore Yhs Christo dove arrivatosi et portosi il Santissimo Sacramento nel altare in sul palco perciò eretto et ornato non solo di lumi quanto di altri acconcimi del Reverendo Padre Monsigniore Lorenzo è stato recitato un deuoto sermone, et essendosi fermo ogni cosa, si cominciò l'orazione da fratelli essendo circa a hora 17 et cosi sonatosi il campanello uenivano li fratelli acciò ordinati et entrati in mezzo a dua fratelli assistenti coperti il viso fatto a piedi del palco orazione con dire il salmo Miserere, baciata la terra salivano al luogho deputato dove secretemente orando stavano lo spazio di una ora tanto che altri in loro luogho uenendo, essi per dreto l'altare scendendo per secreta porta tornavano in compagnia dove di nuovo inginochiatisi fatto di nuovo alcune orazioni et detto il Te Deum Laudamus andavano a spogliarsi; et tale è stato l'ordine; quelli fratelli che sono andati all'orazione sono li la scritta cioè. . . . Essendo uenuto l'hora da potersi celebrar la messa fu celebrata in nostra compagnia sul altare del Palco et alla fine di quella fu per detto sacerdote consumato il Santissimo Sacramento et cantatosi il Te Deum Laudamus et dette alcune orazioni, si rese le grazie a Dio et sonatosi l'Avemaria ciascuno ebbe licenzia con la pace del Signore.

affair that it required 100 participants, 40 torches, and 50 candles and the company had to elect 10 supervisors to plan the proceedings.[149] The focus of the ceremony was on the adoration of the Majesty of Christ, the Heavenly King in their midst, a focus far removed from fifteenth-century sacramentalism, which had stressed the unity of the faithful, the *brotherhood* produced by collective communion. The nature of participation in ritual had changed as well. Although the rite was preceded and followed by processions, the heart of the ritual was the private adoration of the sacrament by individual worshippers.

Sixteenth-century Florentine eucharistic piety was sponsored officially by Cosimo I and his successors. The grand dukes ordered the performance of sacramental processions and paid for the expenses incurred in the celebration of the *Quarantore*.[150] Attendance at all types of religious processions was mandatory for Florentine nobles and members of the court.[151] Corpus Christi was especially important to the grand duke. On Corpus Christi a general citywide procession, in addition to parish processions, was held, led by the confraternities of the city, followed by the clergy. At the center of the procession came the host, carried by the captains of the Parte Guelpha. Surrounding the captains were the pages of the grand duke, all carrying lights and other adornments in order to glorify and focus attention on the sacrament. One might say that the pages performed the same function for the heavenly king that they performed for their earthly prince. Behind the pages marched the grand duke, surrounded by his entire court.[152] Grand Duke Francesco I was absent from Florence for Corpus

149. *CRS*, 1395, (M 93, vol. 5), Compagnia di Santa Maria Maddalena, *Partiti*, meeting record of April 11, 1574:

> Ricordo come il dì di Pasqua che fumo addì 11 d'Aprile a ore 22 si pose in nostra compagnia le 40 ore e leuossi in chiesa il Sagramento e nostri fratelli andorno col nostro crocifisso e con 40 torcie e da 50 candele e funo da cento personi e così venanno e frati con lumi acesi e fa una bella divozione e onore e grolia del nostro Salvadore Dio e le cose andorno quieti e in pacie così tutti li amoreuoli cirimonieri e festaiuoli e così tutti e nostri fratelli negli oratori come s'era ordinato ora per ora che dio ne rendi merito al anime nostro che n'a non di bisogno.

150. See, for example, *CRS*, 1759 (S 6, vol. 2), Sacramento di San Salvatore in Borgo Ognissanti, *Ricordi*, 1569-1578, 69r: "Da lo ilustrisimo ecelentisimo granducha a dì ij d'aprile lire 28 per limosine per comprare cera e pregare idio che gli rendo la sanità ale orazione del 40 ore in San Salvadore." For an elaborate celebration of the Forty Hours ordered by Grand Duke Ferdinand I in 1601, see *CRS*, 4 (A 8, vol. 5), Crocefisso de' Bianchi, *Partiti*, 1576-1626, 39r.

151. Berner, "Florentine Society," p. 224.

152. See Giuliano de' Ricci, *Cronica (1532-1606)*, ed Giuliana Sapori (Milan: Ricciardi, 1972), p. 321, for description of the feast celebrated in 1581.

Christi of 1582. Giuliano de' Ricci chronicled the celebration held in Francesco's absence:

> The Captains of the *Parte,* as they left the Duomo, as is the custom, took the canopy that they carried above the sacrament and brought it as far as San Giovanni, where they gave it to those citizens whom they had selected. And wishing to be the leaders or ministers of the procession, the councillors with their retinue swerved to place themselves in the lead behind the Sacrament, and with shouts, and almost through the use of force, they passed ahead and preceded the [Captains]. And when the Grand Duke was told about this by the interested parties, he rebuked the Councillors and determined that on that day the Captains shall assist the Body of Christ.[153]

The political message of such sacramental processions was not lost on observers or participants. Obedience to the proper processional representation of the heavenly court was linked to obedience to the earthly court. And it was Grand Duke Francesco's prerogative to define that earthly processional order that imitated the kingdom of heaven.

What were the social meanings that participants drew from their participation in the ritual adoration of the Eucharist? The impressions left by descriptions of these devotions and processions suggest one dominant theme: The participant honored Christ the King by serving in His honor guard. That function was perceived not only as honoring Christ but also as bestowing honor on the worshipper. One confraternity, in detailing the behavior appropriate to sacramental processions, described the host in these words: "And when accompanying the Holy Sacrament it should be remembered by our brothers and by all others that they are not accompanying an ordinary person, or even a terrestrial Prince, but the King of Kings, the creator of the universe, in whose presence angels tremble."[154] In the sacramental processions of Medici Florence, one fought for a place in Christ's bodyguard. The politics of divine symbols paralleled the politics at court. The belief of patrician Bernardo Davanzati—that prestige and worth were directly proportional to one's nearness to the duke[155]—could have applied equally to nearness to the Eucharist. The worship of the Eucharist had been transformed from a celebration of ritual brotherhood into the worship of kingly authority. The governors of the seventeenth-century

153. *Ibid,* p. 364.

154. *Capitoli,* 779, *Capitoli della Compagnia del Santissimo Sagramento di San Pier Buonconsiglio,* pp. 23-24: "E nell' accompagnare il Santissimo Sagramento, si ricordino i fratelli, e tutti gli altri che non accompagnano una persona ordinaria ne un Principe terreno, ma il Re de' Regi, il creatore dell' universo al cospetto del quale tremono gli angeli."

155. Leandro Perini, "Un patrizio fiorentino: Bernardo Davanzati," *Studi Storici* 17 (1976): 167. Davanzati is quoted as referring to the "gentuccia plebe" and their affairs in the following terms: "quanto più è vile e lontana dal principe, più son vili e ignobili l'opere sue."

parish confraternity of San Pancrazio even brought the language of the court into their statutes to describe the members' responsibility for correct behavior:

> We ought to observe our statutes with much care if we wish these statutes to preserve for us our position, which is, when we attend to His Most Divine Majesty during the Most Holy Sacrament of the altar, the position of the intimate Courtiers of God.[156]

The confraternities of republican Florence had once provided a ritualized escape from the social order, teaching members the duties of brotherhood and imparting to them a sense of participation in the honors and obligations of the dominant republican culture. During the course of the sixteenth century, citywide confraternities became elite societies, monitored by officials appointed by the grand duke. Poorer Florentines, no longer participants in broader, civic communities, gathered together in companies bound by ties of parish and craft. Class, craft, and neighborhood—the very social bonds that fourteenth- and fifteenth-century organizations had undercut—provided the organizing principles for the religious confraternities of grand-ducal Florence. Counter-Reformation ritual, like fraternal organization, fostered the very structures that Renaissance fraternal ritual had dissolved. The ritual practice of sixteenth-century companies had become a ceremonial recreation of the orders and honors of a courtly society.

---

156. *Capitoli,* 253, *Capitoli della Compagnia di San Pancrazio,* seventeenth-century revisions, p. 7: "Questi [capitoli] doviamo noi con ogni premura osservare se vogliamo che essi conservino noi nel posto di Cortigiani intimi di Dio, che tali siamo, mentre assistiamo alla sua Maestà Divinissima nel Santissimo Sacramento dell'altare."

See also *Capitoli,* 330, *Capitoli della Compagnia di San Francesco,* 1570:

> Come nelle Corti Regali et case signorili si costuma da Signori di quelle eleggersi Maiordomi et maestri di casa che attendino al seruizio di quelle et disponghino le Famiglie che uogliono entrare al servizio del Principe così uogliamo che la nostra compagnia habbia quattro Maestri de' Novizi, l'offizio de' quali sia pigliare informazione di quelli che uorranno essere de' nostri fratelli et ricercare diligentemente se hanno le condizioni che si richieggano a chi disidera essere di nostra santa casa.

Appendix

Confraternal Manuscript Sources Cited in the Text

This appendix consists of a listing of those confraternity manuscripts cited in the text. Confraternities were frequently known by a variety of names. A confraternity might have the name of one or more patron saints, the name of the church in which it met, a name descriptive of its membership, which is especially true of craft fraternities, or a name descriptive of its ritual practices. During its several centuries of existence, the same confraternity might change its name, its meeting place, or its patron saints. An individual confraternity might, therefore, be known by many names. Archival indexes grouped all the records of a single confraternity under one name, usually the last name used by the company, often its eighteenth-century name. I have tried, whenever possible, to use the name of the company that pertained to those specific documents cited, or that name least likely to cause the reader confusion.

Archivio di Stato, Florence

1. Archivi delle Compagnie Soppresse

Archive 1, vol. 4, Santa Maria delle Laudi, called Sant' Agnese, *Partiti,* 1483-1509
Archive 1, vol. 5, Santa Maria delle Laudi, called Sant' Agnese, *Partiti,* 1574-1592
Archive 4, vol. 1, Assunta di Maria e San Bastiano, (del Poponcino), *Partiti e Ricordi,* 1547-1592
Archive 5, vol. 1, San Frediano, *Capitoli,* 1489-1545
Archive 5, vol. 2, San Frediano, *Capitoli,* 1565
Archive 5, vol. 4, San Frediano, *Partiti,* 1436-1470
Archive 5, vol. 5, San Frediano, *Partiti,* 1468-1510
Archive 5, vol. 7, San Frediano, *Partiti,* 1577-1588
Archive 5, vol. 120, San Frediano, *Processo con le monache di San Frediano,* 1556-1685

2. Compagnie Religiose Soppresse (CRS)

Every document in this series is described by two sets of numbers: a general volume number that pertains to the entire *CRS* collection, and a letter and number combination that organizes contiguously numbered documents into subcollections of documents pertaining to the same confraternity. Each subcollection was assigned an inventory letter and number, and each separate confraternity document was assigned a volume number within the subcollection. The parenthetical information provides, first, the letter and number of the subcollection and second, the specific confraternity volume cited within that collection.

CRS volume	Volume of subcollection
3	(A 8, vol. 1), Crocefisso de' Bianchi, in Santo Spirito, called Sant' Agostino, *Capitoli*, 1513-1564
4	(A 8, vols. 4-5), Crocefisso de' Bianchi, in Santo Spirito, called Sant' Agostino, *Partiti*, 1576-1626
107	(A 98, vol. 1), Sant' Antonio Abate, called la Buca, *Capitoli*, 1485
108	(A 98, vol. 4), Sant' Antonio Abate, called la Buca, *Partiti e Ricordi*, 1557-1574
119	(A 98, vol. 34), Sant' Antonio Abate, called la Buca, *Entrature di Fratelli*, 1484
120	(A 99, vol. 2), Santissimi Paolo e Antonio, *Ricordi e Contratti*, 1570-1722
137	(A 132, vol. 1), Sant' Antonio da Padova, *Capitoli*, 1466
141	(A 146, vols. 3-4), Arcangelo Raffaello (il Raffa, comapny of adults), *Ricordi*, 1510-1561, 1572-1601
160	(A 147, vols. 6-9), Arcangelo Raffaello (la Scala, a company of boys), *Ricordi*, 1507-1674
177	(A 149, vol. 2), Santissimo Sacramento dell' Assunta e Pace in San Piero Gattolini, *Libro de' contratti*, 1565-1726
182	(A 151), Assunta e Santissimo Sacramento in San Piero Maggiore, *Contratti*, 1550
183	(A 152, vol. 1) Santissimo Sacramento dell' Assunta in San Niccolò Oltrarno, *Capitoli*, 1581-1755
285	(B 12, vol. 35), Santa Brigida, *Fratelli Defunti*, 1425-1714
316	(C 8, vol. 1, pt. A), Santa Caterina da Siena, *Doti*, 1509
642	(C 21, vol. 5), Santissima Concezione della Beata Vergine Maria, in Santa Croce, *Ricordi*
655	(C 143, vol. 1), Santissima Concezione, in Santa Cecilia, *Capitoli*, 1671-1687
673	(C 68, vol. 1, pt. B), Santa Croce dei Tessitori, *Memorie Diverse*, 1511-1779
1324	(M 51, vol. 1), Madonna della Quercia, *Interesse Diverse*, 1645-1777
1395	(M 93, vol. 5), San Francesco e Santa Maria Maddalena, in Santa Croce, *Partiti*
1430	(M 112, vol. 42), San Michele Arcangelo, *Ricordi*, 1492-1555
1542	(N 22, vol. 5), San Niccolò da Bari, in Santa Maria del Carmine, *Partiti*, 1545-1587
1579	(P 1, vol. 1), San Paolo in Via dell' Acqua, *Libro de' Fondatori*, 1434-1485; (P 1, vol. 2a), *Memorie Diverse* (P 1, vol. 2b), *Processo con la compagnia e San Giovanni Evangelista*, 1763-1782
1582	(P 1, vols. 6-8), San Paolo in Via dell' Acqua, *Partiti e Ricordi*, 1448-1502
1583	(P 1, vols. 9-11), San Paolo in Via dell' Acqua, *Partiti e Ricordi*, 1521-1545, 1570-1585
1591	(P 1, vols. 34-35), San Paolo in Via dell' Acqua, *Libro de' Sette Membri, e Memorie di Fratelli*, 1472-1548, 1563-1704
1592	(P 1, vols. 36-38), San Paolo in Via dell' Acqua, *Campione de' Fratelli*, 1447-1451, 1477-1487, 1506-1514

1594	(P 1, vol. 42), San Paolo in Via dell' Acqua, *Fratelli Morti*, 1452-1477;
	(P 1, vol. 43), *Libro degli Operai*, 1540-1613
1646	(P 30, vol. 8), Purificazione di Maria e San Zanobi, Ricordi, 1518-1575 .
1687	(P 31, vol. 1), Purificazione di Maria Vergine, *Capitoli*, 1482
1690	(P 35, vol. 3), Purità di Maria Vergine, called la Pura, *Ricordi*
1704	(R 2, vol. 6), San Rocco, *Partiti*, 1531-1579
1759	(S 6, vol. 2), Santissimo Sacramento di San Salvatore in Borgo Ognissanti, *Ricordi*, 1569-1578
1769	(S 8, vol. 1), Santissimo Sacramento di Santa Lucia sul Prato, *Capitoli*, 1582;
	(S 8, vol. 2a), *Interesse Diverse*
1869	(S 163, vol. 4), San Sebastiano, *Ricordi*, 1516-1706
1872	(S 163, vol. 14), San Sebastiano, *Fratelli Defunti*, 1483-1770
1880	(S 180, vols. 1-2), Santissimo Sacramento in San Felice in Piazza, *Libro de' Contratti e Testamenti*, 1560-1762
2170	(Z 1, vol. 1), San Zanobi, *Capitoli*, 1326-1480
	(Z 1, vol. 4), *Libro dei Testamenti*, 1313-1518
	(Z 1, vol. 5, pt. K), *Libri Antichi*, 1419-1508
2176	(Z 1, vol. 12), San Zanobi, *Libro dei Fratelli e Memorie*, 1333;
	(Z 1, vol. 14), *Ricordi e Partiti*, 1477-1483
2177	(Z 1, vol. 17), San Zanobi, *Partiti*, 1440-1447

3. *Compagnie Religiose Soppresse*, Capitoli

This collection contains most but not all of the extant confraternal statute books held in the ASF.

3	San Bernardino da Siena, 1569
5	San Leone, in San Leo, 1590-1595
6	Compagnia delle Laudi della Vergine Maria e di Sancto Philippo e di Sancto Gherardo e di Sancto Sebastiano, called San Sebastiano, 1451
22	San Francesco di Pagola, 1595
29	San Paolo in Via dell' Acqua, 1472-1520
30	San Domenico, called il Bechello, 1590-1774
45	Santissimo Sacramento di San Michele Arcangelo della Pace, in Sant' Ambrogio, 1560-1634
53	Santa Maria delle Laudi, in Santa Croce, 1470
62	Santo Stefano, called il Ciottolo, 1568
63	San Giovanni Battista alla Cavalieri di Hierusalem, 1574
81	San Girolamo sulla Costa, 1491
86	San Giovanni Battista, "dello Scalzo", 1579
137	Santa Felicità Maccabea e Sette Figliuoli Martiri, 1507-1532
152	San Giovanni Battista, "dello Scalzo", 1499-1744
154	San Zanobi, 1508
155	San Zanobi, 1555-1756
167	San Giovanni Decollato e Santissimo Sacramento, in Santa Maria in Verzaia, 1743
171	San Iacopo Sopr' Arno, 1589-1643
178	San Iacopo e San Filippo, 1637-1748
179	Corpus Domini di San Frediano, 1573-1674
181	Santa Maria della Neve e Santissimo Sacramento, in San Remigio, 1569-1702
189	San Cosimo e San Damiano dei Medici e Speziali, 1743-1754

190	Santa Croce dei Tessitori, 1644
194	Santa Concordia, 1437-1542
195	San Girolamo sulla Costa, 1441-1730
197	San Martino degli Osti, Albergatori, e Cucinieri, 1681-1749
201	Santissimo Sacramento, in Santa Felicità, 1571-1760
202	Santa Maria della Croce al Tempio, 1586
209	San Donato de' Vechietti de' Merciai, 1575-1579
224	Santissimo Sacramento di San Salvatore in Borgo Ognissanti (company of boys, a Dottrina Cristiana company tied to the adult company in the parish), 1579
253	Santissimo Sacramento, in San Pancrazio, 1668
314	Santissima Annunziata, 1494-1578
330	San Francesco, called il Martello, in Santa Croce, 1570
348	San Giuseppe dei Legnaiuoli, 1654-1772
364	Santo Sebastiano, 1520-1534
369	Santissimo Sacramento di San Silvestro, in San Felice in Piazza, 1715-1750
386	Diecimila Martiri Crocefissi, in San Pancrazio, 1665
439	Compagnia di Disciplina in Santa Maria del Carmine, also known as San Niccolò da Bari, 1431
446	San Niccolò da Tolentino, 1746
452	Purificazione di Maria Vergine, called I Servi di Maria, or di Monte Oliveto, 1297-1610
455	Purità di Maria Vergine, called la Pura, uniting older companies of San Niccolò da Tolentino, Sacrament of Santa Maria Novella, and la Pura, in Santa Maria Novella, 1564-1673
458	San Pietro de' Gabellieri e Stradieri, 1547-1589
492	San Cosimo e San Damiano, 1635-1785
499	Santissimo Sacramento di Santa Lucia de' Magnoli, 1641-1711
516	Santissimo Sacramento di San Salvatore in Borgo Ognissanti, 1565-1726
537	Santissimo Crocifisso e Santa Maria Maddalena, "dei Bianchi," 1531-1691
589	Santa Caterina da Siena, 1518-1620 (damaged in flood of 1966)
595	Sant' Eligio degli Orefici, 1333 (damaged in flood of 1966)
606	Santa Maria della Neve, in Sant' Ambrogio, 1445-1620
608	Santa Maria del Crocefisso del Chiodo (Madonna della Pietà, eventually became Santa Maria del Chiodo de' Tessitori de' Panni Lana), 1566-1767
615	Santissima Annunziata, 1588-1772
620	Santa Maria della Quercia, 1588-1719
623	Sant' Antonio dei Macellari, 1577-1586
635	San Benedetto de' Camaldoli, in Santa Maria Novella, 1385-1431
638	San Bonaventura de' Carcerati, 1605-1640
649	Santissimo Sacramento, in Santa Trinità, 1594-1730
709	Natività di Maria Vergine, 1568-1670 (damaged in flood of 1966)
719	Sancti Martiri Innocenti, 1487-1632
731	Santa Maria de' Poveri (Madonna del Carmine), 1723-1734
745	Sant' Antonio de' Mugnai, 1612-1697
779	Santissimo Sacramento di Santa Maria degli Angeli, in San Pier Buonconsiglio, 1665
793	Oratorio della Meditatione della Passione di Nostro Signore Gesù Cristo, 1590
797	San Matteo de' Muratori
798	Santa Maria dei Raccomandati (la Crocetta), 1628
799	San Giovanni Evangelista e San Michele Arcangelo, dei Tessitori di Lana, 1576-1659 (damaged in flood of 1966)
811	Compagnia dell' Assunta, called Monteloro, 1578
827	Assunta in Via Tedesca, 1575-1641
828	Assunta e Santissimo Sacramento in San Piero Gattolini, 1607-1742

854   Sant' Andrea dei Purgatori, 1466-1471
870   Sant' Andrea dei Purgatori, 1451

4. Conventi Religiosi Soppressi

89   vol. 136, *Capitoli della Compagnia di Santa Trinità de' Ferravecchi, 1560*
92   vol. 390, *Capitoli della Compagnia di San Francesco, 1427*

5. Acquisti e Doni

44   *Capitoli della Compagnia di Sant' Agnese, 1584*

Biblioteca Laurenziana

1. Fondo Antinori

Ms. 24   *Capitoli della Compagnia di San Lorenzo de' Fornai*

Biblioteca Nazionale Centrale di Firenze

1. Banco Rari

Ms. 336   *Capitoli della Compagnia di San Gilio, 1278-1284*

2. Conventi Soppressi

D.3.270   (Santa Croce collection), *Capitoli della Compagnia di San Niccolò del Ceppo, 1563*

3. Fondo Magliabecchiano

VIII, 1500, vol. 6, *Capitoli della Compagnia del Gesù, 1332*

Biblioteca Riccardiana

1. Fondo Riccardiano

Ms. 2204   Miscellaneous sermons and orations
Ms. 2382   *Capitoli della Compagnia di Santa Maria Sopr' Arno*
Ms. 2577   *Capitoli della Compagnia di San Pietro*

2. Fondo Moreniano

Ms. 54   *Capitoli della Compagnia di San Bartolomeo de' Pizzicagnoli, 1509-1579*

Author Index

Subject Index